AF531624

ENCYCLOPAEDIA OF ENTOMOLOGY - 2

INSECT BEHAVIOUR

By

Dr. M. Prakash

Dept. of Zoology
M.M.H. Post Graduate College
Ghaziabad (U.P.)
(India)

DISCOVERY PUBLISHING HOUSE PVT. LTD.
NEW DELHI-110 002

First Published - 2008

Reprinted - 2018

ISBN: 978-93-5056-571-1 (Set)

ISBN: 978-81-8356-288-1

Insect Behaviour

Published by:

DISCOVERY PUBLISHING HOUSE PVT. LTD.

4383/4B, Ansari Road, Darya Ganj

New Delhi-110 002 (India)

Phone: +91-11-23279245, 43596064-65

Fax: +91-11-23253475

E-mail: discoverypublishinghouse@gmail.com

sales@discoverypublishinggroup.com

web: www.discoverypublishinggroup.com

Printed at:

Infinity Imaging Systems

Delhi

Preface

Most insects are exhibitionists. They move about and engage in their daily tasks of acquiring food, courting, and reproduction undaunted by the watchful eyes of an observer. Over the span of human life on this planet people have almost certainly been fascinated and entertained by the activities of insects—what child have never stopped to admire a passing butterfly or sat and watched the coming and goings of a column of foraging ants? From such basic observations we have gained considerable insight into the biology of insects, but only recently have we begun to integrate our knowledge of behaviour, hormones, physiology and ecology into a more complete view.

The present title **Insect Behaviour** has been carefully compiled and edited to meet the long felt needs of increasingly large number of those who have to deal with the different aspects of biology of insects in colleges, universities and research institutes. It provides a balanced and integrated treatment of the entire field of insect Biology. The title is intelligible to the educated layman but it deals with some complex ideas. It is an adequate text for all requirements in this area for most university students. Special efforts have been made to explain ideas in non-mathematical term. The primary aim throughout has been clarity, simplicity and the high standard. It will definitely prove to be a boon to teachers, students and research works in the field of Insect Biology.

The primary aim throughout has been clarity so as to make the text selective and meaningful. We hope also that general Entomologists and students of Agricultural Entomology will find in this book valuable and recent informations about the subject and also allied branch of the subject. The book provides a nucleus around which the teacher can plan a successful course without much bearing on complementary and supplementary readings. The theme of the book is novel and for the first time the various chapters in different volumes have been organised reviewing the available literature. All the topics have been illustrated with line diagrams, graphs and tables wherever necessary.

In the preparation of this book large number of books and research papers have been consulted. So no authenticity is claimed.

The author wishes to express his deepest appreciation to the many people who have contributed in one way or the other to the preparation of this title.

The author expresses his gratitude to Mr. Wasan and staff of M/s Discovery Publishing House for their whole hearted co-operation in the publication of this book.

The author tried hard to be accurate and upto date in statement and realises the impossibility of completely avoiding errors therefore, the author will greatly appreciate having his attention called to any questionable statement.

—Author

CONTENTS

INTRODUCTION

Contemporary animal behaviour is a multidisciplinary approach to the search for answers to a variety of fundamental questions about how and why animals do the things they do. The multidisciplinary nature of the subject is understandable in view of the fact that it is often difficult to separate the basic functioning of anaomical components from behaviour or the physiology of sensory percept on from the basic responses that underlie complex behavioural patterns. Some scientists are interested mainly in the physiological aspects of how stimuli are detected and how responses are initiated. Others are more interested in the patterns of responses, and still others are concerned with the consequences of behaviour. Superimposed over this range of basic interests are the conceptual differences that for a long time separated neurophysiologists, ethologists, and animal psychologists.

Ethology has been defined in a variety of ways; none of which is completely satisfactory. However, it is generally accepted that the emphasis of ethology has been the objective study of the biological significance of behaviour in the context of nature. In the classical sense, as exemplified by the work of European investigators such as *Lorenz*, *Tinbergen*, and *von Frisch,* ethology was concerned with an evolutionary approach to the study of instinct. On the other hand, classical animal psychology was concerned primarily with the evolution of higher mental processes such as learning and problem solving. Animal psychology tended to be more analytical than ethology and concentrated on experiments conducted in a laboratory setting, more often than not with white rats. Ethology tended to be more descriptive, comparative, and field oriented. These differences are not as apparent today as they were during the 1950s, but differences in approach and emphasis still occur depending on the investigator's underlying discipline. Entomologists, as well see, deal with a group of animals that behave mainly instinctively, so insect behaviorists have been aligned more with ethology than animal psychology. However, new tools from neurophysiology, genetics, bio-chemistry, electronics, and statistics have led to a greater unity of purpose and synthesis of thinking among behaviorists studying divergent groups of animals. In spite of the complexity of behaviour, many biologists view it rather simplistically and do not demonstrate much interest in how or why particular patterns of behaviour evolved. In entomology, for example, most textbooks devote little or no space to behaviour. Volumes have been written about the structural and physiological breakthroughs that have occurred throughout over 300 million years of insect evolution and how these breakthroughs have led to the diversity and success of these fascinating animals. Much less of a general nature has been written about the behavioural adaptations that had to evolve along with the structural changes.

Students of biology often lose sight of the fact that the responses that form the basis of behaviour are inherited and, therefore, subject to the same evolutionary processes as inherited structural character-istics; responses that are beneficial or neutral survive, those that are inappropriate are selected against. Clearly, structure and behaviour are largely inseparable in the evolutionary process. If a behavioural response already existed that could enhance the usefulness of a new structural modification, the new structure would be more likely to be retained. Conversely, a new structure with potentially significant uses would not persist in the absence of appropriate behaviour. Under-standing the fundamentals of insect behaviour is, therefore, just as vital to the understanding of the success of the insects as is the understanding of their structure. To the average observer the behaviour of insects seems rather strereotyped in that most individuals of the same species tend to do the same things under similar circumstances. For example, if one moves a hand toward a settled housefly, we can predict with reasonable certainty that the fly will take flight. Likewise, if a stone in the garden is raised, we expect the insects beneath it to run quickly toward and under another stone nearby. Sometimes, these stereotyped behaviours do not seem to make much sense, as when night-flying moths spend an entire evening fluttering around a porch light. But in each of these and many other examples of insect behaviour, we are observing specific genetically programmed responses to stimuli.

Under normal circumstances these basic inherited components of behaviour serve a vital purpose and consequently persist as a characteristic of each species. We call these preprogrammed patterns of response *innate behaviour* or *instinct*. Innate behaviour can be distinguished from learned behavior on the basis that it can be performed with no prior experience. A newly emerged individual can thus respond in a seemingly appropriate manner to both favourable and harmful situations never before encountered. Obviously, the advantage of such a capability to the survival of an organism is immeasurable. However, there are drawbacks, at least for the individual, to behaviour that is entirely preprogrammed, since there is no a opportunity to develop beneficial alternative strategies in recurring situations. Learning, on the other hand, permits the development of behavioural alternatives that in some situations are more beneficial than the basic innate response.

The extent to which the behaviour of a species is dominated by either innate or learned behaviour depends on its capacity to learn and, perhaps, its opportunity to learn. The capacity to learn is determined largely by the complexity of the organism's central nervous system, particularly the number of nerve cells in the brain. The major factor governing the opportunity to learn is the time available to experience events to which alternate responses are possible. Consequently, animals like insects, which have a relatively low number (about 100,000) of nerve cells in their brains and generally have quite short lifespans, must depend almost entirely on innate behaviour. Since insects have relatively few nerve cells, most of them must be devoted to a rather fixed set of responses that lead to the accomplishment of those activities that will assure survival and procreation under normal circumstances. These innate responses may lead to the early death of numerous individuals; yet they seem to assure the survival of the population or species. The speed with which insects must respond to many kinds of stimuli led Wigglesworth to conclude that in the course of their evolution they have sacrificed the refinement of their perception and ability to learn in favour of the ability to react instantaneously to common stimuli.

In addition to not having the longevity conducive to learning, the usefulness of learned behaviour among insects is reduced by the complex life cycles that many of them display. The stimuli that are important at different times in the course of development may be quite different, and the various developmental stages often must respond differently to the same stimulus if they are to survive. This is exemplified well by those species that display a high level of structural and ecological divergence between the adult and immature stages. Clearly, the responses needed for survival may be very different, and the behaviour learned in one stage would be of little value to a subse-quent stage that must live under completely different circumstances. Experiments show,. however, that some insects can and do learn, but when viewed as a whole we find that learned behaviour is not dominant in the insect world. Humans, on the other hand, with brains made up of billions of nerve cells, and having comparatively long lives, display mainly learned behaviour. In fact, crying, smiling, and the suckling response of infants are about the only innate behaviours that can be identified in humans. Because we have a rather remarkable capacity to learn and solve problems through experience and practice, many of the statements we make about the behaviour of other organisms reflect the purpose or emotions we associate with our own actions. These tendencies to attach a purpose *(teleology)* or human feeling *(anthropomorphism)* to behaviour are tempting pitfalls, especially in the interpretation of insect activities, because many, particularly social species, display patterns of behaviour that parallel our own. Furthermore, these kinds of interpretation can obscure the real selective pressures and benefits that led to the evolution of the innate behaviour patterns displayed by many animals.

From the scientists' viewpoint insects are ideal subjects for basic behavioural studies. As pointed out by Eisner and Wilson, many of the sensory cells of insects arise directly from identifiable receptor sites built into the cuticle; these receptors can be manipulated experimentally from the outside with considerable ease. It is possible, therefore, to break behaviour down into basic response components and determine how tightly or uniformly programmed the behaviour is under different circumstances. The fact that learned behaviour does not introduce an unknown variable makes it possible to interpret more accurately the adaptive significance of each response.

Beyond the basic acquisition of knowledge of the way organisms have adapted through evolution, there is a pragmatic reason for studying insect behaviour. The successful management of both beneficial and harmful species depends on a thorough understanding of all aspects of their biology. The list of relevant questions that can be asked seems almost without end, but the answers we obtain could substantially alter a management practice. For example, we might be able to improve the efficacy of pollinators by preconditioning them to the fragrance of the crop we want pollinated. We may be able to explain the success or failure of applied biological control programmes on the basis of the presence or absence of key stimuli in the host's environment. We may be able to avoid crop damage caused by an influx of pests through an understanding of their migratory behaviour. We may be able to suppress a pest population by disrupting a pattern of communication important to its reproduction.

Most insect activities are linked inseparably to some form of stimulus-often several stimuli acting simultaneously. For example, the initiation of walking or flight may be triggered by an interplay of heat and light, and an increase in the intensity of the same stimuli may, in combination with a chemical stimulus, bring about the initiation of feeding. The analysis of these relatively simple components of behaviour and how they are initiated requires a careful study of the physiology of the sensory receptors and the central nervous system - subjects that are beyond the scope of this book.

Insect behaviour has been extensively investigated under natural and laboratory conditions, both approaches being valid, appropriate, and useful. The necessary first step is to describe an insect's behaviour as accurately and completely as possible *(ethogram)*. This should include consideration of the time of appearance of specific behavioural variations associated with physiological state (nutritional, etc.).

Following description, there are three primary objectives

1. Determination of the control of behaviour from the nervous. endocrine, and genetic points of view.

2. Elucidation of the function of the various behaviours in the insect's life, that is, the adaptiveness of behaviour.

3. Determination of the probable phylogenetic origin of behaviour, the rationale being that behavioural traits, like, morphological and physiological traits, are genetically based and represent adaptations that have arisen through natural selection.

One of the pitfalls encountered during the study of insect behaviour has been the temptation to ascribe human pruposiveness or goal seeking to many behaviour patterns. This is commonly referred to as *anthropomorphism* and should be avoided. Anthropomorphic usage tends to obscure the fact that adaptive behaviour is the result of natural selection and anticipation of a goal is unnecessary.

The approach of this chapter is to consider the basic kinds of behaviour characteristic of insects, the control of behaviour (nervous, endocrine and genetic), and the biological functions of behaviour.

KINDS OF BEHAVIOUR

In very broad terms, insects exhibit two kinds of behaviour, innate and learned. *Innate behaviour* to a large extent consists of a more or less fixed response or series of responses to a given stimulus or pattern of stimuli. The "more or less" in the preceding sentence should be emphasized, since innate behaviour is usually somewhat flexible and may be modified by experience (learning). Innate behaviour is generally considered to be based upon the inherited properties of the nervous system. On the other hand, *learned behaviour is* not inherited but is acquired through interaction with the environment during the life of the individual. Obviously, although specific patterns of learned behaviour are not inherited, the potential for learning is. In many instances it is difficult to determine whether an observed behaviour pattern is inherited or learned. There is no evidence of the ability to reason among insects, the observed behaviour patterns being explainable on the basis of innate patterns and learning.

Innate Behaviour

One of the striking features of insect behaviour is that much of it is performed without previous experience and without interactions with other members of the species. Such behaviour is inborn and is called *innate behaviour*. Some innate behaviour patterns seem to be comparatively simple, for example, the *reflexes*. Reflexes may involve only a part of the body, as in proboscis extension, or the whole body, as in the righting reflex, which occurs when an insect is placed on its dorsum. Reflexes can be grouped into two classes, *phasic and tonic*. Phasic reflexes are comparatively rapid and short lived and are involved in rapid movements such as proboscis—extension. Tonic reflexes are slow and long-lived and are involved with the maintenance of posture, body turgor, muscle tone and equilibrium. Reflexes vary in complexity, the simplest being mediated by a afferent impulse from a receptor to an interneuron and then along an efferent neuron to an effector, the *reflex arc*. Probably all reflexes are more complex than this, involving many more neural connections Individuals segmental ganglia may show considerable reflex autonomy. For example, in the silkworm moth *(Bombyx mori)* the oviposition reflex, which results from the ovipositor making contact with a surface, resides entirely in the caudal (last abdominal) ganglion.

More complex innate behaviour includes the various orientation patterns. *Orientation* may be defined as "the capacity and activity of controlling location and attitude in space and time with the help of external and internal references, i.e., stimuli." The terminology used in describing the kinds of orientation is confusing. Frankel and Gunn offer a classification scheme for the various kinds of orientation. They first recognize two broad kinds of orientation· primary and secondary. *Primary orientation is* the assumption and maintenance of the basic body position in space that is, the normal stance-either in a stationary or in a moving insect. For example, reflexes that keep a flying insect on an even course are responsible ffofor the primary orientation. *Secondary orientation is* superimposed primary orientation and has to do with the positioning of the insect response to various stimuli. These stimuli may be external (e.g., light humidity, temperature) or internal (e.g., the presence of a insect particular hormone). Secondary orientation may be of value to an insect by leading it toward potential prey or a potential host, or away from potential danger or an unsuitable environmentm, or toward a favourable one.

In addition to the primary and secondary divisions. Fraenkel and Gunn also offer a classification based on the mechanisms of orientation, dividing them into *kineses, taxes* and *transverse orientations.*

Kineses are undirected lc ocomotor reactions so stimuli, and hence there is no particular orientaigtion of the long axis of the body relative to a stimulus source. For exar ple is tsetse flies, *Glossina spp.*, there is an increase in activity in an arid atmosphere relative to activity in a humid one. This behaviour owould result in the insect "finding" and remaining in a humid atmosphere. The body louse, *Pediculus,* make fewer and fewer directional changes as temperature, humidity and odor increase as the louse mooves closer to a potential host.

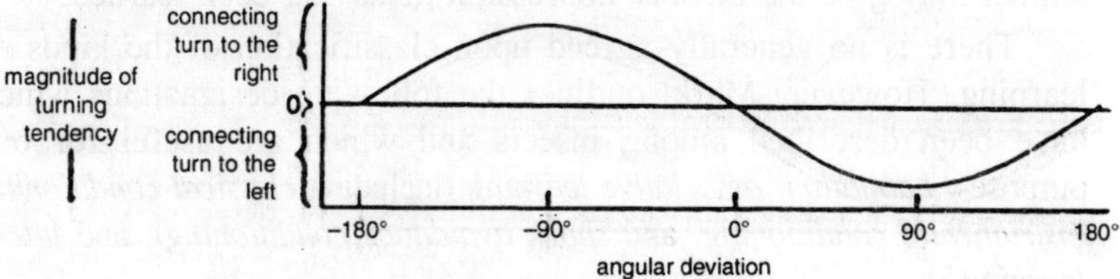

Fig. 1.1. Relationship between magnitude of turning tendency and angular deviation.

Taxes are different frpom wpeses in that they are directed responses relative to a stimuli us source. The long axis of the body takes on a definite orientation relative to the stimulus. The insect may move toward (positive) or away from (negative) the stimulus source. Theoretically, when an insect is maintaining a course relative to a stimulus, angular deviations from this course result in the initiation of a "turning tendency," that is, the tendency for the insect to correct for angular deviation by turning back to its original course. The magnitude of this turning tendency increases with increasing angular deviation. Hence, if the inagkiitude of this turning tendency is plotted as the ordinate and angular deviation as the abcissa, a sine curve is generated.

Taxes may be classified according to the stimuli involved (e.g., *phototaxis,* light; geotaxis, gravity; *Gznemotaxis,* air currents; *rheotaxis,* water currents; and *thigmotaxis*, contact).

A good example of a taxis is *klinotactic orientation.* An insect orienting klinotactically swigs all or part of its body back and forth across a stimulus field and 4ioves rtoward or away from the region of maximum stimulation, depending upon whether it is attracted or repelled by the particular kcind off stimulus. For example, when fly maggots have completed feeding a¢id will soon pupate, they move the head region back and forth until tluey are heading directly away.

Learned Behaviour

Although there are a number of possible definitions of learning, we shall use that of Thorpe: learning is "that process which manifests itself by adaptive changes in individual behaviour as a result of experience." Thus learning involves the accumulation and storage (memory) of environmental information and the subsequent effects of this stored information on an animal's behaviour. Extreme care has been necessary in calling a given pattern of behavior learned, since an innate pattern that appears at some point during the development of an animal may give the distinct impression of having been learned.

There is no generally agreed upon classification of the kinds of learning. However, Markl outlines the following designations which have been described among insects and which are useful for our purposes: *habitation, associative learning* (including *classical conditioning instrumental conditioning,* and *shock-avoidance conditioning),* and *latent learning.*

Habituation has occurred when a stimulus that initially evoked an escape or avoidance response no longer elicits such a response. This type of learning is common in insects and has been demonstrated relative to substrate vibrations, noise, visual stimulation, chemical repellents, etc. The ability of insects to learn in the fashion avoids unnecessary, energy-consuming behavioural responses. Classical conditioning was originally discovered by the Russian scientist Pavolv. In this type of learning, two stimuli are involved. One of the stimuli (the Unconditioned Stimulus, UCs) elicits a response (the Unconditioned Response, UCR). The other,. the Conditioned Stimulus (CS), prior to conditioning, does not elicit the UCR. However, when these two stimuli are repeatedly presented to an animal in very close succession (CS briefly preceding the UCs), the animal gradually begins to respond to the CS in the absence of the UCs. Classical conditioning has purportedly been shown to occur in honey bees. In these insects, the proboscis extension reflex can supposedly be conditioned to respond to the essence, coumarin, in the absence of sugar. In this case, poboscis extension is the UCR, the sugar is the UCs, and the odor of coumarin the CS. However, Alloway explains that the experiments carried out to demonstrate the conditioning of the proboscis extension reflex were insufficiently controlled. Thus, he concludes that classical conditioning has yet to be found among insects.

In instrumental (trail and error) learning, a response or series of responses is induced or inhibited by the presentation of a stimulus or pattern of stimuli [reinforcer(s)]. Maze learning is a good example of instrumental learning. A maze is placed between an insect and its nest, food, or some other strong positive reinforcer; or a negative rein-forcer, such as an electric shock, is applied for an incorrect response. If an insect is capable of learning the maze, the number of errors (wrong turns) will decrease with the number of trails. For example, ants are capable of learning a rather complex maze placed between themselves and their nest (positive reinforcer). Another example of instrumental learning is the "training" of honey bees to associate a particular colour with a sûgar (reward) source. Honey bees can also learn to associate odors with a food reward.

There are many instances where an insect has been conditioned by an inhibitory way. For example, a.mantis can learn not to strike an object it associates with an electrical shock.

Horridge showed that a single leg of a decapitated cockroach suspended above a container of electrified saline solution can be trained to stay above a level where it would receive a shock ("shock-avoidance learning"). The experiments were designed so that a test animal received shocks according to the level of the test leg, while a control animal received the same number and intensity of shocks, but in a random fashion, without regard to leg position. Later investigators demonstrated that even a single isolated ganglion in the ventral nerve cord could medate the shock-avoidance learning of a single leg. Eisenstein provides a review of the literature on this fascinating topic. Latent learning occurs without apparent reward or punishment. Social insects learn characteristics of the immediate vicinity of their nest such that they are able to find their way back from foraging fights. The predatory wasp, *Ammophila,* mentioned above, can find its nest despite forced detours and displacements.

Olfactory conditioning may be a form of habituation of latent learning. An example of this phenomenon is a situation in which exposure to an ordinarily repellent odor during a certain period of development results in the loss of repellencey of this odor to adults. This is the case in *Drosophila melanogaster,* the adults of which are normally repelled by the odor or peppermint oil. However, if the larvae have been reared in the presence of peppermint, they are strongly attracted to its as adults.

PERIODICITY IN BEHAVIOUR

Insects, along with all other organisms, have evolved in an environment characterized by regularly occurring, cyclic changes. Many of the activities of insects (locomotion, feeding, mating, oviposition, eclosion, etc.). also occur at regular intervals. Further, the timing of these recurring activities is adaptive; that is, insects, under natural circumstances, behave in ways that maximize chances for survival. Thus herbivorous (plant-eating) insects hatch from eggs in synchrony with the availability of host plants, insects become dormant and cold-hardly or migrate at a time that favours survival of an upcoming cold or dry season, and so on. The term *periodicity is* applied to such recurrences of behaviour. The patterns of recurrence of particular activities may be every 24 hours, monthly, annually, in coordination with the lunar cycle and so on. Periodicity in behaviour involves both endogenous and exogenous components. Endogenous components arise from within the insect and are ultimately related to its heredity. These include, in particular, rhythms, but the stage in a given physiological-behavioural cycle (e.g., gonotrophic cycle), developmental stage, and other endogenous factors may also play a role. Exogenous components arise from the external environment.

Rhythms are processes that are controlled by an *"innate time measuring sense"* or *"biological clock."* They characteristically conti-nue even when external conditions (temperature, light etc.) are kept constant. Most rhythms that have been identified have a period of approximately 24 hours and are referred to as *circadian* ("about a day") *rhythms*. Several examples of circadian rhythms have been identified in insects.

For example, cockroaches are nocturnally active; *Drosophila* emerge from the pupal stage at down; *Tettigonia* and other orthopterans sing at a particular time of day or night. A number of non-circadian rhythms are known, for example, the lunar emergence of certain chironomid flies and mayflies and the annual emergence of a species of dermestid beetles. A well-known example of non-circadian rhythmicity is found in the species of periodical cicadas *(Magicicada spp),* the various broods of which emerge en masse at 13-or 17-years intervals. These rhythms are sometimes called *gated rhythms* and are evident as population, as opposed to individual, phenomena. Thus, the members of a population are coordinated and reach and pass through a behavioural "gate" at the same time.

Some investigators have maintained that rhythms are under the control of undetected exogenous factors rather than endogenous biological clocks. However, evidence favours an endogenous source, particularly the fact that the phase of a rhythm does not change even if the animal is transported to a place on the earth far from the locality of entrainment ("clock setting"). In addition, two insects can be main-tained on different light regimes in the same room, all other factors being identical. Since rhythmic activities are found throughout the spectrum of living organisms (plant and animal), the general feeling is that the ultimate clock mechanism lies within cells. although its exact nature still remains a mystery.

Although rhythms are not controlled by exogenous factors, some exogenous factors are known to influence rhythms. Particularly signi-ficant are the external time cues *(Zeitgebers),* which set the phase of the rhythmic patterns of the individuals in a population. In a population under artificially constant environmental conditions (e.g., constant illumination) the rhythmic activities of the individuals may be out of phase with one another, but with the introduction of an appropriate time cue, they are set in phase and the activities of the individuals become synchronous. For example, mosquitoes (e.g. *Aedes aegvpti)* held under constant illumination oviposit arrhyth-mically, but when exposed to a dark period, even a very brief one, oviposit synchronously at 24-hour intervals thereafter. Under laboratory condi-tions, the phase of a rhythmic activity can be shifted about at the investigator's will. Among the exogenous factors that may act as time cues are length of the light or dark phase of a photoperiod ("a cycle consisting of a period of illumination followed by a period of relative darkness") light intensity, temperature, time at which food is available an others.

Emergence (probably rhythmic)usually occurs abruptly soon after sunset; it, however, the air temperature falls below 10°C, after larvae have left the water but before ecdysis has begun, some of them will return to the water and emerge the next morning after temperatures have risen again. For these individuals the diel periodicity of emergence has been changed by a short-term response to unfavourable exogenous factors, but the phase-setting of their rhythms has remained unaltered (as evidenced by their attempting to emerge at the normal time). Many external environmental factors display a 24-hour periodicity, which may result in corresponding periodicity in insects without the involvement of biological clocks. Among these are light intensity, moisture, temperature, wind velocity and various possible biotic factors. An example of how one of these factors may cause periodic behaviour is in the swarming of many species of mosquitoes, which is determined by light intensity. These insects continually possess the "drive" to swarm, but do so only under appropriate conditions of light intensity and can be induced to swarm for hours if the light intensity is held artificially at the appropriate level. Under natural conditions, the appropriate light intensity may be periodic (e.g., that which occurs during crepuscular periods). In this situation the mosquitoes would swarm "periodically."

THE CONTROL OF BEHAVIOUR

An insect is continually bombarded with multitudinous stimuli in space and time. Many stimuli provide information pertinent to the insect's life; many do not. In order to survive, an insect must respond to the *"right"* stimuli and do the *"right"* thing at the *"right"* time; escape, locate a food source, feed, locate a mate, copulate, oviposit, migrate, become dormant, and so on. That is, an insect's behaviour must be controlled.

How the environment is perceived and what behaviour is exhibited is a function of the nervous and endocrine systems. The functional characteristics of the nervous and endocrine systems are in turn determined by hereditary mechanisms. In this section, the involvement of the nervous and endocrine systems in behaviour and the role of heredity are discussed.

Nervous Control

Insect are especially good subjects for studying nervous function and behaviour since their behaviour tends to be stereotyped, but with some learning, and their nervous systems contain a relatively small number of neurons.

Aspects of nervous control of several motor patterns (especially flight, walking and sound production) have been studied, but very little is known about the neural control of complex sequences of behaviour. Techniques that have been used include observation of behaviour before and after decapitation, severance of nerves, ablation or destruction of all or parts of ganglia; electrophysiological recording from various nerves and ganglia *in vivo* and in isolated preparations; and use of various stains to elucidate structural connections. A rather ingenious approach has been addressed to the establishment of the location of the sites within the nervous system directly associated with various abnormal (mutant) behaviour patterns. This approach involves the use of genetic mosaics and the establishment of "embryonic faze maps." The operation of the nervous system is dependent upon the properties of individual neurons and the ways these neurons are associated with one another, both spatially and temporally. Behaviour is the result of interactions between sensory input, reflexes, and centrally generated neural patterns. More on reflexes and central patterns will follow.

Behavioural studies provide strong evidence for the filtering of sensory input *(stimulus filtering);* that is, from the many, diverse stimuli impinging on an insect, only certain ones or only certain aspects of a given stimulus are involved in eliciting a particular behaviour. Reflexes depend on sensory input for their occurrence. At one time insect, behaviour was though to be explainable solely on the basis of reflexes where one reflexive response provided the stimulus for the next reflex in line. For example, the repetitive motor patterns associated with flight and sound production were viewed as being controlled by cyclic reflexes, which would continue until inhibited by some other reflex. Although reflexes are undoubtedly important in behaviour, more recent research has revealed evidence for the generation of patterns within the central nervous system independent of sensory input.

It is known from behavioural and neurophysiological studies that patterns of behaviour may occur spontaneously without any external sensory triggering. Thus, the nervous system must be capable of spontaneously generating organized patterns of behaviour from within *(endogenously)*. A decapitated mantid will continuously turn and perform copulatory movements. The central nervous system in a locust with all sensory input from the head and wings removed still produces motor output nearly identical to the motor output recorded during normal flight. These activities are thought to arise from the spontaneous, preprogrammed activity of *neural pattern generators* in central nervous system.

If copulatory behaviour arises endogenously in the maintis, why doesn't the mantis behave this way all the time? How does the locust control flight if environmental conditions (wind, obstacles, etc.) vary? Why don't insects display all of their behaviour patterns simultaneously? Obviously endogenous activity must be regulated. Endogenous activity is thought to be regulated through excitatory and inhibitory stimuli from "higher centers" and by modulating input from peripheral sensilla, and probably directly or indirectly by hormones. In particular, the brain and subesophageal ganglion have both been found to exert excitatory and inhibitory influences on endogenously controlled motor patterns. These patterns seem to reside largely in the particular segments involved (e.g., the thoracic ganglia in flight). Thus, the mantid brain (which was removed with the head in the decapitated individual mentioned above) sends out impulses that inhibit the endogenous activity of the ventral chain ganglia relative to copulation. In the locust, there are wind-sensitive sensilla on the head, which help sustain flight, and also tarsal receptors, which stimulate flight when contact with the substrate is lost. In addition, there are stretch receptors, which aid in the regulation of flight, on the wing hinges and other parts of the wings and pterothorax. Thus, although locust flight patterns is centrally generated, the basic pattern is modifiable by peripheral, sensory input.

Something like neural pattern generators is probably involved in sequences of stereotyped behaviours more complex than simple motor patterns. For example, courtship in-the grasshopper *Gomphocerus rufus* occurs in a very definite sequence of simple behaviour patterns and this sequence is not interrupted by surgical action designed to block potentially controlling sensory feedback. Similarly, in *Drosophila,* an excited male will display all the intricacies of courtship in the presence of an anesthetized, unresponsive female. Thus complex behaviours appear to be programmed into the central nervous system as "tapes" of behaviour sequences and a given insect must have a complete bank of *"tapes"* to be played as appropriate.

For purposes of functional description the nervous system can be considered to have three major functional divisions. In one of these the enormous mass of incoming sensory input is reduced to a small series of sets of information which can serve to drive motor output. The second 'selects' from the sets the one which shall at a given time bee operative, and inhibits others. The third division contains neural generators whose purpose is to produce sequences of motor nerve impulses.

If the brain is involved in excitation and inhibition of the rest of the central nervous system, how is the brain, in turn, excited? Although little is known, there is evidence for excitatory input to the brain from the ocelli, compound eyes and antennae. Spontaneous, endogenous activity and endocrine factors probably also play a role in the levels of excitation of the brain. Little is known about the neurophysiological basis of learning, but destruction of parts of the brain has shown that some long-term memory must reside'there. Also, recall that isolated ganglia displayed shock-avoidance learning. Even habituation, probably the simplest form of learning, is not understood at the neural level. In any case, learning provides a way to modify or "rewrite" behaviour "tapes" through experience.

Endocrine Control

Hormones play major roles in insect behaviour. Through acting directly on the nervous system they can cause major overall changes in patterns of behaviour. Whereas strictly neural mechanisms usually mediate the short-term, sometimes split-second, behavioural responses to rapidly changing external and internal environmental demands (potential attack by a predator, an obstacle encountered during flight, etc.) endocrine mechanisms typically exert . their influence over the longer term, coordinating behaviour with less immediate environmental demands (changing seasons, changes in the availability of food, etc.). Thus strictly neural mechanisms are involved with escape responses, maneuvering during flight, and the like: endocrine mechanisms with development of migratory behaviour or dormancy, changes in feeding behaviour, development of adult behaviour patterns, development of sexual receptivity, and so on. In the terminology of the section on the nervous control of behaviour, hormones are commonly involved in determining which reflexes can be elicited and which behavioural "tapes" are played in a given circumstance.

Interfacing of the nervous and endocrine systems where the latter acts in a "switching" fashion on the former may explain, at least in part, how the very large array of behaviour patterns displayed by insects can be packed into their comparatively small, simple nervous systems.

The determination of hormonal influences on behaviour have usually been based on one or more of the following criteria

1. Correlation of hormone secretion and a particular behaviour pattern.

2. Application of hormone or implantation of active glands inducing a behaviour pattern sooner than it would ordinarily occur.

3. Correlation between removal of an active gland and disappearance of a specific behaviour.

4. A combination of "3" and subsequent restoration of the specific behaviour by hormone application or implantation of active glands.

Obviously, the fourth criterion provides the strongest evidence for hormonal control of a given behaviour.

Riddiford and Truman recognize two categories of hormonal effects on behaviour: hormones can act as *modifiers* or as *releasers* of behaviour.

When a hormone acts as a modifier, it alters the responsiveness of an organisms. Where a given stimulus previously elicited one kind of behaviour, a different behaviour occurs. The hormonal effects on behaviour as described earlier are as modifiers. A recent, excellent example of a hormone acting as a modifier is the influence of ecdysone on the biting behaviour of female *Anopheles fneebomi* (Culicidae, mosquitoes, Diptera). This mosquito does not take blood meals once ovarian development has been initiated. Ecdysone, which is secreted by the ovaries, inhibits biting. This was concluded on the basis that biting inhibition does not occur after removal of the ovaries and is restored by either replacing ovaries or injecting ecdysone.

When a hormone acts as a releaser of behaviour, a specific behaviour pattern occurs within a few minutes of secretion. This situation is analogous to the action of nervous input eliciting a behavioural response, but is much slower in occurring (minutes vs. milliseconds). An example is the *phallic nerve stimulating hormone* in the cockroach *Periplaneta americana*. This hormone can be extracted from the corpora cardiaca and when injected into male cockroaches causes the abdominal movements characteristic of copulation.

The *"eclosion hormone"* (eclosion meaning pupal-adult ecdysis in this context) secreted by the brain (neurosecretion) and corpora cardiaca in the moth *Antheraea pemyii* acts both as a releaser in triggering pre-eclosion behaviour and as a modifier buy "turning on" adult behaviour.

Genetic Control of Behaviour

There are many examples of the demonstration of genetic control of insect behaviour. Not surprisingly, a great deal of work has been done with *Drosophila melanogaster* and other *Drosophila* species as well as a number of other kinds of insects. An extensive treatment of the genetics of behaviour is far beyond the scope of this text. It is hoped that one day we will understand the chain of events occurring between the action of genes in protein (enzyme) synthesis and the expression of behavior. Although there has been some progress, really very little is known. Investigators are approaching genes and behaviour in a number of different ways. A few examples follow. There are several examples of gene mutations in *Drosophila* that change a behaviour pattern. An early example was a sex-linked mutant with yellow body colour instead of the normal gray. Males of these yellow mutants were less successful in mating than the gray wild type.

In are instances, it has been possible through breeding experiments to account for particular behaviour patterns on the basis of the action of single genes. An outstanding example of this is the work of Rothenbuhler. Rothenbuhler studies two inbred lines of honey bees, one that had been selected for resistance to American foulbrood (a disease of honey bee larvae) and another that was susceptible. He noted a distinct behavioural difference between the two lines; the resistant line removed foulbrood-killed larvae relatively soon after death (Hygienic behaviour), and the susceptible line did not (non-hygienic behaviour). Genetic analysis revealed that the action of two sets of dominant recessive genes on different chromosomes would account for the results of breeding experiments between the two lines. One set of

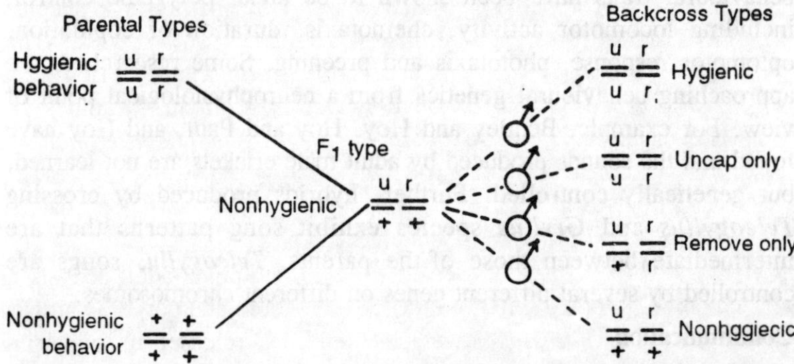

Fig. 1.2. Genetic hypothcaia to explain hygienic and nonhygienic behaviour in the honey bee. u = gene for uncapping (recessive), and r = gene for removing diseased larvae (recessive). + = dominant alleles; that is, no uncapping or no removal of diseased larvae.

alleles involved uncapping of the cells in which diseased larvae were developing; recessive allele, uncapping and dominant allele, no uncapping. Thus homozygous recessives displayed uncapping behaviour. Homozygous dominants and heterozygotes did not. The other set of alleles involved removal of diseased larvae; recessive allele, larvae removed and dominant allele, diseased larvae not removed. Homozygous dominant and heterozygotes did not remove diseased larvae. The "remove only" group was identified by artificially removing the caps from cells containing diseased larvae and subsequently observing the removal of diseased larvae.

Most behaviour patterns are probably under polygenic control, and *directional selection experiments* have been useful in establishing whether a given behavior has a genetic basis. In selection experiments, "individuals are selected at high or low extremes of a distribution in the hope of forming separate high or low lines in subsequent generations". If a trait does not have a genetic basis, then attempts to select for extremes would fail. A good example of a selection experiment is the work of Hirsch and Erlenmeyer-Kimling. They showed that with selection. *Drosophila melanogaster* that had previously been assumed to be negatively geotactic could be separated into both positively and negatively geotactic lines. Following establishment of "extreme" strains, it has been possible in some cases to evaluate the degree of involvement of different chromosomes. For examples, in the case of geotaxis in *Drosophila,* genes on each .,:the three major chromosomes were found to exert an influence. In *Drosophila,* several other behavioural traits have been shown to be under polygenic control, including locomotor activity, chemotaxis, duration of copulation, optomotor response, phototaxis and preening. Some researchers are approaching behavioural genetics from a neurophysiological point of view. For example, Bentley and Hoy. Hoy and Paul, and Hoy have found that the sounds produced by adult male crickets are not learned, but genetically controlled. Further, hybrids produced by crossing *Teleogyllus* and *Gryllus* species exhibit song patterns that are intermediate between those of.the parents. *Teleogyllus* songs are controlled by several different genes on different chromosomes.

Communication

Communication in one form or another is part of every organism's life at all levels of complexity. Thus, for example, the nucleus communicates with the cytoplasm in directing cellular activities; cells communicate with one another as cooperators in a multicellular organism both during development and in the fully developed organism; tissues, organs and organ systems communicate with one another via nerves and hormones; and finally, organisms communicate with one another. At this point we are specifically interested in communication between organisms. At this level, we may define *communication* as the influence of signals from one organism on the behaviour and/or physiology of another organism, with the outcome being beneficial to the *sender, receiver,* or both. It its broadest sense, then, communication involves members of the same *(intra-specific)* or different *(interspecific)* species. Thus a worker honey bee dancing on the hive to give information about the location and direction of a nectar source is communicating, and so is a bug when it releases a repugnant chemical in response to a threatening predator. One could say that virtually any aspect of an organism, even something as basic as colour or form of the body, can be involved in influencing the behaviour and/or physiology of another organism and is hence a means of communication. Communication often involves the use of specialized structures or methods by the sender and/or the receiver. Communication systems have evolved independently many times in insects.

Although systems of communication can be grouped in various ways, such as the type of information conveyed, we will discuss this topic from the standpoint of model of communication utilized by insects, specifically *tactile, acoustical, visual* and *chemical*. Sensory mechanisms are channels of reception. Mechanisms of sending (signal output) include sound and light production and chemicals produced by exocrine gland. Discussions directly pertinent to insect movement.

As mentioned above, communication may be between members of the same or different species. Intraspecific communication is involved in species recognition, sexual recognition, alarm, and social coordination. Interspecific communication is also involved in species recognition (e.g., signals from a plant attracting a pollinating insect) as well as aggression, defense, etc. Tactile communication has been the least studied. This form of communication is limited to situations where direct contact is possible, as during courtship and copulation. Wilson describes a form of communication to explain nest building in termites. Instead of direct touch, information is passed from one individual to another by a product of work. Thus a termite responds to a portion of already constructed nest by adding more material. This response is released by the presence of a physical structure. Wilson includes this form of communication as part of a broader category, *somatectonic communication,* which he defines as "the evocation of any form of behaviour of physiological change by the evidence of work performed by other animals, including the special case of the guidance of additional work."

The ability to perceive sounds is found in several groups of insects.

However, members of at least five orders are known both to "hear" and to produce distinctive sounds: Orthoptera, Hemiptera (both Heteroptera and Homoptera), Lepidoptera, Coleoptera and Diptera. Interspecific acoustical communication tends to be mediated by unpatterned sounds, such as *"warning" sounds,* while intraspecific communication typically involves highly patterned sounds. As intraspecific signals, sounds are involved in aggregation, sexual behaviour, aggression, alarm, and social interactions. Acoustical signals are very effective in that they can operate over relatively long distances, can be modulated in many different ways, can operate in the dark, can provide directional information, and so on. Acoustical signals in insects are monotonal, but vary in intensity and pattern of pulses.

Visual communication is common in insects. Visual signals have a great advantage in that they can provide a large amount of information. Consider the possibilities for variation in all of these parameters. Some insects are bioluminescent and use light production and reception as a mode of communication. However, most insects use light indirectly, that is, reflected or transmitted by something else. Visual signals are involved in reproductive behaviour, aggressive displays (e.g., in territorial behaviour of dragonflies), in defensive startle displays, etc.

Chemical communication is by far the most common form of communication among insects (in fact among animals in general). Chemical signals act over large distances, but they are not easily modulated and thus are used mainly as on-off signals, for example, to indicate sexual readiness in a female. They may also give directional information as in the case of a chemical trail. A given chemical signal may be a single compound or a mixture of compounds and may have been synthesized entirely by the insect or may have been obtained from the environment, especially from food.

Chemical signals can be classified on the basis of whether they mediate intra- or interspecific communication. Chemicals that function intraspecifically are called *pheromones.* For example, when ants are threatened or injured, they may release chemicals that induce dispersal from an area among foragers or aggressive behaviour in the vicinity of the nest. These chemicals are acting as *alarm pheromones.* Chemicals involved in interspecific communication are commonly grouped as *allomones or kairomones.* An allomone is emitted by a member of one species and induced a response that is adaptively favourable to the emitter. For example, the repugnatorial substance released by a bug in response to a predator would be acting as an allomone. A kairomone is adaptively favourable to the receiving organism. For example, the mosquito *Aedes aegypti is* attracted by lactic acid (as well as other compounds) in human perspiration. In this situation, the mosquito (receiver) benefits, and hence the lactic acid is acting as a kairomone. In many ants, bees, wasps, and termites the same chemical can function both as an allomone and a pheromone. For example, in ants formic acid can act as a defensive allomone and alarm pheromone that alerts nestmates to an intruder. Likewise a volatile or mixture of volatiles may act as both a pheromone or a kairomone. In Scolytidae (Coleoptera), for example, the aggregating pheromone may also act to attract predators and parasites of the beetles.

INSECTS IN GROUPS

Insects display many gradations between solitary behaviour and complex, organized social behaviour. However, comparatively few insect species are truly *social (eusocial);* a few thousand perhaps, and these are found in only two orders. Isoptera (termites) and Hymenoptera (ants, bees, wasps and relatives). Matthews and Matthews provide a useful classification of intraspecific insect associations other than sexual interludes. They divide interactions into aggregations, simple groups, primitive societies, and advanced societies *(eusocial* insects).

Group behaviour is thought to provide a number of different benefits; including protection as an result of such things as collective displays and more efficient detection of potential predators, increased efficiency in detection and utilization of food, and moderation of adverse physical environmental factors. Insects that produce defensive secretions and/or display warning colouration no doubt derive increased protection by pooling their defensive capabilities. Wooly apple aphids, *Eriosoma lanigenim* (Homoptera, Eriosomatidae), secrete waxy material, which gives their bodies a whitish, bushy appearance. Disturbance of aggregations of these insects causes them to rhythmically move their bodies at the same time. This collective display gives the impression of a much larger organism. Honey bees are very efficient food users by virtue of their ability to communicate the locations of food sources to one another. During the winter, honey bees form into tight clusters, which provide protection from freezing temperatures. Many insects form into loose, temporary *aggregations* under certain circumstances. These aggregations may result from common attraction to a particular habitat. Attracting stimuli include a particular temperature, light condition, food, an particular chemicals. Aggregations may also result from mutual attraction independent of external conditions. Examples of aggregations are hibernating groups of ladybird beetles (Coccinellidae) commonly found in human habitations during the winter; cockroaches, which are often found in feeding aggregations; and night time clusters of usually conspecific (members of the same species) bees or wasps.

Simple groups are characterized by coordinated movements. Examples are migrating groups of butterflies and locusts. Grouping in the *primitive society* category range from simple parental care of offspring beyond oviposition *(brood care)* to interactions that border on true social behaviour. Reciprocal communication is typical, and cooperation in nest construction and defense is common. Several examples of brood care and nesting behaviour are given in the preceding section. Additional examples of communal nesting include webspinners (Embioptera), which construct and inhabit networks of silken tunnels, and tent caterpillars (Lepidoptera, Lasiocampidac), which cooperate in the construction of silken shelters in which they pass the night. During the daytime, tent caterpillars forage along the branches of the host tree. They communicate by depositing chemical trails in association with feeding success. Other individuals follow these trails preferentially.

Three traits are generally agreed upon as characterizing eusocial insect behaviour.

1. Conspecific individuals cooperate in brood care.

2. There is a division of labour based on reproduction; that is one or more fecund individuals reproduce while essentially sterile individuals serve as a labour force.

3. At least two generations serve in the labour force; that is, offspring assist parents during part of their life.

Behaviour that includes only one or two or these characteristics is viewed as *presocial*. Many of the examples of primitive societies given earlier can be viewed as presocial.

A requisite for the development of social behaviour has been the evolution of systems of communication between the members of a society. In most cases communication in social insects involves chemical signals, although other sensory cues may also be important. Communication makes possible complex levels of behaviour involving groups of individuals, such as construction of complex nests. However, these complex patterns of behaviour result from the integration of relatively simple individual behaviour patterns, which are evident in the behavioural repertoires of solitary and presocial insects. Wilson outlines nine categories of responses to communicatory signals found in social insects. 1. Alarm; 2. Simple attraction (multiple attraction

= "assembly"); 3. Recruitment, as to a new food source or nest sites; 4. Groming, including assistance at molting; 5. Trophallaxis (the exchange of oral and anal liquid); 6. Exchange of solid food particles; 7. Group effect; either increasing a given activity (facilitation) or inhibiting it; 8. Recognition, of both nestmates and members of particular castes; 9. Caste determination, either by inhibitation or by stimulation.

The members of insect societies are divided into forms specialized for different functions within the colony. Differences among the various specialized forms or *castes* vary from solely behavioural (e.g., many bees and wasps) to both behavioural and morphological. Morphological differences, in turn, range from slight to extreme. Further, the particular role played by a given individual may vary with age, *temporal polytheism.* For example, an individual might be involved with brood care and nest maintenance during the first part of its life and with foraging during the later part (e.g., honey bee workers).

In the broadest sense, a social insect colony maybe divided into reproductives and non-reproductives. Reproductives may include one or more fecund females *(queen or queens)* and males. One or more *worker* castes are the numerically most abundant non-reproductives. In addition, forms specialized for colony defense, *soldiers,* may be present. In the termites, there are typically the colony-founding primary reproductives, the *king* and *queen, workers* (immatures in the lower termites and fully differentiated forms in the higher termites), and *soldiers.* The soldiers show a wide array of variation in the structure of the head, especially the mandibles, depending on species. In addition, termites usually have the potential for producing *supplementary reproductives* should the kind and queen be removed.

Whereas the termite worker castes are composed of both males and females, those of the social Hymenoptera are all females. Unlike the termites, male hymenopterans contribute little to the colony save insemination of the queen. In the ants, reproductives (in particular, queens), workers, and soldiers are morphologically well-defined. In a few species workers are divided into morphological subcastes, but in most they are divided into temporal subcastes (i.e., temporal polyethism). Castes are only behaviourally differentiated in most bees and wasps, but in a few species, for example, the honey bee. *Apis mellifera,* there are clear morphological differences between, queens and workers.

Origins of Social Behaviour

Eusociality is considered to have evolved once in the termites and at least eleven times within the Hymenoptera. Although there are many differences between the various groups, there are also many similarities as a result of convergent evolution.

The termites (especially the "lower" termites) have many traits in common with the cryptocercid cockroaches. Outstanding among these similarities is the fact that the lower termites and cryptocercid cockroaches are the only wood eating insects that depend on cellulase-producing symbiotic intestinal protozoans. These symbionts are passed tom one generation to the next by means of anal trophallaxis (trophallaxis is the exchange of alimentary liquids between individuals). This behaviour involves interaction between members of overlapping generations and hence rudimentary social behaviour. Termites may be viewed as "social cockroaches," bound together originally by the contact required to pass along the symbiotic protozoans and subsequently forming into complex societies.

TABLE 1.1. COMPARISON OF ASPECTS OF BIOLOGY. TERMITES VS. EUSOCIAL HYMENOPTERA

	Differences	
Similarities	*Termites Eusocial*	*Hymenoptera*
1. The castes are similar in number and kind,especially betw-een termites and ants.	1. Caste determination in the lower termites is based primarily on pheromones: in some of the higher termites it involves sex, but the other factors remain unidentified.	1. Caste determination is based primarily on nutrition, although pheromones play a role in some cases.
2. Trophallaxis occurs and is an important mechanism in social regulaion.	2. The worker castes consist of both females and males.	2. The worker castes consist of females only.
3. Chemical trails are used in recruitment as in the ants, and the behaviour of trail laying and following is closely similar.	3. Larvae and nymphs contribute to colony labour, at least in later instars.	3. The immature stages (large and pupae) are helpless and almost never contribute to colony labour.
4. Inhibitory caste pheromones exist, similar in action to those found in honeybees and ants.	4. There are no domin-ance hierarchies among individuals in the same colonies.	4. Dominance hierarc-hies are commoplace, but not universal.
5. Grooming between	5. Social parasitism betw-	5. Scial parasitism bet-

individuals occurs frequently and functions at least partially in the transmission of pheromones.	een species is almost wholly absent.	ween species is com-mon and widespread.
6. Nest odor and territoriality are of general occurrence.	6. Exchange of liquid anal food occurs universally in the lower termites, and trophic eggs are unknown.	6. Anal trophallaxis is rare, but trophic eggs are exchanged in many species of bees and ants.
7. Nest structre is of comparable complexity and, in a few members of the Termitidae *(e.g. Apicotennes. Macrot-emtes)*, of conside-rably greater comple-xity. Regulation of temperature and humidity within the nest operates at about the same lavel of precision.	7. The primary reproductive male (the "king") stays with the queen after the nuptial flight, helps her construct the first nest, and fertilizes her intermittently as the colony develops; fertilization does not occur during the nuptial flight.	7. The male fertilizes the queen during the nuptial flight and dies soon aferward without helpling the queen in nest construction.
8. Cannibalism is widespread in both groups (but not universal, at least not in the Hymenoptera).		

Two possible evolutionary pathways to eusocial behaviour among the Hymenoptera have been envisioned. The *para-social* sequence (which may have been followed by most social bees) began with *communal* behaviour involving cooperation in nest construction, but with separate brood rearing. Subsequently, cooperation in brood care was added (i.e., *quasisocial* behaviour). This was followed by the development of a non-reproductive worker caste *(semisocial* behaviour). With the development of cooperation of two or more overlapping generations the path to *eusocial* behaviour was complete.

The *subsocial* sequence of evolution of eusocialism has been envisioned for ants, social wasps, and a few species of: social bees (and also applies to termites as described above). In this'.'pathway, the female first remained with brood for a time following oviposition, but departed before eclosion *(primitively subsocial)*. Subsequently, the female remained with a newly hatched brood, and an overlap in generations occurred *(intermediate subsociall)*. In the next stage, the first generation offspring aid in the rearing of the next generation of brood *(intermediate subsocial II)*. Differentiation into reproductive and non-reproductive castes then led to complete sociality.

The "prime mover" in the evolution of social behaviour among Hymenoptera is considered to be *haplodiploidy*. The term *haplodiploidy* denotes that female Hymenoptera arise from fertilized eggs and are diploid, whereas males arise parthenogenetically and are haploid. As a result of haplodiploidy, female Hymenoptera are more closely related to their sisters than to their daughters. That is, on the average, sisters share 75% of their genes with each other but only 50% with their daughters. This fact has been advanced to account for the tendency for Hymenopteran societies to be characterized by *altruistic behaviour* between sisters. An example of altruistic behaviour is a honey bee "sacrificing" its life to protect the hive. When a honey bee stings, the barbed sting apparatus remains embedded in the victim and is ripped away from the bee's body; the bee subsequently dies. The notion of altruistic behaviour is linked to *inclusive fitness, a* central concept in the rapidly developing area, *sociobiology*. *Fitness,* in Darwin's original view, is a measure of the reproductive success of an individual, that is, an individual's relative contribution of genes to the next generation. Inclusive fitness is more encompassing than Darwinian fitness in that the contribution of an individual to the reproductive success of close relatives *(kin) is* considered in addition to an individual's own reproductive success. In this view, then, it is possible for an individual to be fit in the evolutionary sense without reproducing directly. Thus, the honey bee worker is not really making such a "sacrifice" after all since the act of apparent altruism actually enhances the reproductive success of her younger sisters, with whom she shares most of her genes and from among whom future queens will arise. The study of insect societies is playing a major role in the development of sociobiology.

2

PATTERN OF BEHAVIOUR

Insects are often said to exhibit *programmed behaviour,* which means that they are born with the capacity to behave in certain set patterns on receipt of appropriate stimuli. They are also *specialists;* that is, they are programmed to do certain things with great efficiency; other thing, not at all. The gardener's potatoes, may be defoliated by Colorado potato beetles, and perhaps, the eggplants too, but the gardener may feel confident that these insects will not touch the carrots or the strawberries. Female moths of the fruittree leafroller, a, pest of apples and other fruits, produce a volatile pheromone that attracts males of their own species from a considerable distance -yet the males do not respond to the pheromones of closely related species even though they differ only slightly in molecular configuration. A tiny parasitic wasp called *Aphytis holaxanthus,* when introduced from Hong Kong to Israel, virtually, wiped out the red scale insect of citrus in that country- a specialist *par excellence,* programmed to find and consume a specific host insect and no other. That is not to say that all insects are highly specialized feeders or that all behaviour is fully programmed - matters we shall consider shortly-only that these are two of the more striking features of insect behaviour features that we may sometimes turn to our own advantage.

INNATE BEHAVIOUR

Behaviour is the result of interactions between on organism and its environment by way of receptors (eyes, sensory setae, and the like) and effectors (muscles, exocrine glands). What an insect does at a given time is the result not only of the cues it is receiving from the outside but also of such internal factors as patterns inherent in the nervous system, physiological states (such as hunger or fatigue), kind and level of hormones circulating the blood, and learned information.

One of the striking features of insect behaviour is that much of it is performed without previous experience and without interaction with other members of the species. Such behaviour is inborn, or *innate*. Innate behaviour may be fairly simple and straightforward, as when a mated female imported cabbageworm butterfly, responding to specific cues, lays her eggs on a farmer's broccoli. Or it may be complex and capable of being switched from one behaviour pattern to another, as when a worker yellowjacket chews wool pulp from a fence post, mixes it with saliva, and applies it to the covering of a paper nest, all the time coordinating its behaviour with that of other workers and with the needs of the colony. There are several questions we may ask of such behaviour-none of them easy to answer, but all of them the subject of much current research:

1. How is innate behaviour inherited?
2. How is such behaviour stored so as to be called on when needed?
3. To what extent can behaviour be modified in response to environmental variables?
4. Can insects learn, and if so, what is the relationship between innate behaviour and learning?

Inheritance of Behaviour

Students of behaviour often use the term *fixed-action pattern* for segments of behaviour that are performed in a stereotyped, species-characteristic manner. Much of the performance of insects consists of fixedaction patterns, often following one another in series, guided by internal and external cues. These patterns are in large part coded in the genes and expressed by specific nervous pathways that link receptors and effectors. Much behaviour is polygenic, that is, under the control of numerous genes, each of which may code other aspects of development.

The effects of single genes on behaviour are known in a few cases. For example, the mutant *yellow* in the fruit fly *Drosophila melanogaster* causes males to vibrate their wings in courtship at a lower frequency than normal and thus reduces their success in mating.

These same mutants are also more strongly attracted to light than the wild type. Even complex behaviour has sometimes been shown to have a rather simple genetic basis. Certain strains of honey bees are resistant to the bacterial disease called American foulbrood. The workers of these strains uncap cells containing diseased larvae and pupae, remove them, and clean the cells. By appropriate crossing, Walter Rothenbuhler, of Ohio State University, showed that the switch from "hygienic" to "non-hygienic" behaviour was controlled at two loci, one affecting uncapping and the other removal of diseased offspring. The underlying behavioural mechanisms may well be under the influence of many genes, but in this case two pairs of alleles control the expression of hygienic behaviour.

Cricket Acoustic Behaviour

When a male field cricket reaches sexual maturity, he begins to sing a "calling song," a series of chirps familiar to everyone who has lived in the country. This song serves to attract females, who approach the male and mate with him. Males of each species of cricket produce a pattern of chirps characteristic of that species, and in each case the female is programmed to respond to the appropriate pattern; in this way the integrity of each species is maintained. When male crickets of a given species are reared from the egg in isolation, or with exposure only to the songs of alien species, they nevertheless produce their own species-specific song when they reach maturity. Thus, these songs are the output of fixed action patterns. Crickets of different species can sometimes be induced to mate in the laboratory, and in some cases the hybrids are fertile and can be backcrossed with the parental stock. As might be predicted, first generation males produce songs intermediate in pattern between the two parental species, and first-generation females are most attracted to these intermediate songs. With appropriate backcrossing, it can be shown that the song patterns shift in a manner corresponding to the proportion of genes inherited from each species. The different element (number of chirps, chirp interval) do not segregate independently, suggesting that many genes are involved in determining the neural basis of song production.

Cricket songs are produced by movements of the fore wings, in which a "file" on one wing is moved over a "scraper" on the other wing and sounds are amplified by a resonating membrane on the partially elevated wings. It is possible to insert very small electrodes into the nerves and muscles of a cricket through small holes in the cuticle, without interfering in any important way with the cricket's behaviour. It was found that only the first two thoracic ganglia are required for generation of the calling song, but the song is elicited by a "command neuron" emanating from the central body of the*protocerebrum).* This interneuron has complex interconnections with interneurons. and motor neurons within the ganglia, and the latter produce appropriately rhythmical contractions of the longitudinaland dorsoventral muscles -the same muscles that under a different nervous regimen produce flight.

The circuitry necessary for production of the calling song develops gradually through the several molts of the immature cricket, and premature activation of any part is prevented via inhibition fromthe brain. During development, new cells are added and new dendritic and synaptic connections are developed. A single motorneuron of an adult insect may have an enormously complex dendritic branching within the ganglion. The construction of this neuronalprogramming network is genetically determined, much as an electronic transistor might be built from blueprints and templates.

Inhibitory Centers

The importance of central inhibitory centers has been demonstrated in many insects, and it is probable that much behaviour is initiated by removal of inhibition rather than by stimulation. Destruction of inhibitory centers often results in abnormally high activity levels. Lesions in the

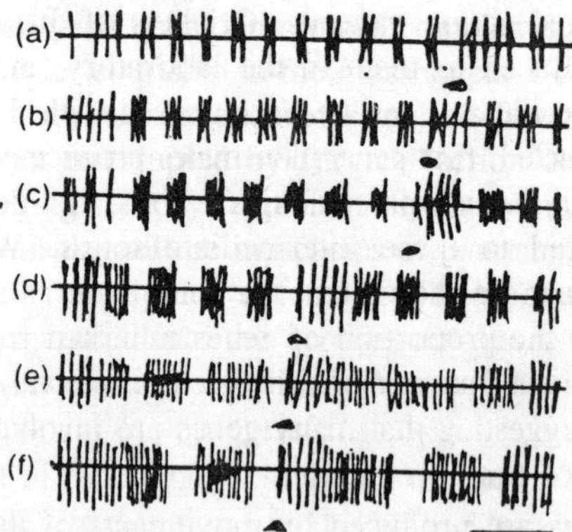

Fig. 2.1. Song patterns of two related species of crickets (a and f) and Fi hybrids (c and d) and backcrosses (b and e). Patterns shift in proportion to the ratios of genes inherited from each species.

protocerebrum of the brains of many insects produce an increase in locomotor activity that may last for hours. When a male cockroach is decapitated and electrodes placed in the nerve trunk to the genitalia, activity of the neurons climbs steadily and remains high for several hours. Such cockroaches show much movement of the tip of the abdomen, including the genitalia. In the praying mantid, this behaviour may have strong survival value, for the female mantid commonly attacks her mate and begins feeding on him from the anterior end. Kenneth Roeder and his colleages at Tufts University have shown that removal of inhibitory centers in the head of the male mantid produces greatly increased firing in the nerves supplying the genitalia. The result is that when the female has eaten the head of the male, the abdomen of the latter undergoes more vigorous movements than occur in the intact male. These result in prolonged copulation and implantation of a spermatophore in the female.

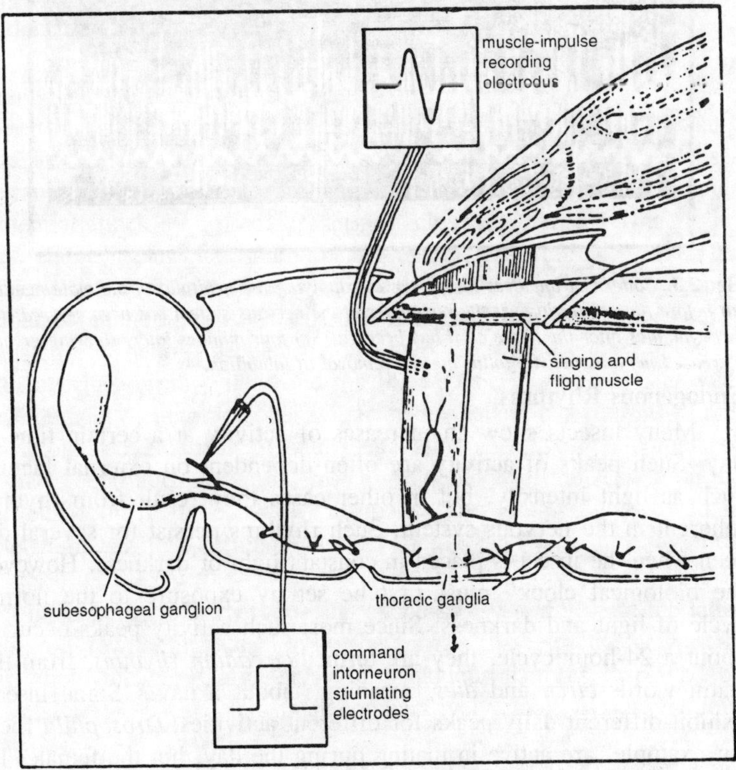

Fig. 2.2. Anterior part of a cricket nervous system with electrodes implanted to elicit and record impulses responsible for the song. The two shaded ganglia are sufficient for generating the song, via the thoracic muscles. Stimulation of the command interneuron induces singing been shown to possess daily rhythms of spontaneous firing. Though synaptic connections with neurosecretory cells, these may provide the generators of rhythmic activity. But for the present these matters remain in the realm of hypothesis.

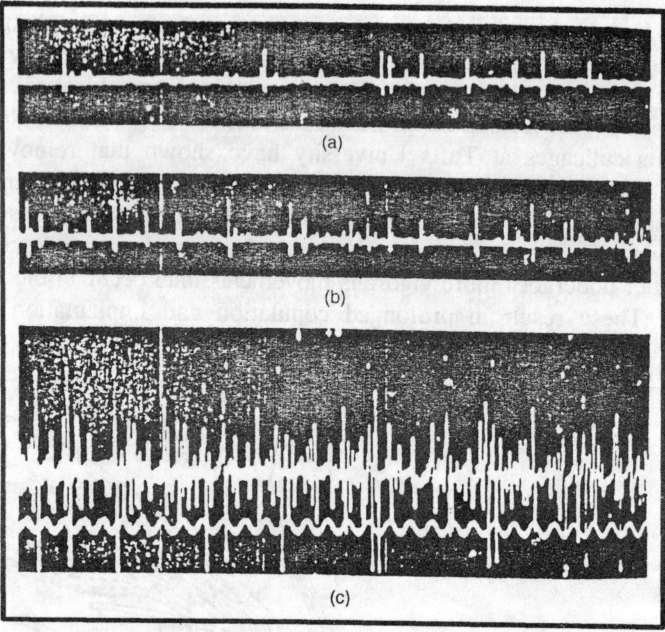

Fig. 2.3. Pattern of impulses in the nerves supplying the genitalia of the male mantid: (a) before the connection wit the remainder of the nervous system has been severed: (b) three minutes after the nerve cord has been cut: (c) four minutes later, showing greatly increased nervous activity following the removal of inhibition.

Endogenous Rhythms

Many insects show an increases of activity at a certain time of day. Such peaks of activity are often dependent on external factors, such as light intensity, but in other cases they result from rhythms inherent in the nervous system. Such rhythms persist for several day seen when the insect is placed in constant light or darkness. However, the"biological clock" must first be set by exposure to the normal cycle of light and darkness. Since most such activity peaks occur on about a 24-hour cycle, they are termed *circadian rhythms,* from the Latin words *circa* and *dies,* meaning "about a day." Some insects exhibit different daily peaks for different activities: *Drosophila* flies, for example, are active in mating during the day, but the females lay most of their eggs in the evening. Endogenous rhythms are normally independent of temperature, at least within the normal temperature range of the species. They are also largely independent of hunger and other physiological states. Indeed, little is known regarding the control of endogenous rhythms. Cells in certain parts of the brain have

Any basic response that can be performed spontaneously the first time an appropriate situation presents itself is clearly *unlearned* and is referred to as *innate behaviour*. Often, a number of inherited responses are combined into complex patterns of behaviour that, although having the appearance of a learned reaction or procedure, are not the result of prior experience. On the other hand, a simple response maybe modified by experience and thereby qualify as *learned behaviour*. Consequently, in the absence of experimental evidence, the distinction between innate and learned behaviour can be difficult.

INNATE BEHAVIOUR

Innate or inherited behaviour consists of a wide range of responses; some involve meovement and some do not. The responses are most commonly classified as *reflexes*, *Kineses*, *taxes* and *transverse orientations*.

REFLEXES

The simplest form of innate behaviour is called a reflex. The rapid involuntary withdrawal of your finger from a hot object is a typical reflex reaction. This simple form of response involves a receptor

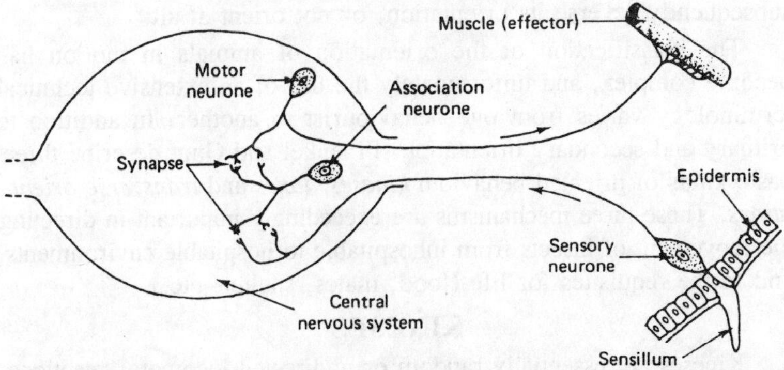

Fig. 2.4. A simple reflex are of the type involving an association neuron.

organ complete with at least one sensory neuron as well as a motor neuron connected to an effector organ, in this case a muscle. When dendrites of the sensory neuron are excited, an impulse flows along the nerve to the end of its axon. The impulse is then transmitted across a synapse either to an association neuron and then across another synapse to a motor neuron or directly to a motor neuron; the axon of the motor neuron terminates in a muscle fiber. This simple pathway of stimulus reception and response, called *a reflex arc*. Some physiologists divide reflexes into two functional groups. *Phasic reflexes* are rapid, short-lived responses, involved in the rapid movement of one part of the body or the entire body. For example, many insects respond to a threat by suddenly taking flight, a reflex also known as an avoidance reaction. *Tonic reflexes,* on the other hand, are slow, long-lived responses that maintain posture, the position of the body is space, muscle tone and so forth.

Reflexes vary in complexity and usually occur in sequences or patterns coordinated within the ganglia of the central nervous system. The most apparent reflexes are those involved in the orientation of the body in space or relative to specific sources of stimulation. Jander defined orientation as "`the capacity and activity of controlling locating and attitude in space and time with the help of external and internal references, i.e., stimuli." The maintenance of the position of the body is often called *primary orientation,* whereas directional responses to stimuli are called *secondary orientation.* Most studies of individual behaviuor are concerned with secondary orientation. Such studies reveal a great deal about the stimuli that dominate behaviour but may be complicated by the current physiological state of the individual; the same individual may orient toward a stimulus at one time, but subsequently reverse its orientation, or not orient at all.

The classification of the orientation of animals in motion has become complex, and unfortunately the use of an extensive technical terminology varies from one behaviourist to another. In addition to primary and secondary orientation. Fraenkel and Gunn describe three basic kinds of oriented behaviour *kineses, taxes* and *transverse orientations.* These three mechanisms are exceedingly important in directing the movement of insects from inhospitable to hospitable environments, and to the requisites for life (food, mates, shelter, etc.).

KINESES

Kineses are essentially random or undirected locomotor reactions, the intensity of which varies with the intensity of the initiating stimulus; no particular orientation of the along axis of the body results. The simplest type of kinesis, called an *orthokinesis (orthos, straight; kine,* movement), is basically a movement response to a stimulus. For example, an insect that is inactive in total darkness may start to stir when exposed to a low level of light intensity. As the light intensity is increased slowly from darkness, an intensity is eventually reached at which the insect becomes active; this intensity is the threshold for the light stimulus for the individual being observed under the prevailing conditions. If the light intensity (the strength of the stimulus) is increased further, the rate of movement will increase as well, until some upper stimulus threshold is reached and activity ceases. In other words, there is a direct or straightforward relationship between the intensity of the stimulus and the intensity of the response, between a lower and an upper threshold.

Whereas an orthokinesis may lead to aggregations of individuals that have simply entered a zone of low-level stimulation and become inactive, aggregations are more likely to result from *klinokineses (klinein,* bend; *kine,* movement). Klinokinetic responses are characterized by a change in the frequency of random turns in relation to changes in the strength of the stimulus. When a stimulus is diffuse or occurs as a gradient, a responding insect may display orientation behaviour characterized by a number of random directional changes. This kind of orientation can assist an insect in the location of a stimulus source and can prevent entrapment in a zone where unfavourable conditions prevail. For example, an insect could locate food by following the odor gradient emanating from it; the orientation is straight while the intensity of the stimulus is constant or increasing, but when the stimulus is constant or increasing, but when the stimulus declines the insect makes a random turn. This pattern of alternating movements leads the insect to the source of the stimulus. Conversely, a klinokinesis in a temperature gradient could prevent an insect from being trapped because the turns would result in its leaving a zone where extreme temperature could cause immobilization.

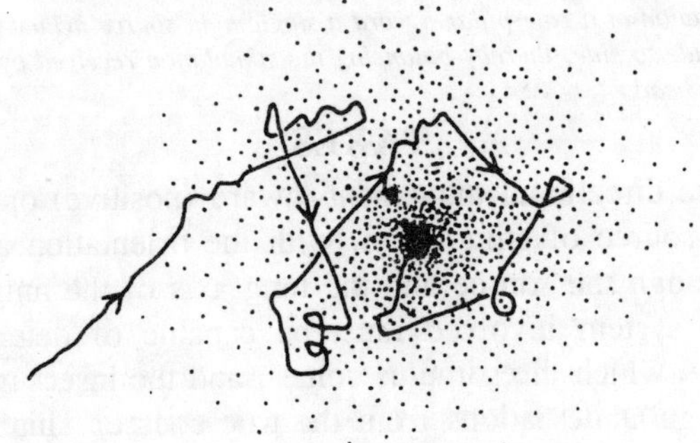

Fig. 2.5. The hypothetical track of inset orienting toward the center of a concentration gradient such as for an odor stimulus. The track remain straight as long as the strength of the stimulus remains constant or increase, but random turns are made whenever the strength of the stimulus declines.

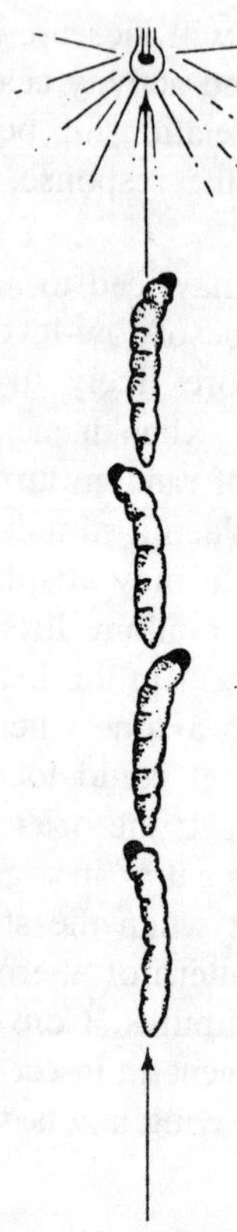

Fig. 2.6. Orientation of a caterpillar toward a single light source achieved by swinging the head from side to side, thereby balancing the stimulation received by the ocelli on each side of the head.

TAXES

Taxes are directional movement toward (positive) or away from (negative) a source of stimulation, with the orientation along a line that runs through the source and the long axis of the animal's body. The sensory system involved must be capable of determining the direction from which the stimulus comes, and the insect must be able to correct angular deviations from the true course. This is achieved by a turning tendency that increases in magnitude directly with increased angular deviation. A taxis, therefore, provides an efficient means of orientation. Taxes *(taxi,* formal arrangement) in general are classified according to the type of stimulus that initiates them [e.g., phototaxis (light), skototaxis (darkness), geotaxis (gravity), amenotaxis (air current), rheotaxis (water current), thigmotaxis (contact), and so on]. They are also classified according to the manner in which the animal deals with differences in the strengths of stimuli, stimuli from more than one source, or mixtures of stimuli.

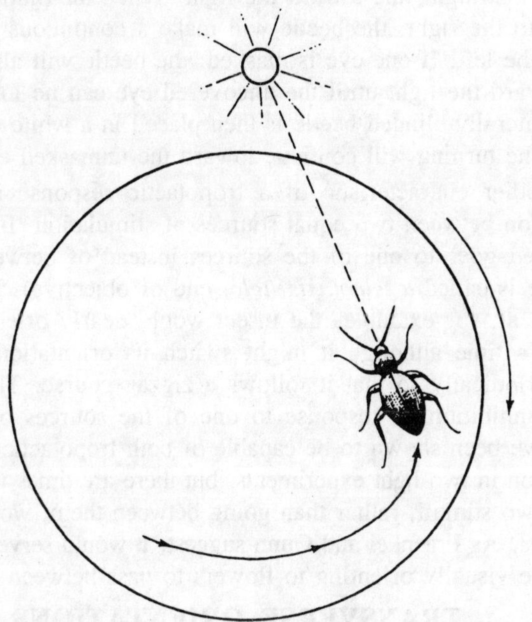

Fig. 2.7. The curved track of a photopositive beetle orienting to a fixed single-light source while walking on a slowly rotating platform.

Klinotaxes are orientation reactions to or away from a source of stimulation involving regular alternating deviations as a necessary component of the orientation. An insect displaying a klinotactic orientation swings the anterior portion of its body back and forthacross the field of stimulation because the receptor(s) are not equally accessible to multidirectional stimulation but move more or less directly to or away from the source of stimulation.

Tropotaxes (tropo, change) are characterized by a path that is straight and directly toward or away from the source of stimulation by the sue of paired receptors, one of which is located on each side of the animal's body. Insects responding in this way to light have been described as moving "as if spitted on a light ray." The sensory receptors must be arranged so they are not usually stimulated equally. In a light response, for example, if one eye is stimulated more than the other, the insect will turn toward the more intensely stimulated eye until a balance between the impulses from the two eyes is established in the central nervous system. A phototropotaxis can be demonstrated experimentally is several ways. If a photopositive beetle is placed on a platform is front of a point source of light, it will soon begin to walk in a straight line toward the light. When the platform is slowly rotated to the right, the beetle will make a continuous compensatory turn to the left. If one eye is masked, the beetle will also continue to turn toward the light until the uncovered eye can no longer see it. If the unilaterally blinded beetle is then placed in a white arena lit from above, the turning will continue toward the unmasked eye.

Another characteristic of a tropotactic response is a balanced orientation between two equal sources of stimulation. If an animal so stimulated goes to one of the sources instead of between them, the response is called *a teleotaxis (telo,* end or objective). In a two-light experiment, for example, the insect would dearly orient toward one light at a time although it might switch its orientation to the other light periodically so that it follows a zigzag course. This suggests a central inhibition of response to one of the sources of stimulation. Bees have been shown to be capable of both tropotactic and telotactic orientation in two-light experiments, but there are times when choosing one of two stimuli, rather than going between them, would be clearly beneficial. As Fraenkel and Gunn suggest, it would serve little purpose for a bee visually orienting to flowers to pass between them.

TRANSVERSE ORIENTATIONS

Transverse orientations result in an alignment of the body at a fixed angle relative to the direction of the source of a stimulus, but they do pot necessarily involve locomotion. The dorsal (ventral) light reaction, displayed by many insect, is an example in which locomotion is not psually involved. Yet it is important as a means of maintaining primary orientation. The dorsal (ventral) light reaction is one means by which freeswimming aquatic insects maintain their normal position; back swimmers, *Notonecta,* depend upon a ventral light reaction for maintenance of their seemingly upside-down position, whereas the position of the water boatmen, *Corixa,* is maintained by a dorsal light reaction.

The most common form of transverse orientation involving locomotion is the *light compass reaction*. Since the locomotion is ocquently oriented at a fixed angle, relative to a light source, it is an nportant aspect of navigation. Several simple'; experiments can be conducted to demonstrate this type of orientation. If a small black container is placed over an ant carrying food back to its nest (provided that it is not following a chemical trail) and is left there long enough for the position of the sun to change substantially, the ant, when released, will set out upon a new direction displaced by an angle equal to the angle of change in the sun's position, Similarly, if the image of the sun is blocked from the view of an insect navigating by a sun- compass reaction and a mirror is situated so that the insect sees a reflected image in a new position, it will change direction. The new track will be oriented at the same angle relative to the reflected image as the original track was to the real sun.

The sun, moon, and perhaps stars make particularly good navigational reference points because they are‘ so distant that some insects are able to maintain a constant orientation angle and travel in a straight line for a long distance. If the light source is close, its angle of incidence on the retina changes after the insect has traveled in a straight line for only a short distance, and the insect can only maintain its transverse orientation if it continually turns toward the source. This places the insect on a spiral course that ultimately ends at the light itself. It is in this manner that moths are though to fly into the flame of a candle. Many more example of responses to a variety of separate environmental stimuli could be presented, but they would serve little purpose.

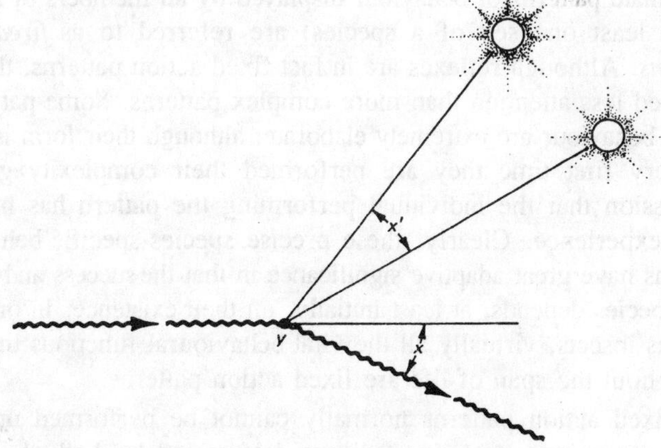

Fig. 2.8. Course followed by an ant employing sun compass navigation. After spending 2 hours in a dark box at pointy, the released ant changes the direction of its track by an angle (x) roughly equal to angle (x) subtended by the arc through which the sun traveled during the period of captivity.

Under natural circumstances, insects are not exposed to a single dominant stimulus as they so often are in laboratory experiments conducted to gain an insight into a specific response. In nature, insects are exposed to a variety of stimuli to which they must respond in an integrated way, and most species display what appears to be a great deal of response compatibility. For example, foliage dwelling insects that are- negatively geotactic are usually positively phototactic, whereas insects that live in the soil, are usually thigomtactic and display a negative phototaxis, a positive geotaxis, and a hygrokinesis.

COMPLEX INNATE BEHAVIOUR

Many behaviourists recognize three kinds of external stimuli, each of which has a different effect. There are stimuli that *arouse* the individual, stimuli that *elicit* a response, and stimuli that tend to *orient* the individual during its response. In some instances, different intensities of the same stimulus may arouse, elicit a response, and orient an individual.) found that when a resting male cabbage looper detects a low concentration of the female's sex attractant, it begins to move its antennae and vibrate its wings (arousal); if a higher concentration of the sex attractant is detected, the male moth takes flight (elicitation), and then follows the concentration gradient to its source (orientation). More commonly, however, a series of different external stimuli are involved in the completion of such complex patterns of behaviour.

Innate patterns of behaviour displayed by all members of a species (or at least one sex of a species) are referred to as *fired action patterns.* Although reflexes are in fact fixed action patterns, they have attracted less attention than more complex patterns. Some patterns, of innate behaviour are extremely elaborate; although their form is typical, the very first time they are performed their complexity gives the impression that the individual performing the pattern has had some prior experience. Clearly, these precise species-specific behavioural patterns have great adaptive significance in that the success and survival of a species depends, at least initially, on their existence. In organisms such as insects, virtually all the vital behavioural functions that occur throughout the span of life are fixed action patterns.

Fixed action patterns normally cannot be performed unless the organism is in a state of readiness determined by both the internal and external environments. This prevents the organisms from responding spontaneously to some stimulus when harm might result. When a state of readiness exists, however, the fixed action pattern is performed in a response to some specific form of stimulus called *a releaser.* For example, a newly emerged female with no ripe eggs in her ovaries would probably not be in a state of readiness for egg laying and, consequently, normal oviposition stimuli would not release ovposition behaviour. Similarly, the stimulation of stretch receptors in the gut, caused by the presence of food, often inhibits the release of a normal feeding response; when the ingested food has been digested, the inhibition is lost and normal responses to food are displayed. There is a range for most physical environmental parameters within which an insect is ready and able to initiate various patterns of behaviour. When some condition (e.g., heat) falls below a lower threshold or rises above an upper threshold, the insect will remain inactive even if the releaser stimulus is present. When the external environment is suitable and the insect is in a state of readiness, it may engage in activities that increase the likelihood of encountering a releaser stimulus. Most commonly, this so-called *appetitive behaviour* consists of an increase of locomotion. Some bark beetles that have completed their migratory flight above the forest canopy will begin to fly about within the stand where the chances of coming in contact with chemical cues produced by others of their own kind are greatly increased.

Often, the inhibition or release of normal patterns of response are under the control of inherited, internal rhythms that induce behavioural periodicity. The diurnal rhythms displayed by many insects provide ample evidence of some internal "biological clock." For example, cockroaches are usually active during the hours of darkness and inactive during daylight hours. However, if the time of light and dark periods are transposed, the roaches may still be active at about the same time, even though it is light. The original rhythm may persist for several days before any adjustment to the new light-dark cycle occurs. The subject of activity rhythms will be considered in more detail in the next chapter.

There must be a large amount of coordination between both basic responses and various complex fixed-action patterns so that adaptive behavioural sequences are established that serve the organism's day to day needs. Often such sequences involve both inhibitory and releaser stimuli. Even in a rather simple process, such as feeding, a wellcoordinated sequence of responses may be necessary. For example, blood-sucking flies will orient toward a host in response to the host's silhouette, odor, moisture, and temperature; as it approaches the host, the fly may extend its pro1 oscis in responses to an intensification of the same stimuli. A probing response may then be stimulated by odor, and the actual feeding by taste; feeding would stop when the fly was disturbed by a threat stimulus (perhaps some avoidance reaction on the part of the host) or when stretch receptors associated with a full gut inhibited the normal feeding response.

TABLE 2.1

A SUMMARY OF THE CHARACTERISTICS OF ORIENTED BEHAVIOUR

Response	*General Description*	*Type of stimulus Required*
Kineses	Undirected or random locomotion response, involving no orientation of the long axis of the body relative to the stimulus	A gradient of intensity
Orthokineses	The speed of locomotion, directly dependent on the intensity of the stimulus	A gradient of intensity
Klinokinesis	Frequency of turning, Direetly dependent on the intensity of the stimulus; can lead to aggregation	A gradient of intensity
Taxes	Directed reactions involving an orientation of the long axis of the body in line with the source of stimulation; toward stimulation-positive; away	A source of stiumulation that generates a beam or a steep gradient
Klinotaxis	Orientation reactions involving regular alternating deviations of all or a part of the body across the field of stimulation	A beam of light or a steep gradient
Tropotaxis	Direct orientation to or away from stimulation by simultaneous comparison of intensities of stimulation to each side of the body	A beam of light or a steep gradient
Telotaxis	Direct orientation to a light source as if a goal; if two sources are present, orientation is directly to one source	A beam of light from a point source
Transverse Orientations	Orientation of the body with or without locomotion at a temporarily fixed angle relative to the source of stimulation	A point source of light, directed light or gravity
Dorwal (or ventral)	Orientations so that light is maintained perpendicular to both the long and transverse axes of the body	Directed light light reaction
Light-compass reaction	Locomotion in a direction temporarily fixed relative to the source of stimulation	Light from a small source

Other patterns, however, involve complex successions of responses, among which the nest-building and provisioning activities of solitary wasps and bees provide excellent examples. In some species the sequence can be interrupted only up to a certain point, where as other species always seem to be able to resume an interrupted sequence here it was broken, and still others can switch from one sequence to another without apparent confusion. The potter wasp *Eumenes will* repair a hole made in its small earthen nest as long as it is under construction. But, once the wasp completes the nest and starts to provision it, she will not interrupt the latter part of the behavioural sequence even though the food she delivers may fall through the hole. The solitary leaf-cutter bee *Megachile* also engages in an elaborate sequence of nest-building steps. The female must first locate a nest hole of appropriate size. She then leaves the nest site in search of a source of leaves and petals of a kind suitable for the construction of the individual larval cells. The cell are constructed or oval pieces of leaf or petal, cut to precision with the mandibles, and carried separately to the nest. When the first cell is complete, it is provisioned with 7 to 12 loads of pollen and topped with a load of nectar. An egg is then laid on the store of food, and the cell is capped with several discs of plant material. One such cell may take from 1 to 4 days to construct and provision, depending on the weather and the availability of resources. A series of such cells will be made sequentially, the number depending upon the depth of the nest tunnel. Each step in this process involves different stimuli, plus navigation to and from the nest, and each act must be done in the appropriate sequence.

The nest-building behaviour of the solitary wasp *Ammophila campestris is* even more remarkable.. The sequence begins with the construction of a vertical burrow in the ground that, upon completion, is sealed with several appropriately sized pebbles. The female wasp then leaves the nest site in search of a caterpillar to serve as food for her larva. When she finds a caterpillar, the wasp stings it in successive segments to paralyze it and carries the immobilized prey back to the nest. The small stones blocking the entrance are removed so that the caterpillar can be dragged into the burrow, after which a single egg is laid upon it. The wasp then leaves the burro wand temporarily seals it with the same pebbles selected earlier. The female then collects additional caterpillars, temporarily sealing the nest after each one has been added. Only after the burrow is fully provisioned does the female engage in the final nest closing, which includes concealing the entrance by smoothing the dirt over it. What seems even more amazing is that

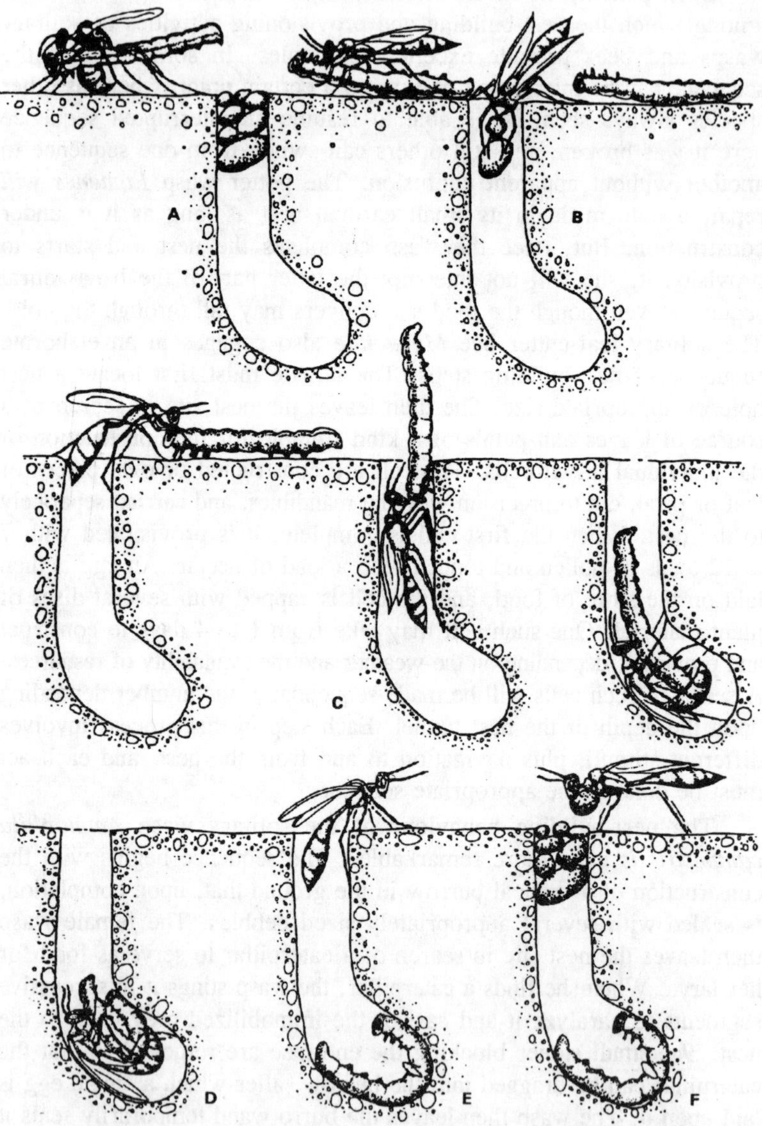

Fig. 2.9. The successive acts in the provisioning of a previously constructed nest by the solitary wasp Ammophila campesnis. After returning to the nest with a paralyzed caterpillar (A), the female removes the stones she has placed in the entrance (B) and drags the prey into the nest (C). The female then lays an egg on the caterpillar (D), climbs out of the nest (E). and replaces the stones (F).

A. campestris may have several nests in different stages of provisioning and can switch from one to another without any apparent confusion; in each case the sequence of steps dictated by the current status of each nest is adhered to rigidly.

LEARNED BEHAVIOUR

Learning has been variously defined, but almost any definition that implies some beneficial adaptive change in behaviour as a result of experience is acceptable. Learning implies some storage and retrieval of information (memory) that has a subsequent effect on the animal's behaviour. Learning, therefore, improves the chances that an individual will be successful by eliminating unnecessary expenditures of energy, increasing the likelihood of obtaining a reward or reducing some form of punishment. Consequently, it is not possible to measure learned behaviour directly but only to determine the extent to which the learning process has progressed. Among the insects, it is not a simple matter to determine what is innate behaviour and what has been learned, because their complex patterns often appear to have a well-defined purpose. Some behavioural acts of insects even give the impression of insight; the use of a pebble by a female *Ammophila* to tamp and smooth the soil over her nest provides a good example. Not all behaviourists are in agreement as to how different kinds of behaviour should be organized, and entomologists are not in full agreement as to the kinds of learning displayed by insects. Alloway, for example, identifies *conditioning instrumental teaming, shock avoidance learning* and *olfactory conditioning* as four examples of learned behaviour experimentally demonstrated among insects. However, other behaviourist claim that insects also display *habituation, latent learning imprinting* and even *insight learning*.

TABLE 2.2

CLASSIFICATION OF LEARNED BEHAVIOUR WITH INDICATION OF CURRENT EVIDENCE OF LEARNING IN INSECTS

Type of Learned Behavour	*Comments Regarding Insects*
Habituation	Probably common among insects (e.g., reaction of mosquito larvae to shadows)
Associative learning	Some experimental evidence of insect capability
Classical conditioning	(e.g., proboscis extension by blowflics)

Instrumental learning	Some experimental evidence of insect capability (e.g., maze experiments with ants; feeding studies with honeybees; shock avoidance reaction of cockroach)
Latent learning	Some evidence from inseects (e.g., orientation flights and homing among nest-building hymenopterans)
Insight learning	Circumstantial evidence only for insects; probably refined innate behaviour
Imprinting	No good evidence of imprinting in insects

HABITUATION

Habituation is recognized as the simplest form of learning. Unlike other forms of learned behaviour, it involves the loss of a fixed action pattern rather than the development of some new response. Basically, an organism learns not to respond to a stimulus that has neither reward nor punishment associated with it. Insects are routinely exposed to many stimuli, the response to which would result in a wasteful expenditure of time and energy; learning not to respond would therefore be beneficial. For example, mosquito larvae often spend considerable time at the surface of the water, periodically wiggling their way downward as an escape response to a shadow cast by an object overhead. However, they learn not to respond to the frequent passage of shadows that pose no threat, for example, those cast by overhanging foliage swaying in the breeze. Many such examples of habituation must occur throughout the Insecta.

ASSOCIATIVE LEARNING

Classical Conditioning

Classical conditioning, also called conditioned reflex or respondent conditioning, was first described by Pavlov following his now famous study in which dogs were conditioned to salivate in response to the sound of a bell by repeatedly ringing the bell immediately before a food reward. In all examples of classical conditioning presented since, an Un-Conditioned Stimulus (UCs) that elicits an Un-Conditioned Response (UCR) is provided immediately following a Conditioned Stimulus (CS) to which the *animal* would normally show no response. However, when the UCs and CS are presented in sequence over and over again, the animal becomes conditioned to respond to the CS when it is presented alone. Studies involving honeybees have long been cited as evidence for classical conditioning in insects. When offered a mixture of a sugar syrup reward (UCS) and the chemical coumarin (CS), the bees respond by extending their proboscses. Studies have purported to show that when the usual UCS with withheld, the test bees would still display the reflex response to the coumarin. However, most insect behaviourists have considered the results of these studies to be inconclusive. Nelson provided more convincing evidence of

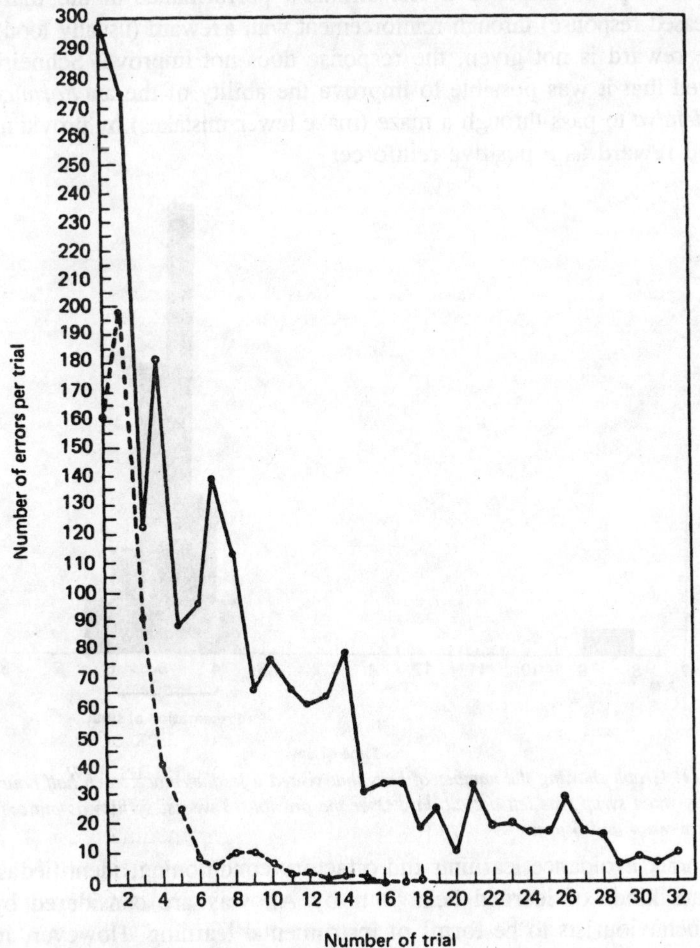

Fig, 2.10. The learning curve for the ant Formica pallide- fulva *in a six-point maze (solid line) compared to that for hooded rats (broken line).*

classical conditioning in insects with his carefully controlled experiments involving proboscis extension by blowflies.

Instrumental Learning

Instrumental learning, also known as instrumental conditioning and learning by trial and error, involves the modification of fixed action patterns through the application of *positive reinforcers* (rewards) and/or *negative reinforcers* (punishment). The most common form of instrumental learning involves the use of a maze. The basic technique is to attempt to improve a test animal's performance in the maze (increased response) through reinforcement with a reward (usually food); if the reward is not given, the response does not improve. Schneirla showed that it was possible to improve the ability of the ant *Formica pallidefulva* to pass through a maze (make fewer mistakes) by providing a food reward as a positive reinforcer.

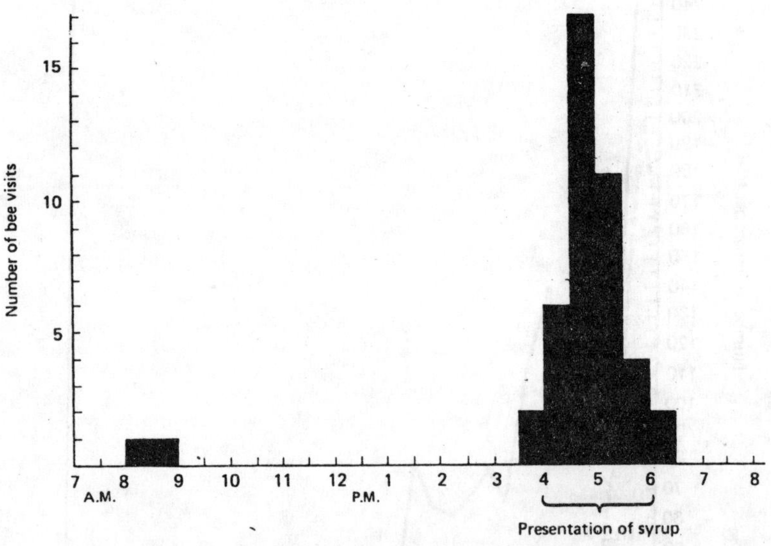

Fig. 2.11. Graph showing the number of bees that visited a feeding place. each half hour on a day when syrup was left out all day. Over the previous 3 weeks, syrup was put out only between 4 and 6 p.m.

Shock avoidance learning and olfactory conditioning, identified as separate kinds of learned behaviour by Alloway are considered by most behaviourists to be forms of instrumental learning. However, in some respects they bear more similarity to habituation than learning by the process of trial and error. Horridge provided the best evidence for insect shock avoidance learning. He was able to train cockroaches not to lower one leg beyond a certain level by attaching the leg to an electrical circuit that generated a shock (negative reinforcement) when it was lowered into a saline solution. The olfactory conditioning demonstrated in *Drosophila* also suggests learning. When larvae were reared in the presence of peppermint oil, normally an adult repellant, the resulting adults were attracted to it.

The experiments conducted to demonstrate the colour and chemical senses of bees have also provided insight into their learning ability. When a dish containing a 50 per cent sugar solution is set among similar dishes containing distilled water on a checkerboard of coloured squares, foraging bees will soon aggregate at the dish containing sugar. If that dish is subsequently switched with a water dish on a different coloured square, the bees will continue to visit the dish on the coloured square where they previously found the syrup. This association of a stimulus (colour) with a reward (sugar syrup) clearly qualifies as learning.) If a few bees are marked when they visit a feeding station placed on one square of a coloured checkerboard, it is possible to construct a learning curve similar to that for the ants traversing a maze. The more experience each marked bee obtains, the fewer wrong landings it will make even when the position of the learned coloured square is changed. Bees also seem to be capable of learning the association between the time of day and the availability of food. When presented with sugar syrup at a feeding station at a particular time for several consecutive days, they learn when to visit the station at the appropriate time. If food is subsequently made available all day, the bees will only visit the feeding station at the time food has been there previously until they learn the new situation. Under natural conditions, this time memory is believed to be important in enabling the bees to visit certain flowers only during those hours when they make their pollen and nectar available.

Latent Learning

Latent learning has been defined by Thorpe as '...the association of indifferent stimuli or situations without patent reward." Although this definition suggests a special variant of associative learning, the lack of an obvious reward or some immediate benefit creates an interesting distinction. Many insects, particularly the nest-building hymenopterans, make reconnaissance flights during which they display a capacity to learn the position of their nest relative to landmarks and celestial cues. Subsequently, these insects are able to locate their nests without difficulty following foraging trips at some distance.

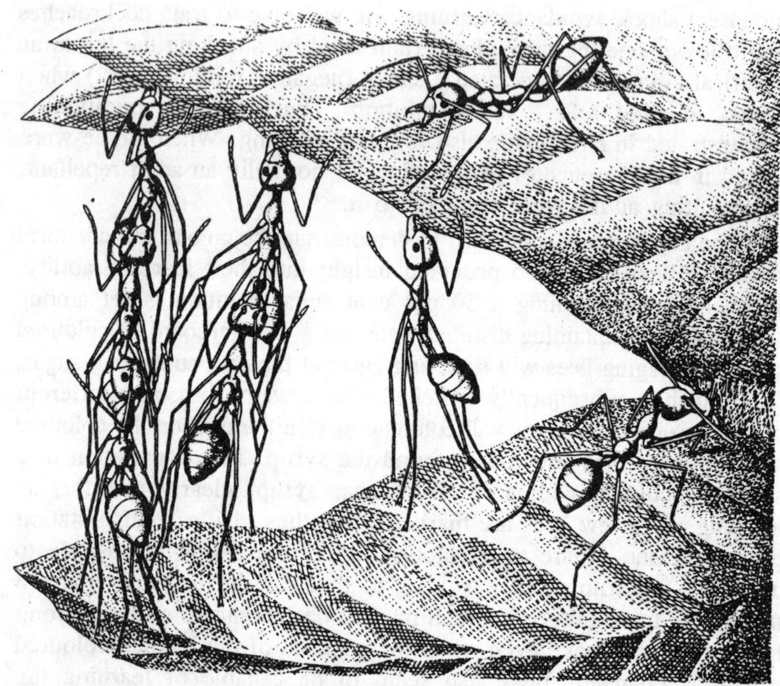

Fig. 2.12. Workers of the ant Oecophylla srnaragdina *drawing together leaves that are tied in place with silk produced by the larva held in the mandibles of the worker on the tight.*

Insight Learning

Behaviourists recognize insight learning to be the most advanced form of behaviour. The employment of insight, or solving problems by reasoning rather than trial and error, is a technique that humans take for granted. As a result, when we see an individual of another species solve a problem too rapidly to have conducted any trials, we conclude that insight was involved. Insects often display behaviour that creates the impression that they are capable of insight. For example, a female *Ammophila* returning to her nest on foot, with a caterpillar slung beneath her, will almost instantly detour around obstacles placed in her path.

The use of a tool to perform some task is usually considered an example of insight learning, and there are at least two examples of tool using among the insects. As noted earlier, *Ammophila* females have been seen to use a small pebble held in the mandibles to smooth the ground over their nests, and the ant *Oecophylla smaragdina* holds one of its own larvae in its mandibles and uses the silk the larva produced to tie leaves together as a nest. However, if all or a reasonable percentage of a species engage in the same behaviour, it is clearly a fixed action pattern even though it may appear to be insight. There seems to be little doubt that the behaviour of insects is dominated by inherited reflexes and response patterns and that innate behaviour serves the insects well. There is also little doubt that some species of insects are capable of modifying their behaviour on the basis of experience. Obviously, we have much yet to learn about the behaviour of insects. With careful experimentation and sophisticated new techniques, the years ahead will almost certainly reveal some remarkable discoveries.

Maze Learning

Considering the fact that associative learning is widespread in insects, it is not surprising that some insects are capable of learning to run a maze containing a terminal reward or an initial punishment. One of the first persons to demonstrate this behaviour was C.H. Turner. Turner's maze was a simple, homemade one, built of copper strips over a pan of water. An overhead light served as a negative stimulus: a jelly glass "home" at the end of the maze, as a reward. After only a few trials most cockroaches greatly reduced the time required to complete the maze. Turner also performed some of the earlier experiments on maze learning in ants. These studies were extended by the late T.C. Schneirla and his colleagues at the American Museum of Natural History. When ants were compared with white rats in the same maze, all of the rats ran the maze with only a few errors after 6 trials; and with no errors at all, after about 12 trials. However, the ants continued to make a few errors after 30 trials. Nevertheless the contrast between the two groups is less than one might have predicted, considering the vastly more complex nervous system of the rat. The contrast is greater when the animals are asked to run the maze in reverse. Rats show a considerable transfer of learning from the original running whereas ants perform as if tit were a wholly new problem. Similarly rats quickly accommodate to a small change in the maze, while ants again act as if it were a different maze. These and other experiments reveal that insects have little capacity for *transfer learning* that is, learned patterns cannot be readily transposed to a different situation.

Locality Learning

Insects that have a nest in which their brood is reared must be

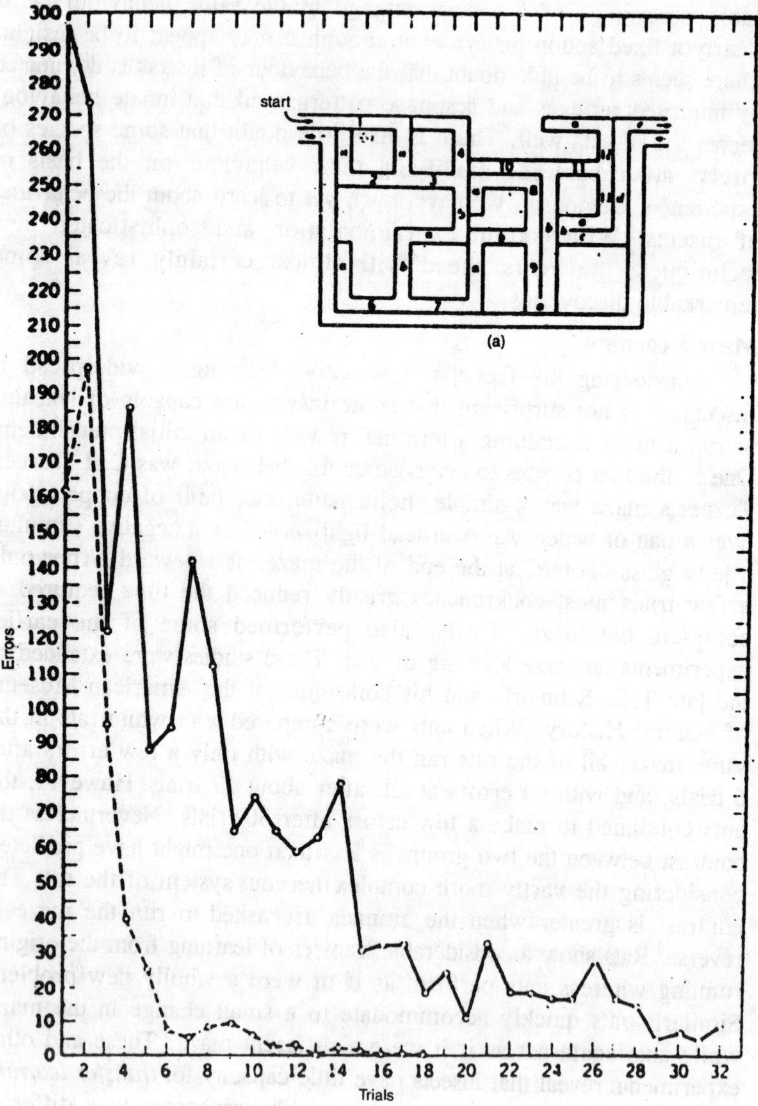

Fig. 2.13. (a) Maze used for testing ants and hooded rats, the ants being rewarded with their nest at X: the rats, with food. (b) Performance of the ants (solid line) compared with that of the rats (broken line).

able to leave the nest to hunt and to return quickly and with a minimum of errors, even though there may be small changes in the environment during their absence (for example, a change in the angle of sunlight or disturbance to landmarks by wind or other factors). Such insects perform an *"orientation flight"* or *"locality study"* on leaving the nest, during which they learn a configuration of cues at, surrounding, and often some distance from the nest entrance. Such *locality* or *exploratory learning is* a form of *latent learning,* in the sense that the insect is not rewarded until somewhat later, on the return flight.

The ability of bees and wasps to learn a complex configuration of landmarks quickly and to return without error from a considerable distance is a continual source of amazement. In *Philanthus* digger wasps, an orientation flight of 6 to 10 seconds is sufficient to ensure safe return to the nest. Many wasps prepare a series of nests in the course of the season, each time learning the necessary configuration of landmarks. Most remarkable are certain species *ofAmmophila* that maintain three to five nests at one time, each at a different stage of development of the egg or larva in the nest. In this instance the female visits each nest in the morning (remembering the precise location of each), inspects the cell contents, then supplies each nest with the needed number of prey or closes the nest permanently if the larva is mature. In the latter case she no longer visits that site but prepares a new nest and remembers its location until its larva has reached maturity. The nature of homing behaviour varies considerably depending on the terrain and whether the insect returns over the ground or in the air. Species of *Ammophila* digger wasps that bring their caterpillar prey to the nest by walking over the ground appear to have an intimate knowledge of the area in which the nest is located. In the bee-wolf, *Philanthus triangulum,* a species that flies with its prey, the Dutch behaviourist Niko Tinbergen and his co-workers found that cues close to the nest entrance are all-important, and returning females can be n0led by displacement of landmarks. Further experiments showed that the wasps do not learn individual landmarks as such, but their configuration the displacement of one or a few objects may cause only temporary disorientation. Members of a related genus, *Bembix, ofte 1* nest in broad expanses of bare sand yet return successfully to them nests. They do so by learning subtle cues in concentric circles from the nest, including even the profile of the distant horizon. O' they usually return successfully even when there are major disturbances to a portion of their nesting area. Wasps have been known to fotage as much as 3 kms from their nest and to return successfully after many hours delay. Honey bees, when their hive is displaced, will remember its previous location as much as 12 days later.

Homing is by no means entirely dependent on memorization of landmarks. Many ants, for example, lay odor trails, which colony members follow to food sources and back to the nest. As we have seen, manyy insects are able to navigate by maintaining a constant angle with the direction of so3filibht, or even with the plane of polarization of light, if they cannot see the sun directly. Even these basic mechanisms of orientation may involvelearning. For example, honey bees have an excellent *temporal memory;* that is, they are bale to compensate for the passage of time and Consequent change in angle of the sun's rays while they are foraging. Honey bees can be taught to fly to a food source at a certain time of day; infact, they are able to remember over a period of days the location and time of presentation of several different food sources. Accurate, tune compensation for sun compass orientation may always require experience. Ants tested early in the spring, without much experience with the sun, maintain a constant angle with the sun regardless of the passage of time; but later in the season they are able to adjust their angle of progress in accordance with changes in the sun's position.

Insect Memory

There is evidence that insects readily forget learned behaviour when the training period is quickly followed by performance of a different task. Foe example, when cockroaches are trained to avoid shock and then immediately forced to run a treadmill, they tend to lose their learned ability to avoid shock. But if they are forced to remain quiescent for a period right after training, there is no such loss of memory. Thomas Alloway, of the, University of Toronto, showed that when yellow mealworm beetles were trained to run a maze, both learning and retention were enhanced when the beetles were exposed to cold (1.7°C) between training sessions and during retention periods of 1 to 10 days. Evidently reduced activity improves then entrench.nent of learned behaviour. Some learned behaviour is, however, deep-seated and less readily extinguished by performance of other activities. Even after ether anesthetization, honey bees are able to find their hive readily, and as we have seen honey bees remember over several days both the location and the time of presentation of food sources. Such learning is evidently more firmly fixed in the memory and not readily extinguished. Perhaps the existence of two "levels" of memory, short

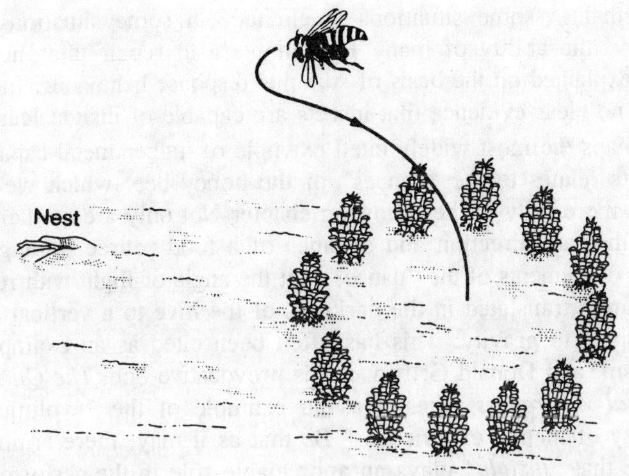

Fig. 2.14. The bee-killing digger wasp Philanthus uses physical landmarks to recognize its home nest. In an experiment, Tinbergen allowed wasps to become accustomed to a circle of pine cones around its nest entrance; hen then moved the circle while the sasp was away, and on its return the wasOp sought the entrance of its nest in the circle of pine cones as before.

term and long term, helps to explain why some learned responses are easily extinguished, while others persist much longer, as in insects with a permanent nest (such as the honey bee), which are able to remember over many days not only nest location but place and time of food availability. Evidence of the role of the mushroom bodies in memory was reviewed in the previous chapter.

Mental Capacities of Insects

In summary, one may say that insects are able to learn many things, from simple reflex behaviour (such as shock avoidance) to the complex homing behaviour seen in various social insects. It is not surprising to learn that some persons have maintained that insects are capable of *insight learning* that is, the ability to combine processes learned from previous experience to meet a new problem. One example that is often cited is "tool using" in the differ wasp *Ammophila:* When the female has completed a nest, she fills the, burrow and then ponds the soil in place with a small pebble held in her mandibles and later discarded. Recent students of *Ammophila* have concluded that this behaviour is by no means "intelligent," as sometimes claimed. Rather these wasps are performing inherited patterns capable of the usual find tuning to the precise environmental situation. In some species of this genus, "tool using" is optional -that is, this behaviour is a latent pattern that in some situations is elicited, in some situations not. Similarly, the ability of many Hymenoptera to repair their nests is readily explained on the basis of stimulus response behaviour. In sum, there is no clear evidence that insects are capable of insight learning.

Perhaps the most widely cited example of higher metal capacities in insects relates to the "dances" of the honey bee, which we shall describe more fully in the following chapter Not only are worker bees able to indicate direction and distance of a food source by angle an duration of elements of the "dance," but the angle of flight with respect to the sun is translated in the darkness of the hive to a vertical angle with respect to gravity. This has often been cited as an example of symbolism, and Donald Griffin, in his provocative book *The Question of Animal Awareness,* cites it as an example of the "evolutionary continuity of mental experience." Be that as it may, there is no real evidence that `*Insight"* plays an appreciable role in the performance of this remarkable behaviour. Rather, it is a supreme example of the process of evolution achieving startling results with a nervous system of limited capacity. In general, insect learning is highly adaptive but limited to matters directly related to their specialized, programmed lives. What and how well they learn is related to the capacities of their sense organs and their nervous system, and ultimately to their genes. Honey bees learn to fly to feeding stations with blue or yellow markers in only 2 or 3 trials; but 7 to 12 trials are required if the markers are blue-green or black. They can be trained to arrive at a food source 24 hours later, but not at some other time interval- Perhaps it is unfair to ask what "human" traits insects cannot perform when it is clear that they can perform a great many insectan traits that are far beyond our capability.

RESPONSE TO THE ENVIRONMENT

We have been looking at the insect from the "inside out," asking questions about its equipment for dealing with the environment. We now change our focus slightly, asking what environmental cues are important, how they are received and processed, and how the insect responds on the basis of its internal state.

Much insect behaviour can be thought of in terms of *stimulusresponse,* although this simple statement conceals a multitude of variables. Response in influenced by many factors in the internal environment, as we have seen. *Stimuli* are those elements in the environment capable of eliciting a response. A stimulus for one species may be totally ignored by another -for example, a speciesspecific sex pheromone. Or a stimulus attractive to members of one species may repel members of another; for example, mustard oils repel many plant-feeding insects but are stimulants for larvae of the imported cabbageworm. Failure to respond is often an indication that a stimulus is not being received. A medieval control for fleas and bed bugs in churches was to declare them excommunicated. That they failed to leave was not a reflection of their religious beliefs; they simple were unable to detect the modulations of the human voice. On the other hand, certain insects are supremely capable of detecting and responding to certain sounds-female crickets to the songs of the males, moths to the ultrasonic cries of bats. In these and many other cases a built-in response mechanism, often called *a releasing mechanism, is* essential for survival and reproduction. The stimulus itself is in this case called *a releaser*.

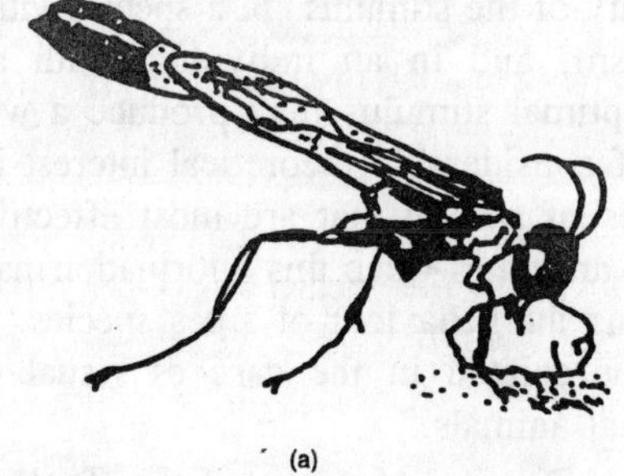

(a)

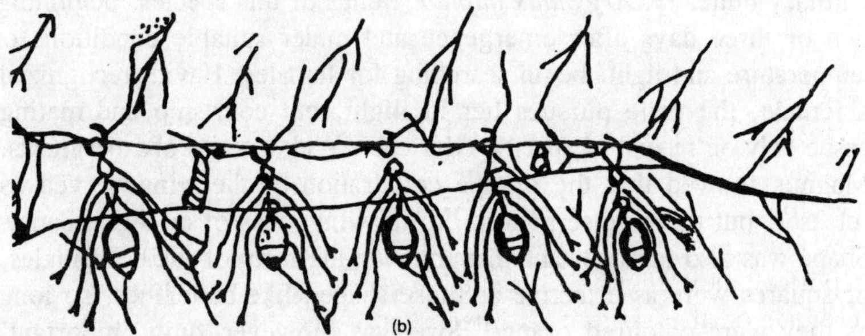

(b)

Figure. 2.15. Two examples of "tool use" in insects: (a) Ammophil: *digger wasp pounding the soil in her nest entrance with a stone (b) worker weaver ants using their larvae as "shuttles" to weave together leaves to make their nest (the larvae spin silk, but the adults lack silk glands).*

Insect often respond to stimuli that we cannot perceive except with special equipment: volatile pheromones, secondary plant substances, ultrasound, ultraviolet, and so forth. Of course, they often also respond to images and sounds within our own perceptual field. But any one species is likely to respond to only a few key stimuli; other stimuli elicit no response and often are no received at all. *Sensory filtering* is a term applied to the many instances in which only a few environmental cues pass through the "filter" provided by the insect's sense organs and releasing mechanisms. Moths' specialized receptors for ultrasound- and their deafness to sounds having no biological meaning for them - provide a superb example.

Stimulus Quality

Not all insect receptors are as "finely tuned" as the moth tympanic organs to the ultrasound of bats. Yet most behaviour is triggered by certain *sign stimuli* to which the insect is specially tuned to receive and to respond. Response will vary depending on the internal state and on the precise quality of the stimulus. In a species with an appropriate releasing mechanism, and in an individual with a high level of motivation, a suboptimal stimulus may produce a weak response or none at all. It is of considerable theoretical interest interest to know the precise qualities of stimuli that are most effective in eliciting a response -and there are times when this information may have practical value in manipulating the behaviour of a pest species. Stimulus quality is perhaps best appreciated in the case of visual cues, since we ourselves are "visual animals."

Some years ago Dietrich Magnus, of the Zoological Institute at Darmstadt, West Germany, made a study of sexual releasers in a fritillary butterfly, *Argymnis paphia*. Males of this species, beginning two or three days after emergence and under suitable conditions of temperature and light, begin searching for females. Having recognized a female, the male pursues her in flight, but courtship and mating ensue only on receipt of specific odor cues. With a series of experiments, Magnus showed that the orange colouration of the wings served as releaser, but the precise pattern on the wings was of no significance. Shape was also unimportant; Dummies in the form of circle, triangles, or squares were as effective as those shaped like butterflies, so long as they were coloured orange. Size was, however, quite important. Models smaller than the usual size of the female (surface area about 22 square centimeters) produced fewer approaches. But those larger than the female, in fact up to four times her surface area, were still more effective in eliciting a response. Magnus also showed that speed of wing flutter was important. When given a choice between a slow alternation of orange and black and one twice as fast, males showed a

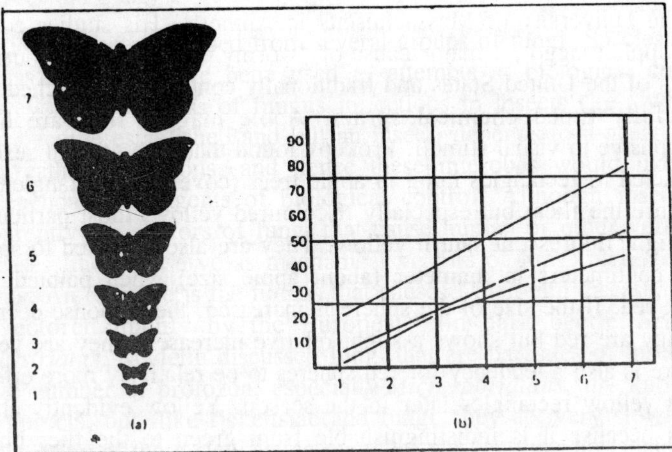

Fig. 2.16. Experiments on the effect of size of female on approaches by males of the butterflyArpnnis paphia: *(a) relative size of the seven models used, the third from the top being the normal size; (b) percentages of approaches by male (ordinate) to models of the seven size (abscissa).*

preference for the faster speed of flicker-up to about 75 alternations per second, which taxed the resolving power of the butterflies' eyes. But in nature females do not move their wings anywhere near this rapidly. Thus Magnus and discovered two ways in which visual stimuli could, be made *supernormal*: by increasing the size or by increasing the speed of flutter well beyond the normal. One might expect evolution to produce larger females with more rapid wing movements, since these qualities are more successful in attracting males. However, there are many other selection pressures operating to maintain the present size and speed of wing movement.

Magnus noted that fritillaries of both sexes approach objects coloured blue or yellow, since these are the colours of the flowers they visit for nectar. Niko Tinbergen and his colleagues, working on another species of butterfly, the grayling, found that in this species colour is of little importance in sexual pursuit, but hungry individuals of,both sexes show a strong response to blue and yellow. Similarly, the imported cabbageworm butterfly selects blue and yellow flowers for feeding, but the female selects green objects for oviposition.

Obviously stimulus quality cannot be evaluated except with reference to the internal state of the animal.

A striking example of the practical importance of understanding stimulus quality has recently been provided by Ronald J. Prokopy,now at the University of Massachusetts in Amherst. His studies concern the apple maggot, a major cause of "wormy" apples throughout many parts of the United States and traditionally controlled by a schedule of carefully timed chemical sprays. Apple maggot flies are highly responsive to visual stimuli. Prokopy found that flies of both sexes are attracted to rectangles hung in apple trees (covered with tanglefoot to capture the flies) but especially if coloured yellow, most particularly daylight fluorescent saturn yellow. They are also attracted to spheres 7.5 centimeters in diameter (about apple size) when painted tartar dark red. If the size of the sphere is increased, the response decreases if they are red but shows a slight relative increase if they are yellow. There is also a tendency for red spheres to be relatively more effective than yellow rectangles later in the season. Yellow evidently attracts flies because it is indistinguishable from green to the flies but has higher reflectance. Thus, it attracts them to apple foliage, which is a source of honeydew for the flies, while the red spheres possible oviposition sites for the females and mating sites for the males.

The possibilities of using these supernormal stimuli, either singly or in combination (red spheres on a yellow rectangle), for monitoring

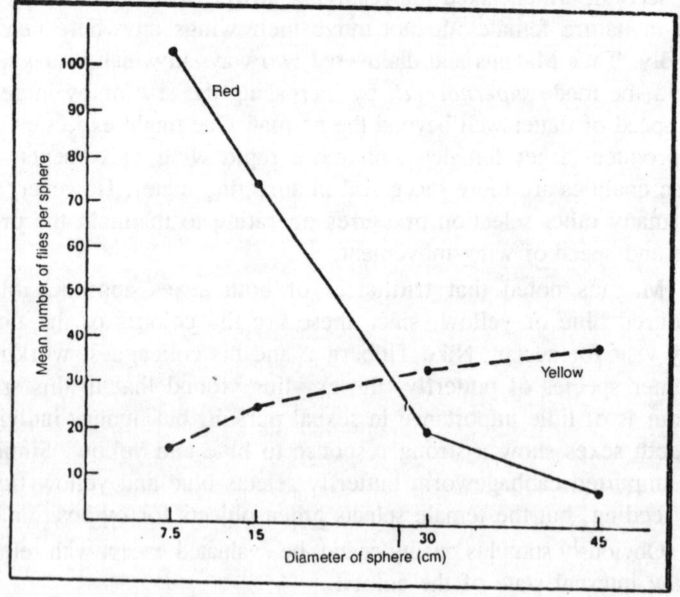

Fig. 2.17. Response of apple maggot flies to red and yellow spheres of various sizes. under orchard conditions.

or for reducing apple maggot population, is intriguing. In his own orchard, Prokopy placed 469 sticky-coated spheres in 81 unsprayed apple trees. He captured about 10,000 apple maggot flies on these spheres and discovered that the infestation of apples by maggots that season was 1% to 3% as compared to 97% to 98% in nearby unsprayed and entrapped orchards. While conditions in this isolated orchard may have been somewhat unusual, there is reason to hope that these techniques may be further refined and may someday be employed against some of the other serious pests in the fruit fly family (Tephritidae).

Reaction Chains

In nature, insects do not often perform isolated bits of behaviour but rather perform acts in continuous series, each act commonly dependent on completion of the preceding one and on receipt of appropriate stimuli. A comparison might be made with a car passing along a street with a traffic light at each intersection. Each block must be traversed before the next one can be started; at each comer one must have the appropriate stimulus in this case a green light and eventually one reaches a goal -in this case perhaps a supermarket. The goal in an insect might be copulation, oviposition, return to the nest with food, or some other essential act. Orientation will be especially important in the appetitive behaviour preceding attainment of the goal; and as we have seen, even taxes may be sequential. Use of the term *goal* does not, of course, mean that the insect purposefully proceeds to a perceived goal. Rather, goal orientation is a result of natural selection, which has produced a series of responses that, over time, have resulted in maximum survival and reproduction.

Such chains cannot often be short circuited by presenting a stimulus out of place. For example, if suitable prey is presented to a digger wasp while it is digging its nest, the wasp will show no reaction-such a reaction would of course be non-adaptive at that stage. If prey is presented right after a temporary closure but before the initiation of the hunting flight, it may also be rejected-but not necessarily so it the wasp's larva is large and hungry, for then the wasp's threshold of response may be low. If prey is removed from a fully stocked nest, before final closure is begun, the female may be induced to bring in additional prey to fill the nest before the closure is made. An attempt to outline the major steps in the nesting cycle of a typical solitary wasp, but in fact each step is capable of further analysis. Consider, for example, *'prey found."* Tinbergen has shown that in the bee-wolf this in itself is sequential and involves three different sensory

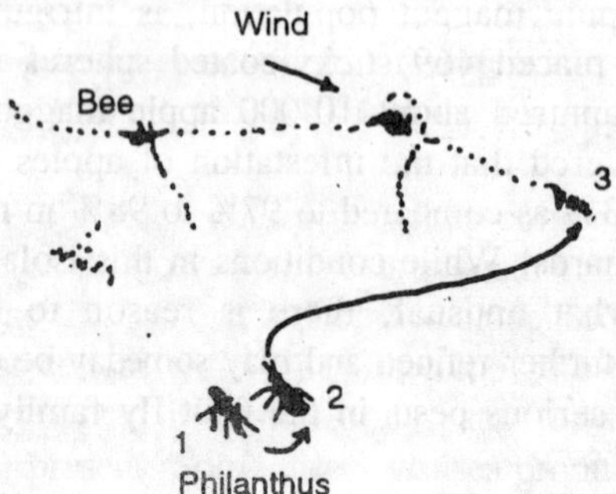

Fig. 2.18. Sequence of hunting behaviour of the bee-wolf, Philwukw.

modalities. The first response is to a visual stimulus, which must be moving and of about the right size at this stage there is no response to the odor of the normal prey even when it is presented close to the wasp. Having spotted potential prey, the wasp flies downwind of it, and at this point odor becomes the dominant stimulus;

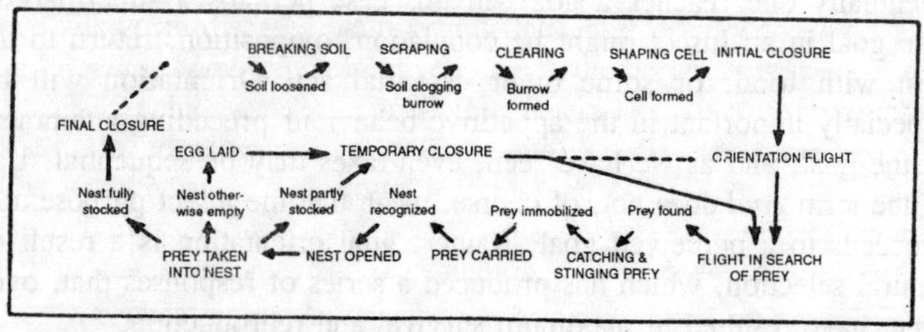

Fig. 2.19. Model of the reaction chain of a nesting female digger wasp. Fixed-action patterns are shown in capitals,; resumed releasers, in small letters.

dummy prey are not approached unless supplied with bee odor. Finally, the wasp flies to, seizes, and stings the prey, evidently employing tactile stimuli.

It is convenient to think of reaction chains as of two general types: *insect-environment* (including both physical and biological factors, other than members of the same species), and *insect-insect* interactions. Examples of the first include the nest preparation and hunting behaviour of the digger wasp just considered; the search for and discovery of a host plant, and subsequent oviposition, by a moth or butterfly, and the like. Exchange of signals between members of the same species is properly termed *communication* and is considered in greater detail below. To be sure, many reaction chains include interactions both with conspecifics and with the environment – for example, the mating swarms of midges, in which individuals come and stay together by means of common responses to landmarks and to air currents and other physical factors, at the same time responding to one another in complex ways. It is nevertheless convenient to consider communication a separate topic, since it involves a precise, sequential change of signals between two or more individuals.

COMMUNICATION

Communication is defined as the production of a signal by an individual that influences the behaviour of another individual and that is mutually beneficial. Commonly both individuals are of the same species, but not necessarily so. For example, a person may communicate meaningfully with a dog, or ants with aphids that they guard and from which they obtain honeydew. But interactions that are not mutually beneficial (such as predator-prey) are not usually said to be communicative.

Insects communicate in all sensory modalities, and members of any one species may employ several modalities. The queen butterfly employs chemical, visual and probably tactile signals; crickets employ acoustic, tactile, and in some species chemical signals; water striders communicate by patterned sequences of surface waves produced by leg movements. The messages conveyed are diverse: alarm, attraction, recruitment to food Sources, information on conditions within the nest, readiness to mate, and so forth. Reproductive behaviour includes some of the finest examples of elaborate, species-specific behaviour. We have already mentioned examples among crickets, silkworm moths and butterflies. We consider here a few somewhat different examples as well as a few general concepts.

Effective communication between members of the opposite sex may serve several functions:

1. Signals may be used to draw members of the opposite sex from a distance.

2. Mates must recognize one another as members of the same species, thus avoiding wastage of gametes, as well as time and energy, by inappropriate matings.

3. Signals may be used to bring the partner to a state of readiness or to cause it to remain quiescent during copulation.

3

MIGRATORY BEHAVIOUR

Orientation is, of course, a constant background feature of any animal's life. The term can respond to the mechanisms whereby animals respond to the basic physical qualities of their environment. In addition to migratory movements, insects move around a great deal within what can be called their *home* or *action range. For* a given species the nature and purpose of these movements are much more variable than for migratory movements. As stated already migrations are characterized by the straightening of the individual's track' resulting from a suppression of its responsiveness to appetitive stimuli. Trivial movements, on the other hand, are characterized by frequent responses to appetitive stimuli. However, both trivial and migratory movements require some degree of orientation and some ability to navigate. The need to navigate and return to a specific location varies from species to species. Conversely, species that travel great distances independent of the wind, like some butterflies, must have some means of maintaining an appropriate course. Likewise, within their home range some species may need only to recognize the boundaries of their range, whereas others, particularly those that utilize nests may need to navigate with considerable precision.

The fact that trivial movement involves the search for mates, oviposition sites, food, and so forth, suggests that stimuli associated with these basic requisites will often influence an individual's orientation. Within its home range then, we should expect to observe much behaviour dominated by the orientation to spec stimuli such as host odors or the auditory call of a mate. In this chapter we will examine the means by which insects find their way within their home range, including their repeated return to nest sites and how they navigate during migration. What will be presented will, by necessity, be a mixture of experimental evidence and conjecture. Much of the work done on insect homing in the field has produced some solid results, but such is not the case for long-distance migrations.

NAVIGATIONAL CUES

Stimuli to the kinds normally associated with feeding and reproduction have a pronounced influence on orientation after the migratory drive has been satisfied and the individual is engaged in the search for food, mates, or reproductive sites. Appetitive stimuli would seem to be less important to navigation and homing. These latter processes would be served best by more reliable (in the sense of more accurately identifying location) reference points such as celestial cues (sun, moon and sky polarization), landmarks (visually discernible fixed objects and patterns), electromangnetic fields and in a few instances currents of flow patterns. For homing insects, chemical trail markers can also be important.

Celestial Cues

Most of insects are capable of maintaining the alignment of the long axis of their body at a fixed angle relative to a source of stimulation. These so-called transverse orientations may or may not involve movement. A commonly displayed example involving move-ment is called the light-compass reaction. Celestial cues such as the sun, moon, stars, and the polarization of the sky are particularly good reference points for a light-compass reaction because they are so far away that orientation relative to them can result in travel along a straight line for long distance. The innate nature of transverse orientations is an explanation for the seemingly self-destructive behaviour of insects flying into a candle flame of light fixture. When the artificial light source is close at hand, the insect can only travel in a straight line for a short distance before it must change direction to maintain its fixed angle to the source of stimulation. The insect travels along a logarithmic spiral the ultimately leads to the light source.

Light-compass orientation can be demonstrated by several simple experiments first conducted many years ago. While working with ants foraging in featureless deserts of Tunisia, Santschi shaded workers returning to their nest from the sun and provided them with a mirror image of the sun projected from the opposite side of their track; the ants turned 180 and headed away from their nest. Brun placed a worker of the ant *Lasius* in a small light-tight box on its homeward journey and held it captive for 12 hours. When released, the ant traveled in a new direction, 23.5° from its original path. As the sun had traveled through an arc of 22.5° during the same time, it can be concluded that the ant was using a sun-compass orientation but was not capable of time compnsation. The lack of a time-compen-sation mechanism would make celestial orientation ineffective for any insect that may forage away from its nest for some time and could be prevented from returing, as happens when bees are grounded by a drop in temperature associated with passing clouds. However, Jander demonstrated time-compensated orientation for experienced *Formica* wokers, and a similar capability has been ovserved in the honeybee. The ability to navigate relative to the position of sun it, of course, best known in the honeybee, which has evolved an elaborate communication system based on the sun as the key reference point.

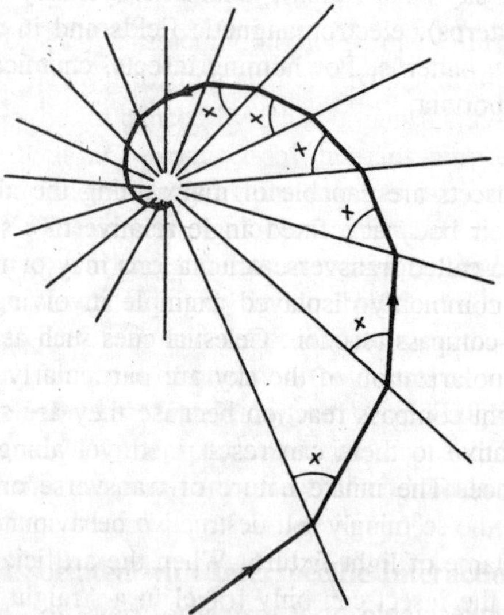

Fig. 3.1. The spiral track followed by an insect orienting to a nearby point source of light. The "logarithmic spiral" results from the fact that the insect is actually employing light-compass orientation and attempts to maintain a line of travel at a fixed angle (x) the light.

The phases of the moon and the ease with which it is obscured by clouds would seem to make the moon a less useful navigational cue for nocturnal insects than the sun is for diurnal species. Stars also would seem to be marginally useful reference points for insects. Many night-flying insects do display a light-compass response, however, and a moon-compass orientation has been demonstrated in the ants *Monomorium* and *Formica.*

Huffman (unpublished) has worked extensively with the water-boatman, *Trichocorixa reticulata,* to determine the basis of its escape orientation away from the shoreline toward deeper water. One might assume that the escape could be achieved readily by following the slope of the bottom or by utilizing depth receptors, but both were ruled out experimentally. Huffman has shown that during the day the sun and to a lesser extent polarized skylight are the main orientation cues, whereas at night there is strong evidence of moon-compass orientation. Since shore birds that prey upon *Trichocorixa* are active on moonlit nights, the moon-compass orientation provides an escape a mechanism not needed when the moon is absent. It is tempting to conclude that the light-comapss orientation of many nocturnal species represents and evolutionary carry-over that may be beneficial when the moon is bright enough to provide a navigational reference point.

Some insects can also detect polarized light and therefore orient relative to the position of the sun even though they may not be able to see its actual disc. The light waves produced by the sun vibrate in all directions at right angles to their direction of travel, but as they pass through the earth's atmosphere, the light is scattered and some planes of vibration are eliminated until each wave tends to vibrate in a single direction at each point in the sky. The resulting pattern of polarized light varies according to the relative position of the observer, the position of the sun, and the portion of the sky being viewed. The area of maximal polarization forms a band across the sky at approximately 90° to the sun's angle above the horizon and centered about the opposite point on the compass. For example, when the sun is 45° above the southeast horizon, the maximum plane of polarization would stretch across the northwest quadrant of the sky approximately 45° above the horizon. Consequently, the plane of maximum polarization shifts as the sun moves across the sky. Although the phenomenon of atmospheric light polarization has been known since before the turn off the century, it was not until the late 1940s that Karlvon Frisch discovered that honeybees navigate by polarized light. Only very recently has the mechanism of polarized light perception in insects been determined.

The early work of von Frisch stimulated a number of insect haviourists to reevaluate insect light reactions. In retrospect, the studies

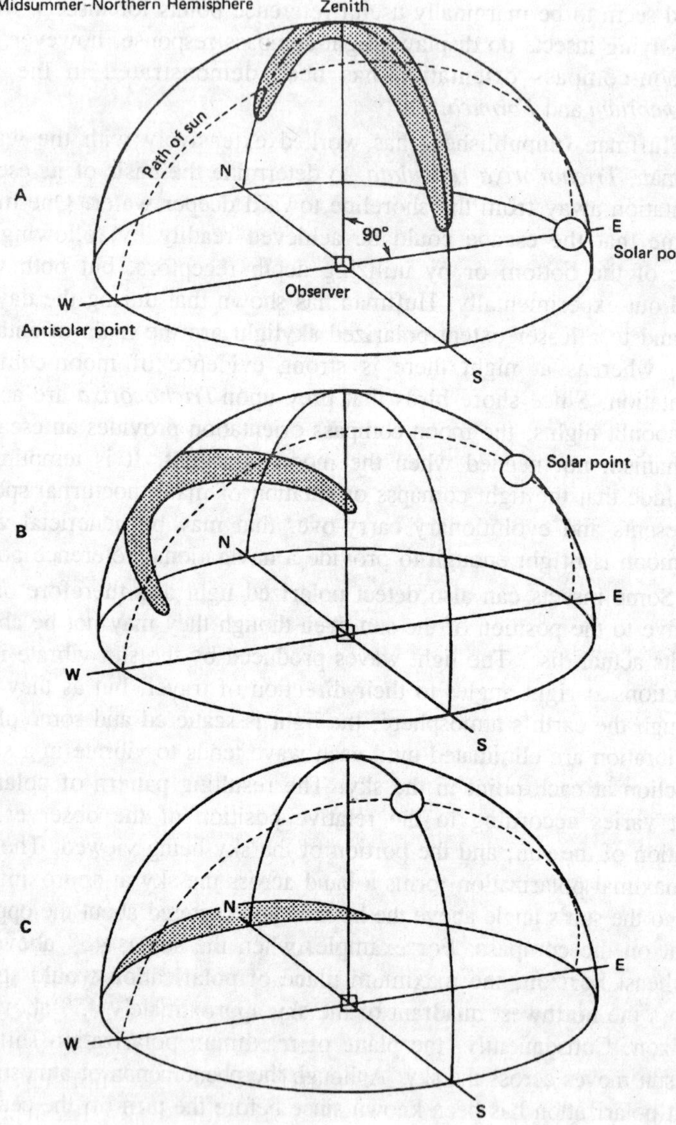

Fig. 3.2. Changes in the location of the area of maximal polarization relative to the position of the sun and the observer. (A) When the sun is near the horizon, the area of maximum polarization is directly overhead. (B) About midmorning when the sun is about 45° above the horizon, the area of maximum polarization drops below the zenith to the northwest. (C) When the sun is overhead at noon, the area of maximum polarization is just above the northern horizon.

of Wellington *et al.* and Wellington are of considerable interest in that they involved sawfly and moth larvae. These investigations extended the phenomenon of polarized light sensitivity not only beyond the adult Hymenopterans, but also to organisms not possessing compound eyes. Both the sawfly and lepidopterous larvae were able to orient to the plane of polarized light, but the latter were more precise. The question remains as to how insects can navigate unambiguously by polarized light when any given plane of polarization can be found at different points in the sky. Since insects can always view the zenith where the solar meridian extends at right angles to the plane of polarization, they can determine the path followed by. the sun across the sky. However, additional cues would be necessary for an individual to disinguish between the two arcs of the meridian. Experimental evidence suggests that these cues are obtained from a view of a large area of sky. Wehner found that the honeybee could accurately communicate the direction to a food source by performing the waggly dance on a horizontal surface when a large portion of the sky was in view. However, when the dancers' view of the sky was limited to a small patch with a single plane of polarization, they danced alternately in two directions - one right and one wrong. It is interesting that the wrong direction was consistent but not that which would be predicted from the plane of polarization viewed.

The disc of the sun would seem to be a most suitable and reliable navigational reference point except that it may be obscured by clouds or may be out of sight during those periods when it is low in the sky. The ability of insects to view an area of polarized sky must provide a valuable alternative cue. Furthermore, Wehner found that the desert ant, *Cataglyphis,* oriented erratically when the sky was depolarized with a filter even though the sun was visible. He theorized that the position of the sun may not be identified as the brightest spot in the sky but rather as that area lacking polarized light; this could not be discerned when the entire sky was depolarized. Obviously, we have much more to learn about celestial navigation.

Over the past few years Wellington has been concentrating on the importance of polarized light in insect behaviour rather than just how it is utilized. His findings have proved quite interesting. Wellington noted that insects use two kinds of informationn for finding their way around familiar territory. They can traverse it directly by utilizing polarized light as a navigational aid or follow a zigzag pattern from one familiar landmark to another. Transients unfamiliar with the local terrain can be caught aloft by the passage of a cloud dense enough to obscure their view of the plane of polarized light and must settle until their solar reference is restored, whereas local residents can change their mode of orientation and remain active. Nevertheless, the pattern of activity and behaviour was markedly affected by changes in the availability of polarized light to serve as a guide. For a period of time on either side of solar noon, polarized light cannot be seen in the overhead sky. During this period Wellington found that the passage of transients through the experimental area abated, as did the activity of residents in the open spaces; the resident flies, bees, wasps, and butterfies either restricted their activity to small localized territories or moved about from one route marker to the next. Wellington noted a parallel change in navigation of foraging western bumblebess, *Bombus tenicola*. When polarized light was present overhead, the workers would spiral upwad from their foraging site and fly, directly back to their nest in a staight line. When the polarized light overhead failed, the workers returned by a zigzag course dependent on landmarks. Coating portions of the compound eyes and the dorsal ocelli with an opaque substance revealed that the ocelli were important in navigation by polarized light during twilight when the light intensity was too low for the compound eyes to perceive landmarks.

It is obvious from the foregoing discussion that landmarks provide an important alternative to celestial navigational cues for a variety of insects. Beekeepers are familiar with the orientation flights of workers after a hive has been moved to a new locale; the workers fly around the hive in expanding circles, returning to the hive entrance and then flying off again as if to reconnoiter the immediate surroundings. When a number of hives are placed in a row in featureless terain, the workers will tend to drift with the prevailing wind toward the hives at one end of the row. This can be prevented quite easily by painting a few hives different colours or adding banners or some other artificial landmarks. Many solitary wasps make similar circular orientation flights after having completed a subterranean nest. Just what landmarks some of these insects use can be a mystery. Desert ants and the solitary wasps that nest in sand dunes occupy a seemingly featureleass terrain, where shifting sand constantly changes even the subtle surface features. The Nobel prize winning behaviourist Tinbergen conducted an extensive study of homing in digger wasps, the essence of which is presented along with numerous other obser-vations of wasp behaviour in Howard Evans' *Wasp Farm*. Tinbergen noted that the bee-wolf, *Philanthus,* upon completion of its nest, flies upward and then circles the nest site several times. If identifying objects were removed from around the nest opening while the wasp was away foraging, the wasp would have difficulty fording the opening, and upon leaving again would engage in another study of the immediate vicinity-behaviour not necessary when the identifying landmarks were left undisturbed. Tinbergen also found that moving landmarks would result in the returning wasps missing their nest openings.

It is seen that *Ammophila* females make similar reconnoitering flights after completing a nest. However, these wasps disguise the nest opening before they leave and return with their prey on foot, often over a considerable distance. Evans described the return of a female that had just captured a caterpillar in his vegetable garden as follows: "The *Ammophila* proceeded straight down between two rows of peas with her caterpillar slung beneath her. When she reched the end of the garden, about twenty feet away, she made a right angle and followed a plow furrow for another five feet. Then she ascended the far side of the furrow and entered a patch of weeds where, with scarcely a hesitation, she dropped her caterpillar and began to dig." The dune-inhabiting *Bombix* apparently are able to recognize landmarks consisting of no more than minor depressions in the sand. Some of these wasps hunt over considerable distances and return to their nests periodically even if their search for prey has been unsuccessful. It has been theorized that these wasps are able to memorize the location of larger and more distant objects and their relationship to the small ones near their nests.

Electromagnetic Fields

Electromagnetic fields would seem to be an ideal navigational cue. An insect orienting to such a field could navigate equally well during both day and night, and travel long distances without need for the time compensation necessary in celestial navigation. There is evidence that insects can perceive electromagnetic fields. The honeybee, for example, responds to the earth's electromagnetic field in a way that incorporates systematic errors in the straight run of the waggle dance performed on a vertical comb. Lindauer and Martin were able to eliminate these errors by placing the dancing bees in an artificial magnetic field. Furthermore, a honeybee swarm transferred to a cylindrical container oriented their comb in the same direction as combs in the hive from which they were taken; this has been considered the result of magnetic field imprinting. Although Gould *et al.* discovered the presence of magnetic material in the abdominal region of honeybees, there is still no behavioural evidence that they use the perception of the magnetic field in their navigation.

Chemical Trails

For social insects the establishment of chemical trails to aid in orientation to a food source and back to the nest provides a very effective aid to navigation. Such trails are used primarily by ants but also by a few species that forage on the wing. The termite, *Zootennopsis nevade-nsis,* also produces a trail pheromone. South American bees of the genus *Trigona* are known to mark a trail from a food source by depositing a droplet of mandibular gland secretion every few meters on their way back to the hive. Many ants establish one or more well-traveled trails between their nest and their foraging site. Sometimes these routes are so well trodden that they are easily followed once established. At least to begin with, the route back to the nest may be determined by celestial cues or by followinng landmarks, but often it consists of a well-marked pheromone trail. Chances are that any dense column of ants traveling back and forth across some featureless terrain such as an area of pavement is following a chemical trail. Often it is possible to demonstrate that such is the case by obliterating a section of the trail with soap and water. If a chemical trail exists, the ants arriving at either end of the obliterated portion will begin to mill about at random until several individuals reunite the divided column. The literature on the chemical trails of ants has grown rapidly in recent years and now includes species belonging to a variety of strategy groups. The trail pheromone is commonly a secretion of Dufour's gland, as it is in the harvester ant, *Pogonomyrmex badius,* and the fire ant, *Solenopsis saevissima.*

In some insects including the fire ant, worders go out alone in search of food. Successful workers returning to the nest extrude their sting and leave streaks of pheromone along the ground. In this species the trail substance both activates and guides other foraging workers. However, the pheromone is highly volatile, and the trail declines to a non-detectable level in about 2 minutes. Since only ants returning to the nest with food add to the trail, when a food source is depleted recruitment ceases; thus foragers are not distracted by encounters with old useless trails.

CONCLUSIONS

Studying the orientation and homing of insects within their home range or as they travel back and froth between their nests and places where they find their food is much easier than studying the navigation of long-range migrants over many miles of variable terrain. Mark and recapture experiments with migrant butterflies such as the monarch, *Danaus plexippus,* leave no doubt that these insects can and do fly up to 2000 miles. Not only do monarchs fly great distances, but after their southward migrations they end up at predictable locations that would seem to require rather precise navigation. Just how they accomplish this has not been demonstated convincingly. They problem is that single individuals have not been followed over long distances, so the ability of migrants has been inferred from observations made as they pass through a series of localities along their route. Some butterflies and moths traverse specific mountain passes with seasonal regularity, whereas others seem to follow the coastline or other prominent topographic features. Certainly, insects are capable of using celestial cues, but, with the variable direction and velocity of winds they encounter along their way, how do they know when they have gone far enough ?

Obviously, insects can find their way by perceiving and respond-ing to a variety of cues including some, like polarized light, that have little meaning in terms of our own sensory systems. We should not assume that insects function in accord with human experiences, since their homing ability would certainly seem to surpass our own. Bees can communicate the distance between a nectar source and the hive by means of what Wilson called "a ritualized and miniaturized imitation of their journey." Ants can be trained to travel a specific distance from a source of food to their nest; when displaced from the nest area they will travel that distance in a straight line and then begin to search for the nest entrance. Many foraging species that hunt back and forth over a large area are capable of returning to their nests with considerable precision. Some behaviourists feel that insects employ kinesthetic memory (the ability to keep track of both the distance and directional changes on a journey and then to translate the information into a more direct return trip), but such feelings are supported mainly by negative evidence. Nevertheless, insects seem to be capable of navigational feats that we can perform only with the aid of a computer.

Communication

Insects, employ tactile, visual, auditory, and chemical methods of communication, and in many species a combination of methods is involved in patterns of behaviour that fulfill a single biological function. For example, a special odor or sound may be produced to bring together a number of scattered individuals to mate and reproduce. Once in close proximity, pairing may result from visual recognition, and courtship behaviour also may involve visual cues. Once paired, the male may induced the female to copulate by releasing a volatile aphrodisiac or by exciting her tactilely. Because so many of the behavioural sequences engaged in by insects involve more than one method of communication, as just illustrated, it is desirable to begin with a discussion of the basic means of communication before considering their integration and the functions they serve.

Chemical Communication

In the broadest sense, among insects chemical communication involves the transfer of information by way of the detection of chemicals present in the environment, particularly insect- produced compounds collectively called *pheromones*. Pheromones can be likened to hormones in that they are of a specific composition, produced by special glands, to be released at specific times. Furthermore, they inhibit or stimulate specific biological functions. Whereas hormones coordinate the physiological and behavioural processes within the individual, pheromones coordinate the physiological and behavioural activities between individuals of the population. The rapidly expanding field of research involving the chemical control of insect behaviour has been reviewed by a number of authors, including Karlson and Butenandt, Butler, Shorey, and Sdorey and McKelvey. Pheromones are now thought to imfluence behaviour, both directly and indirectly, and most workers now use the terms *pheromone, allomone* and *kairomone.*

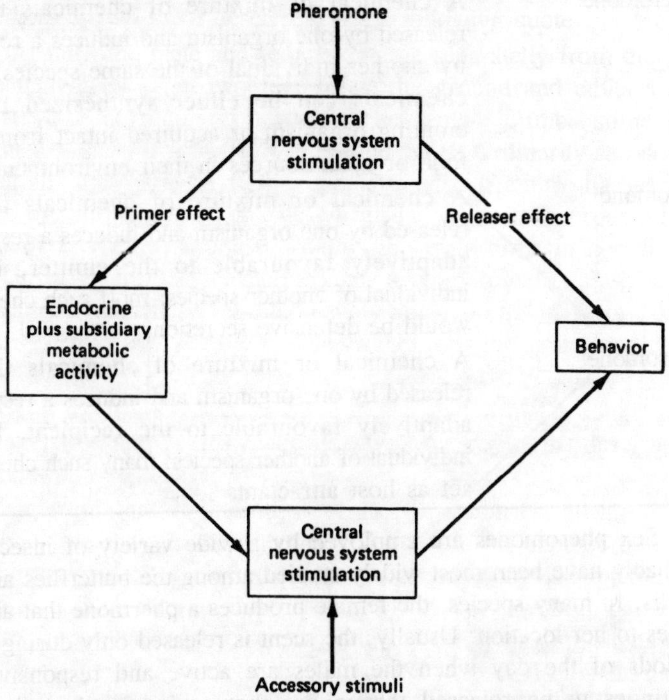

Fig 4.1. Schematic diagram of the direct and indirect influences that pheromones have on the behaviour of insects. If a pheromone stimulates an immediate change in b haviour, it is said to have a releaser effect. If it has a long term physiological effect fiat later influences a response to some accessory stimulus, the pheromone is said to hove a primer effect.

Insect pheromones can be variously grouped according to the kijad of behaviour or activity they coordinate. Some pheromones action over long distances as sex attractants or as population aggregators, whereas others function only over short distances, as is tie of some sex stimulants. Consequently, pheromones can be important in stimulating reproductive behaviour, producing aggregations at sources of food, stimulating mass defensive tactics, regulating population density, aiding navigation, and so on. Among social insects, pheromones are particularly important in coordinating members to perform all of the activities necessary for the survival of the colony as a whole.

TABLE 4.1.

DESCRIPTION OF TERMS CURRENTLY USED IN THE CHEMICAL CONTROL OF INSECT BEHAVIOUR

Pheromone	A chemical or mixture of chemicals that is released by one organism and induces a response by another individual of the same species; these chemicals can be either synthesized by the emitting organism or acquired intact from their food or other sources in their environment
Allomone	A chemical or mixture of chemicals that is released by one organism and induces a response, adaptively favourable to the emitter, by an individual of another species; most such chemicals would be defensive secretions
Kairomone	A chemical or mixture of chemicals that is released by one organism and induces a response, adaptively favourable to the recipient, by an individual of another species: many such chemicals act as host attractants

Sex pheromones are employed by a wide variety of insects but probably have been most widely studied among the butterflies and the moths. In many species, the female produces a phermone that attracts males to her location. Usually, the scent is released only during those periods of the day when the males are active and responsive but continues to be released throughout that period until mating has occurred. In species that mate several times, the female will release her pheromone for severral days, thus ensuring the receipt of sperm from several males. In the moths the pheromone molecules are perceived by thousands of olfactory receptors located on the large plumose antennae of the males. These special receptors are capable of detecting a single pheromone molecule, and the excitation of only a few hundred receptors at one time by a pheromone concentration of only a few hundred molecules per cubic centimeter can cause the male moth to respond with a basic change in behaviour, which may lead into a complete behavioural repertory. When the antennal receptors of a-resting male intercept the scent of a "calling" female, the male will often respond by vibrating its wings and then taking flight. The male will fly into the odor-bearing airstream until he locates the female or can no longer perceive her scent. If the male loses the scent, he will engage in a random flight that increases his chances of intercepting the trail again. In this way, widely separated males and females are effectively brought together; in one experiment more than one quarter of the released males of the saturniid moth, *Arctias selene*, were able to locate canged females about 7 miles away.

TABLE 4.2

CATEGORIES OF BEHAVIOUR MODIFYING CHEMICALS BASED ON THE TYPES OF BEHAVIOUR THEY INDUCE

Locomotory stimulant	A chemical that causes kineses that, in the absence of orientation cues, often cause animals to dispeise from an area by increasing their speed of locomotion or appropriately affecting their rate of turning
Arrestan	A chemical that causes kineses reactions that, in the absence of orientation cues, often cause animals to aggregate near the chemical source by decreasing their speed of locomotion or appropriately affecting their rate of turning
Attractant	A chemical that causes an animal to make oriented movements toward its source
Repellent	A chemical that causes an animal to make oriented movements away from its source
Feeding, mating, or ovipositional stimulant	A chemical that elicits one of these behavioural reactions
Feeding, mating, or ovipositional deterrent	A chemical that inhibits one of these behavioural reactions

Chemical communication between mates is particularly important for bisexual species in which the females are flightless. Such is the case with a number of mothes belonging to the families Saturniidae and Lasiocampidae, in which the females are either extremely sluggish or have short, non-functional wings. In some of the tussock moth, for example, a newly emerged female sits on her empty cocoon, releases the pheromone that attracts a male, mates, and then lays her eggs in the immediate vicinity; the young larvae then migrate. Sex pheomones not only serve to bring males and females together but theymay also cause some sexual excitation that facilitates copulation. Sometimes a low concentration of a pheromone will only agitate the male, but a higher concentration will stimulate oriented flight, and an even higher concentration will result in courtship and copulation. In some species the females need a little stimulation as well, and the males produce a scent that acts as an aphrodisiace. For example, the male of the grayling butterfly, *Eumenis semele,* has a patch of special scent scales on the upper surface of the forewings, which are exposed to the female by the spreading of his wings during courtship. When the female encounters the pheromone, she is stimulated to engage in copuloation.

Some insects release a mixture of chemicals that attract both sexes. This is common among the bark and ambrosia beetles, which use pheromones not only to attract members of the opposite sex but also to create an aggregation of individuals collectively large enough to overcome host resistance or, in the case of susceptible hosts, to maximize the utilization of contagiously distributed resources. In the genus *Dendroctonus,* the females initiate the attack of the host tree and subsequently release a sex-aggregating pheromone. In those genera such as *Ips,* in ''hich the brood gallery is started by the male, the male produces the pheromone. As more beetles are attracted to the host and attack it, more pheromone is released, strengthening the stimulus. Obviously, such a procedure cannot go on indefinnitely. As the host material approaches an optimal level of occupancy, the chemicals released by the host and the beetles change, and the attraction of new individuals slows doewn. Subsequently, the fully occupied host becomes unattractive as the production of the attractant compounds ceases, and the production of an antiaggregation pheromone, which acts as a deterrent to late arrivals, takes its place. Thus chemical communication can serve to optimize spacing and reduce intraspecific competition.

Many ant species lay chemical trails that assist them in traversing the distance between their nests and sources of food they have located. Ant trails are frequently marked by the release of small droplets of pheromone at regular intervals along the travelled route. In addition to marking the way, the released pheromones serve to recruit other individuals to gather food from the same source. As numerous ants travel back and forth over the same route, leaving spots of pheromone as they go, the spots blend together to form a continuous trail. The fact that ant trails involve chemical communication can be readily demonstrated by rather simple experiments involving the disruption of an established trail by replacing a portion of it with unmarked soil. It is also possible to create artificial trails with a crude extract of the ant's Dufour's gland, where the pheromone is produced. Termites mark their trails with a pheromone produced in special glands located in their abdomens. In the primitive species, and odor trail is used to recruit workers to damaged portions of nests that need to be repaired. In some more complex species, however, the same pheromone is used to recruit workers to food gathering, as in the ants. Some primitive bees also use spots of pheromone laid down at regular intervals to create a trail even through they folage on this wing.

Chemical communication serves a veriety of other function among non-social insects, both within and between species. Some parasites mark their prey with a pheromone that discourages oviposition by another female of the same species. For example, the braconid *Microphanums* that parasitizes the eggs of the green vegetable bug, *Nezarq* marks each parasitized egg by depositing a pheromone with a circular motion of the tip of her abdomen. If another female locates the same bug egg mass, she will parasitize only those eggs that are not marked;; in this way intraspecific competition is avoided. Some parasitic hymenopterans also use pheromones to mark the territory they have traversed in search of prey and there by avoid repeating the search of the same area. As one might expect, chemical communication is not restricted to members of the same species. There are many examples of insects using the chemical characteristics of other organisms as a means of identifly them as suitable hosts. Nowhere is this more apparent than in the relationship between insect herbivores and their food plants. There are examples, however that involve one species keying on the pheromone communication of another.

Although in a relatively short. time investigators have come to realize that chemical communication among insects is widespread and serves many functions, much remains to be learned. Workers investigating the chemical communication systems of pest species such as bark beetles are discovering that mixtures of different pheromones released in different concentrations elicit different responses. The integration of chemical communication with other methods of communication is even more complex, as we will discover a little later in this chapter.

Audio Communication

Sound is also an effective means by which insects are known to

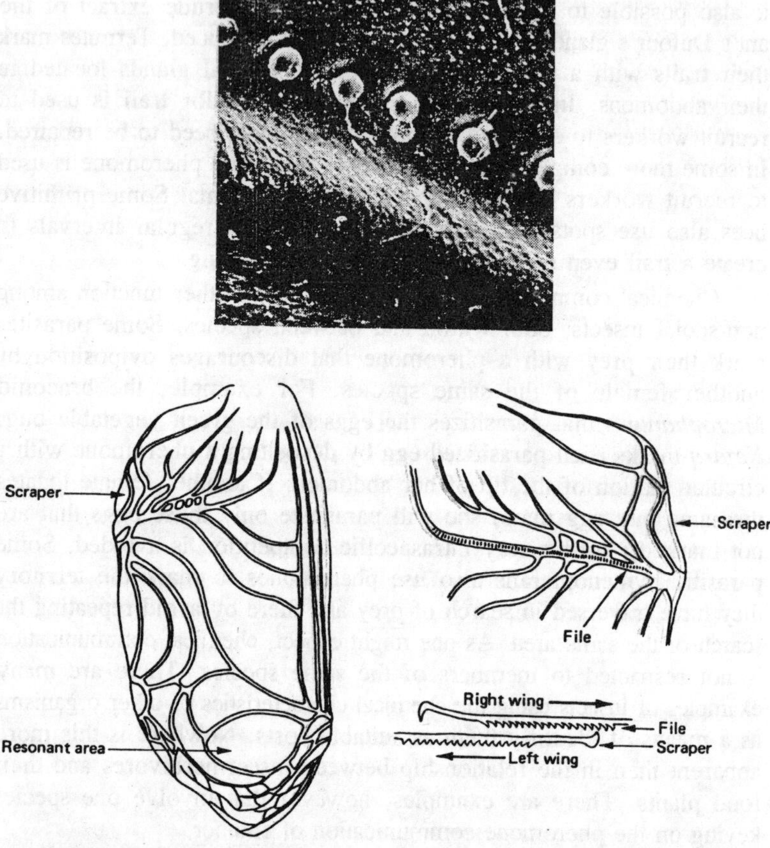

Fig. 4.2 (A) A scanning electron micrograph of the inner surface of the hind femur of a grasshopper showing the structure of the stridulatory file. (B) Diagram of the stridulatory apparatus of the cricket Acheta.

communiacte over a wide range of distances, but not over the long distances described for some pheromones. Sound is perceived by specialized inechanoreceptors, which may or may not be grouped together into ears. Since these receptors can detect any sound within their range of receptivity, sound itself does not necessarily provide a specific means of communicating any more than the detection of some common chemical does. However, some insects produce specific sound squences or "songs" that form a functional parallel with the specific molecular mixtures of pheromones. Insects may produce sound as a by-product of another activity, such as flight, by striking their substrate, by rubbing two parts of their body together, by activating a vibrating membrane, or by pulsing an airstream.

The sound produced by the beating wings is used by some insects to ocate other individuals and to bring the sexes together. A swarm of small flies is clearly audible to other individuals in the area. Males of the *mosquitoAedes aegypti* are attracted to the flight tone of sexually mature females, whereas immature females have a different tone to which the males do not respond. A variety of insects produce sound by striking the substrate with some part of their body. Some grasshoppers strike the ground with their hind tibiae. Because both sexes engage in the activity, it probably serves to bring individuals together by way of a response to low frequency vibrations through the substrate. Individuals of the termite *Zootennopsis* rock back and forth on their middle legs so that the mandibles tap against the floor of their tunnel. This behaviour is initiated by a disturbance near one part of the nest and warns other members of the colony to move elsewhere.

Sbidulation is the term applied to the production of sound by the rubbing together of two body surfaces. The mechanism, which is used by many different insects, can be likened to running one's thumb nail down the teeth of a comb. Usually, a ridgelike structure, the *scraper,* on one part of the bnody is moved back and forth over a ridged surface, the *file,* on an adjacent part. Variations of this type of system are common among the grasshoppers, crickets, katydids, true bug, and beetles. In the grasshoppers, a row of pegs along the inside of the hind femora is rubbed back and forth over the edge of the parchmentlike forewings. In katydids and crickets, the cubital vein of each forewing is toothed. When the wings are folded at rest, a ridge near the base of the left wing overlaps the file on the right wing. When these incects sing, their wings are repetitively opened and closed part way and the sound is produced by a vibration of the adjacent wing membrane.

Beetles use many different parts of their well-sclerotized bodies as stridulatory organs, but the *elyt a* are most commonly involved. male bark beetles of the genus *Dendroctonus* have an abdominal Scraper that is moved back and forth across an elytral file to produce a clearly audible chirping sound. The function of the sound is not understood but commonly occurs when the male is sitting in the entrance to a female's gallery while the host tree is under attack.

The production of sound by a muscle-driven membrane, or *Cymbal,* occurs among a few moths and homopterans. The most thoroughly studied mechanism of this type is that of a well-known insect chorister, the cicada. In these insects, the first abdominal segment is highly modified for sound productio. There are a pair of dorsolateral structures that resemble drumheads; each consists of a thin disc of cuticle, supported by a thicker cuticular rim. These discs form the cymbal, which are protected by tymbal covers composed of regular cuticle. Each tymbal gives rise to an apodeme on its inner surface, to which the tymbal muscles are attached. When the muscles contract and cause an inward buckling of the tymbals, there is an associated click. When the muscles relax, the tymbls return to their normal shape and produce a second click. The succession of clicks associated with a cycle of rapid muscle contraction and relaxation produces the familiar trill of the cicada.

The only known case of sound produced by a pulsed airstream occurs in the moth genus *Acherontia,* which draws air in through its proboscis by dilation of the pharynx. The in-rushing air causes a flaplike epipharynx to vibrate and to produce a pulsed airstream and a related low-pitched sound. This is followed by a high-pitched whistle as the air is expelled. Insect-produced sounds can serve a variety of functions, such as the stridulatory sounds that accompany defensive displays or occur in response to agitation. I have a cerambycid beetle in my garden that produces a loud startling buzz when touched. More important from a behavioural standpoint, however, are sounds used for communication within species. Functionally, acoustic behaviour is most important to activities associated with territoriality and reproduction and, consequently, plays a role in speciation. Some specific examples will therefore be presented when these topics are dealt with later on; however, Haskell presented a general outline of acoustic signals in reproductive behaviour, which are paraphrased here : A calling song produced by either the male or the female stimulates locomotor activity and brings the sexes together, provided the recipient of the song is ready to court. A courtship song which may be divided into several distinct accoustic signals, such as a serenade and nuptual song, may lead to the actual joining of the genitalia. During copulation the male may continue to calm the female with a copulatory song. Following copulation the pair may go their separate ways or there may be some postcopulatory singing, which in crickets apparently discourages dislodgement of the spermatophore.

A spectacular form of audio communication among insects is the seemingly synchronized singing called chorusing. Such behaviour occurs in populations of male cicadas, crickets, and katydids, and results in the attraction of females and sometimes recruits additional males to the chorus. A number of hypotheses suggested to explain this behaviour failed to recognize the current view that natural selection operates principally at the level of the individual. Alexander discussed the problems of interpreting chorusing behaviour and concluded that the phonoresponses involved can be explained primarily as competitive interactions between neighbouring males.

Audio communication also seems to be important in predatorprey systems involving insects. According to Haskell, insect predators can locate prey both on land and in the water by responding to the vibrations created by their prey; some hymenopterous parasites are believed to locate hosts lying beneath the substrate in a similar manner. One of the most highly evolved interspecific audio communication systems occurs between some moths and insectivorous bats; these bats are able to locate flying insects by orienting to the source of the echos of their own ultrasonic chirps. The owlet moths have evolved a countermeasure in the form of a pair of tympanic organs that detect the hunting bat's cries. The moths respond with evasive fligh maneuvers, which substantially reduce the chance of capture. Some arctiid moths have gone one step further; they also produce trains of ultrasonic clicks, which for some reason cause bats to swerve away at the last moment.

Visual Communication

Visual communication among insects is common and highly variable. Unlike chemical and sound communication, visual communication requires a direct line of sight between individuals and is only effective over relatively short distances. Within its effective range, vision can be important as a means of bringing individuals together and also in the sometimes elborate patterns of courtship behaviour.

The females of mayflies, caddisflies, and midges are attracted visually to swarms of males engaged in dancelike up-an-down flights in compact groups. Male butterflies frequently pursue appropriately colored females and can be persuaded to chase pieces of coloured paper moved in a manner that imitates a female's fligh. Once butterflies have paired, visual displays become an important part of the courtship behaviour without which copulation may not occur. The most spectacular visual displays encountered among the insects involve luminescence. In some insects, luminescence is incidental and serves no specific communicative function. Some collembolans, for example, give off light as a by-product of their metabolism as do many bacteria; insect larvae infected by such bacteria may also appear luminescent.

The most brightly luminous insects are beetled belonging to the familes Elateridae, Phengodidae, and Lampyri~ le; variously know as fireflies lightning bugs, and glowworms. The lampyrid, *Photinus pyralis,* which is common in the southern United States, has been studied extensively. Both adults and larvae have light-producing organs-the larvae and females have single pair, whereas the males have two pairs. The flashing signals produced by these organs seem to be a species specific means of communication widely recognized as a mechanism that brings the sexes together.

The behaviour of *Photinus pyralis* has been described by McDermott and Mast as follows; "At duck the male and female emerge from the grass. The male flies about 50 centimeters above the ground and emits a single, short flash at regular intervals. The female climbs some slight eminence such as a blade of grass and perches there. She ordinarily does not fly at all and she never flashes spontaneousloy as does the male but only in response to a flash of light which is produced by the male. If a male flashes within a radius of 3 or 4 meters of the female she usually responds after a short interval by flashing. The male then turns directly toward her in his course and soon glows again. Following this the female again respond., by glowing and the male again apparently takes his bearings, turns and directs his course towards her. This exchange of signals is repeated usually not more than 5 or 10 times until the male reaches the female and mates with her."

In *P. pyralis* the female flashes about 2 seconds after perceiving the flash of the male, and this apparently aids in sexual recognition. A number of individuals flashing within a small area at the same time would seem to produce a confusing situation, but perhaps it is unscrambled,. at least in part, by the critical response distance displayed by the males relative to a flashing female. Synchronized flashing by male P. pyralis is rare, but it is reportedly commonplace among some tropical species. How this synchronous behaviour is triggered is unclear, and it raises the same fundamental questions regarding selection as does the synchronous chorusing mentioned earlier.

Tactile Communication

Coiurrunication by touch obviously can occur only after other means of communication bring individuals together. Nevertheless, insects engage in rather elaborate forms of contact behaviour for courtship and sexual stimulation. In *Drosophila,* for example, the male is attracted to the female visually, but final species recognition results when the male taps the female with his forelegs. In many species the female is not immediately receptive to the male's copulatory advances and will only allow the male to mount after some appropriate foreplay. In a few insects the male appeases the female with an offer of food and then copulates with her while she eats his offering. Male scorpion flies of the genus *Panorpa* (Mecoptera) secrete droplets of saliva that harden and serve as a snack for the female during copulation. The males of other species appease their mates with seeds or nonedible objects such as a brightly coloured petal.

The appeasement behaviour of males would seem to guard against exciting a female to respond to a mate as a potential attacker or prey. In the mantids the male carefully approaches the female from behind, over a protracted period, but even then the female responds by grabbing him violently with her forelegs and then proceeds to remove his head with her mandibles during copulation. The outcgme, however, is vigorous copulatory activity resulting from the severing of the male's subesop-hageal ganglion.

Communication Methods

In the foregoing discussion the four main methods of communication used by insects have been treated separately. However, we must realize that they are not used independently. Each has its special attributes. Odors, for instance, are carried great distances on the wind and, if detectable in low concentrations, can provide a way by which insects beyond the range of sight or hearing can communicate effectively. At closer range, other forms of relaying information may be more. appropriate. Furthermore, boilogical functions are frequently fulfilled by way of complex behaviour patterns composed of a sequence of responses. Such is often the case with those functions served by communication.

For mating to occur, individuals may have to come together over considerably distances. The danger of attack by natural enemies is considerably lessened when individuals can communicate while they remain concealed. Odor and sound would seem to serve this strategy well. Once individuals have been able to gain proximity, visual cues would become useful as a means of species recognition. Finally, tactile stimulation can serve to provide the excitation required before the female submits to copulation. A behavioural sequence of the type just described involving several types of communication, is relatively simple compared to the communication that must take, place among the subsocial and a social insects. In truly social species, the survival of entire colonies depends upon the intergartion of the relatively simple incividual patterns of communication and response into a coordinated system of mass behavioural phenomena. An examination of communication within a colony of honeybees therefore serves as probably the best example of cooperative behaviour mediated by various forms of communication.

The coordination of life and behaviour within a beehive-involves communication of each of the types discussed. Since social bees return to their nest at regular intervals, mechanisms for long- distance communication have been replaced largely, but not totally, by elaborate communication in an around the nest site. Although visual, sound, and tactile communication occurs between members of a hive, chemical communication predominates. In addition to chemical communication, as discussed previously, bees exploit chemical signals in the from of special substances in the food that is exchanged between individuals. The following diswtion, therefore, will be organized according to the function served by communication rather than by the method employed. The discussion will of necessity be shorter than the subject justifies, but interested students are referred to the outstanding treatment by E. O. Wilson for further details.

Wilson divides social communication funcationally into alarm. and assembly recruitment, recognition, food exchange, grooming and group effects. A brief examination of the kinds of communcation used in the regulation and coordination of these functions in only a single species should provide some perspective of the complex nature of this subject over the entire range of social insects.

Alarm and Assembly

Alarm and assembly can be used for both defensive and foraging purposes. An initial sting by a honeybee may provoke other bees in the vicinity to become aggressive. Because the worker's sting is barbed, it catches in the victim's skin, and, as the bee attempts to fly away, the poison gland and *Dufour's gland* are often left behind. The act of stinging releases the compound isoamyl acetate, produced by secretory cells that line the sting pouch. This highly volatile substance attracts other bees to the source, and some subsequent stinging may occur. However, it does not stimulate the release of the substance by other bees not engaged in stinging, so, as the danger passes and the alarm pheromone dissipates, behaviour returns to normal.

Much more important in honeybee behaviour is the chemical communication that leads to other forms of assembly. Worker bees release a mixture of chemicals produced by their *Nasanov glands*. The substance is often released by bees located near the hive entrance during swarming, and when new food sources are first located. Individuals that have been isolated from their nest mates for a period of time will also release the scent as a means of reestablishing contact.

The scent continuously laid down around the entrance to the hive assists the foraging bees to locate the nest on their return. However, this hive odor does not serve to distinguish one colony from another, as was once though. During swarming, the Nasanov substance stimulates the assembly of workers that ultimately leads to the familiar cluster of bees around their queen.

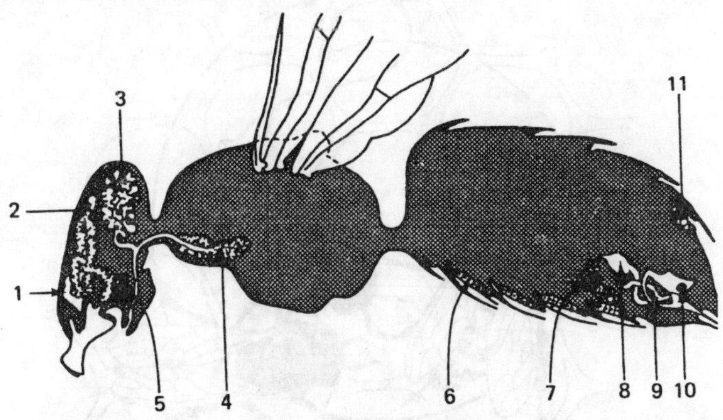

Fig. 4.3. Chemical producing glands of the worker honeybee Apis mellifem (1) mandibular glands, (2) hypopharyngeal gland, (3) head labial gland, (4) thoracic'labial gland. (5) hypostomal gland, (6) wax glands, (7) poison gland, (8) vesicle of the poison gland, (9) Dufouras gland, (10) Koschevnikov's gland, (11) Nasanov's gland.

Another assembly pheromone consists of a-group of chemicals, commonly called *queen substance,* produced by the mandibular glands of the queen. This secretion and another from *Koschevnikov's gland* are at least partially responsible for the formation of the cluster of *"court bees"* that constantly surrounds the queen. Also, when a colony swarms, the workers are attracted to the queen in flight and follow her trail of evaporating pheromone to the settling site located by the scout bees. Once the queen settles, she releases another mandibular gland secretion that tends to settle the nearby workers. The first group of settled workers dispense their own Nasanov secretion, which stimulates the rest of the swarm to cluster.

Recruitment

Recruitment involves the gathering together of nest maters at a particular place for purposes of applying a joint effort to a specific task, such as nest construction or food retrieval. The most elementary form of recruitment communication in the honeybee involves the recognition of food sources from the scent that adheres to the bodies of foraging bees and the nectar they regurgitate upon return to the hive. When a particular food source is abundant and near the hive, this simple form of communication is quite adequatew. In fact, investigatiors have increased pollination by training the bees on sugar syrup tainted with the odor of the crop.

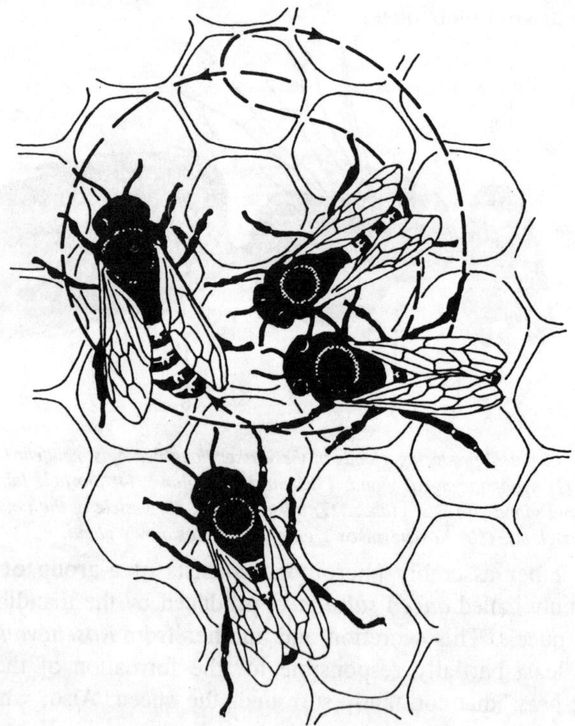

Fig. 4.4. The round dance of the scout honeybee that is thought to communicate the presence of a nectar source near the hive.

Ants forage for food on the ground and so are able to leave well-marked trails to recruit their nest mates to the task of exploiting a food source. Bee, on theother hand, forage on the wing, so they must have some other means of communicating the exact location of food to their colleagues. Some bees do lay odor trails, however. As discussed previously, the South American genus *Triogona* having established a course from the hive to a food source, will stop every few meters on the homeward flight and deposit a droplet of mandibular gland secretion at each point. Other bees then follow the odor trail.

The honeybee employs a rudimentary form of odor trail used for short-distance orientation in the immediate vicinity of the hive. The trail is laid down by workers returning to the hive over a short distance on foot; the chemical is referred to as the *footprint pheromone*.

Fig 4.5. The waggle dance of the scout honeybee that is believed to communicate both the direction and the distance to nectar sources away from the hive.

The honeybee communicates the distance and the direction to good foraging sites by an elaborate method of communication widely know as *the bee dance*. Different races behave slightly differently, but usually, if the source of pollen or nectar is rairly close to the hive, returning workers perform the *round dance. As* indicated in the figure, a worker that has just returned from a successful foraging trip penetrates the hive to where there are other field bees and engages in an excited circular pattern of running. Other field bees follow and in the course of the dance pick up odor information about the source of food. This

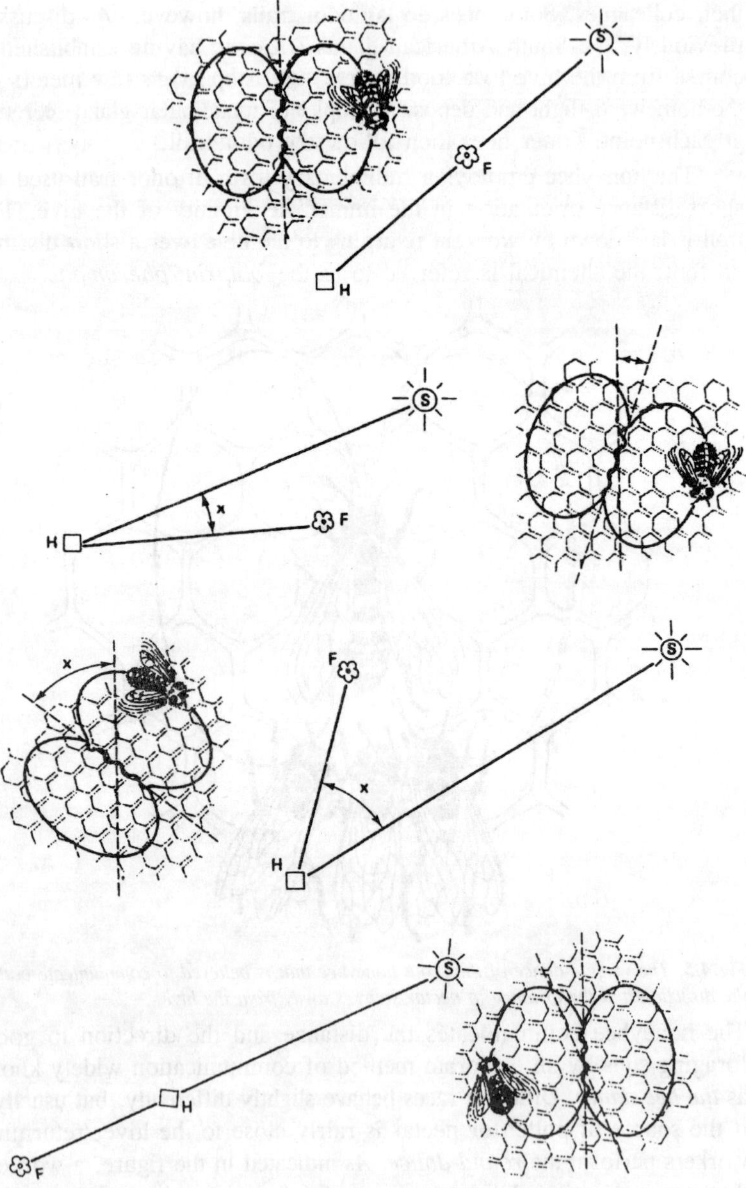

Fig. 4.6. Diagrams showing the orientation of the straight run of the waggle dance relative to the position of the hive (H), the forage site (F), and the sun (S).

simple form of the bee dance recruits other workers to search for pollen or nectar of a certain kind in the immediate vicinity of the hive. If the food source is more than *50* meters or so from the hive, the information transmitted by the round dance would be of little use. As the distance to the foraging site increases, the round dance becomes modified by the incorporation into it of a straight run, during which the performing worker waggles its abdomen from side to side. The new pattern of behaviour that results is called the *waggle dance.* After much painstaking study, von Frisch was able to decode this remarkable means of communication.

When a scout bee returns to the hive after having made several successful trips to and from a forage site a considerable distance away, she penetrates deep into the hive, regurgitates nectar from her crop, and begins to perform the waggle dance on one of the vertical honeycombs. The sun is used as the key reference point for the communication of direction. If the forage site is located on a line between the hive and the sun, the straight run of the dance will be up the comb. If the -direction is directly away from the sun,, the straight run will be down the comb. The straight run is followed by a circle to the right, another straight run followed by a circle to the left, and so on. Likewise, if the forage site is located 30° to the right of the sun, the straight run of the dance will be performed at an angle 30° to the right of the vertical. The compound eyes of the honeybee are so sensitive to ultraviolet radiation that they can detect the position of the sun and communicate the direction to forage sites, even on lightly overcast days, and navigate using polarized light.

The communication of the direction to more-distant food sources is highly beneficial, but foraging efficiency would clearly be enhanced by some communication of distance as well. This information is

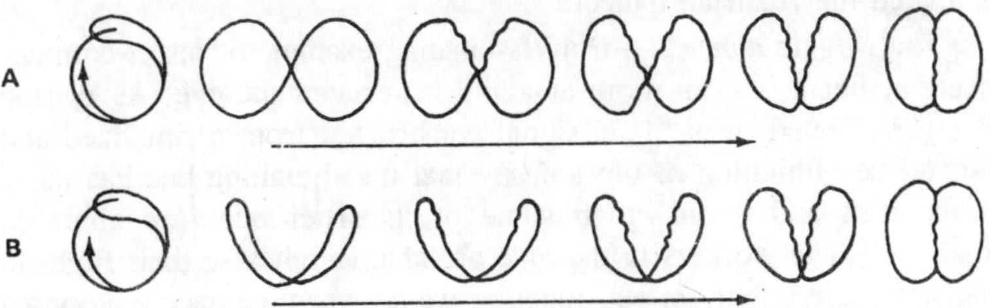

Fig. 4.7. Changes in the round dance that occur as the distance between the hive and the foraging site increases. (A) Changes characteristic of the Austrian strain. (B) Changes characterristic of the Italian strain.

provided by the duration of the straight run and the speed with which the dance is performed. During the straight run, the dancing bee waggles her abdomen form side to side with a frequency of about 13 to 15 vibrations per second, at the same time producing an audible buzzing sound by vibrating her wings. By observing the dance of scout bees returning from feeding platforms placed at different distances from the hive, von Frisch was able to decode the dance language. The further the food from the hive, the longer was the duration of the wagging portion of the dance a44 the fewer were the number of complete cycles of the dance per unit of time. Apparently, the duration of the staight run is not based on the absolute distance to the foraging site but on the energy that must be expended to get there. If the trip involves a flight up a steep slope or against the wind. The straight run performed in the hive will be longer. Furthermore, different genetic races of honeybee have incorporated variations into their dance that have been referred to as dialects.

For example, the transition from the round dance to the waggle dance differs between the Austrian variety and the Italian variety; the flattened figure-eight pattern or *sickle dance* of the Italian race is used when the nectar source is t an intermediate distance from the h:ve, the opening of the sickle f cing the source of food. A study of the dance behaviour of three wild species of *Apis,* in addition to the Austrian and Italian races of the honeybee, revealed substantial differences in the correlation between the rapidity of the wagging motion and the distance to the nectar source. *Ir Apis mellifera* there is even difference between the dialects of the varieties, which results in misinterpretation of the dance language in, a mixed group. Experiments with colonies containing both Austrian and Italian workers revealed that the Austrian strain cpnsistenlty overestimated the distance communicated by Italian dancers, whereas Italian foragers underestimated the Austrian dancer.

The *waggle dance is* a truly fascinating example of insect communication, but it is even more amazing than meets the eye. As Wilson so clearly stated, it is "... a signal constructed from a ritualized and minaturized imitation of the journey that the signalling bee has taken in the past and upon which some of its sister bees are abnnt to emabark." The workers in the hive are able to rehearse their flight in miniature before they set out, much as we do when we trace a proposed plane trip on a map. In 1967, Wenner and Johnson challenged von Frisch's interpretation of the bee dance as the major means of communication for foraging. They contended that the bees could adequately achieve recruitment with the odor of the nectar brought to the hive and the recruitment pheromone left by foragers in the field. This stimulated additional research. The results indicate that the two hypotheses, although in conflict, are not mutually exclusive, as pointed out by Gould. Gould concluded that von Frisch and Wenner were simply examining different parts of the same process. The elaborate dance language is of great value in the rapid recruitment of foragers to remote isolated patches of food, but, when an extensive supply of food is available, recruits can use odor alone. A Gould pointed out, the honeybee evolved in areas where a means of exploiting spatially and temporally discontinuolls food sources that were also sought by other species would have been a significant advantage.

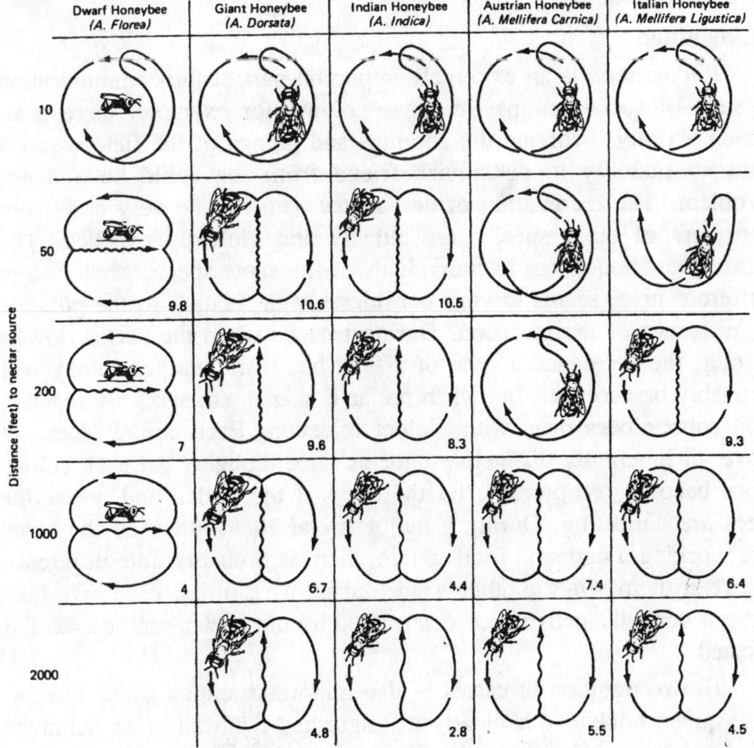

Fig. 4.8. Dialects in the dance language of several different species and strains of the honeybee genus Apis. The dwarf honeybee dances on a horizontal surface whereas the others all dance on a vertical surface. The more rapidly the wagging portion of the dance is performed, the shorter the distance to the forage site. The values in the corner of each square represent the number of wagging runs in 15 seconds for each distance for each variety of bee.

Honeybees engage in other dance variations that have yet to be studied as thoroughly as the waggle dance. One called the buzzing run initiates swarming. During the warm part of a suitable day, one or several workers begin running through the colony in an excited zigzag pattern, vibrating their wings and abdomens as they go. The sound produced is quite distinctive and may be part of the total pattern of communication. The dance is highly contagious, and many workers join in. Within minutes, the bees near the hive entrance rush out and are followed by a mass of workers and the absconding queen. Wilson believes that this form of communication may be unique in that the initial signal stimulates others to produce the same signal in the form of a chain reaction.

Recognition

Recognition is an extremely important part of the communication system of social groups. In a bee colony, for example, there is so much activity involving the comings and goings of the field workers that an inability to distinguish friend from foe could be a major problem. The recognition of nest mates seems to be very casul, but intruders of other species are quickly and violently expelled. The reaction of honeybees to individuals of the same species, but from a different hive, seems to very considerably in relation to the possible significance of the intrusion. During periods when the nectar flow is strong, the accidental arrival of a field bee from another colony will probably be accepted. But when nectar is scarce, strangers are repelled and robber bees meet with violent rejection. Each colony does not have an inherently distinctive odor as once thought, but each colony does become recognizable by the odor of the pollen and nectar the bees are collecting. During a mojor nectar flow, when all the hives are working a common food source, there is probably little difference between them. On the other hand, during hard times, each hive may have a very distinctive odor determined by the nectar source each has located.

The recognition of castes is also important among social insects. The queen honeybee is clearly distinguished from all other members of the colony and is treated with apparent respect. The workers not only recognize the queen on the basis of the odor substances she secretes but are also able to determine when she is becoming reproductively ineffective. After the old queen leaves a colony with a swarm, the first virgin queen to emerge communicates audibly with other young queens who have not yet emerged. If the first queen to emerge killed

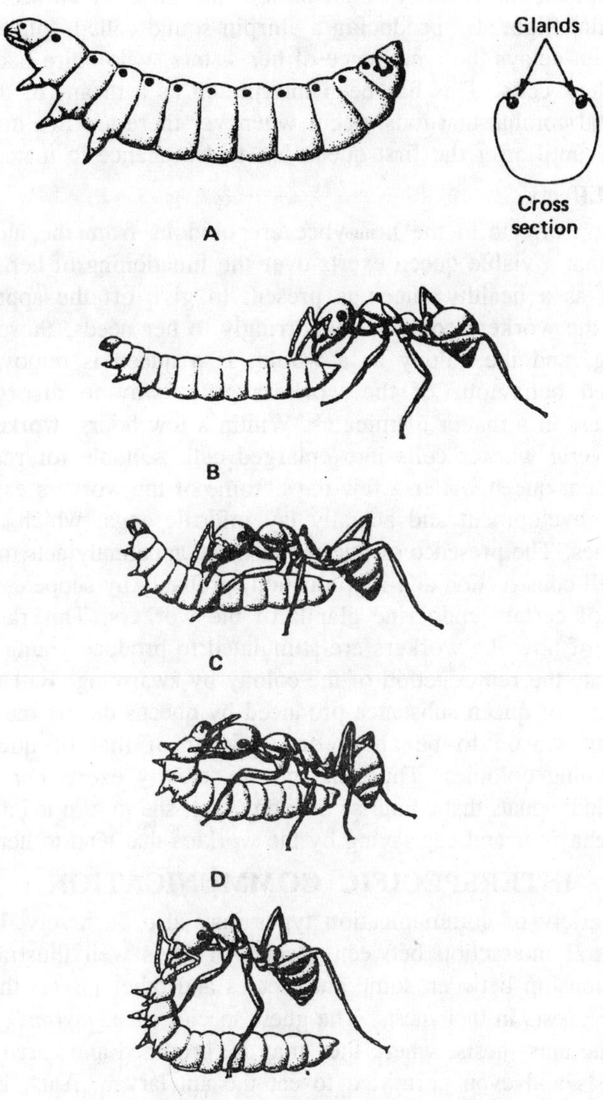

Fig 4.9. Chemical communication between a beetle larva and its ant host. (A) The position of the glands of the beetle larva that produce an attractant substance. (B) The worker ant is attracted to the beetle larva and (C) *is stimulated to engage in grooming. (D) The tactile stimulation causes the beetle larva to rear up and, if the larva makes mouth-to-mouth contact with the ant, (E) the ant regurgitates a droplet of liquid food.*

all the others, the coloney could be left queenless by an accident on her nuptial flight. By producing a chirpin sound called "piping," the first queen delays the emergence of her sisters, who chirp back from within their cells. This has been interpreted as a means of delaying the mortal combat that must occur whenever there are two queens in a colony until after the first queen has had a chance to mate.

Group Effects

Group effects in the honeybee are obvious from the incredible control that a viable queen exerts over the functioning of her colony. As long as a healthy queen is present to give off the appropriate signals, the workers contribute unerringly to her needs, those of her offspring, and the colony as a whole. If a queen is removed, the organized behaviour of the workers gives way to disorganized restlessness in a matter of minutes. Within a few hours, workers will draw several worker cells into enlarged cells suitable for rearing a replacement queen. After a few days, some of the workers exprience ovarian development and actually lay infertile eggs, which develop into drones. The presence of queen substance apparently acts to inhibit queen cell construction and reproduction, probably by supperessing the activity of certain endocrine glands of the workers. This raises the question of how the workers are stimulated to produce young queens to facilitate the reproduction of the colony by swarming. Butler found the amount of queen substance produced by queens during the normal swarming season to be about one quarter of that of queens of nonswarming colonies. Thus, the queen clearly exerts her control over all individuals that comprise a colony, yet, she in turn is influenced in her behaviour and egg laying by the workers that tend to her needs.

INTERSPECIFIC COMMUNICATION

A variety of communication types may also be involved in the behavioural interaction between species. This is well illustrated by the relationship between some ant species and other insects that they treat like guests in their nests. The guest species called *myrmecophiles,* live in the ants' nests, where they may be groomed and cared for by their hosts and even permitted to eat the ant larvae. Ants, like the honeybee previously discussed, have an elaborated communication system that coordinates nest construction, food gathering, brood rearing, and defense of the colony. The fact that the ants allow some alien species full access to the benefits of their society suggests that the guests have, in the words of Holldobler" . . . broken the ants' code, that is, attained the ability to 'speak' the ants' language which involves a diversity of visual, mechanical and chemical cues." Holldobler reports that the larvae of the rove beetle, *Atemeles pubicollis,* which live in nests of *Formica polyctena,* produce a secretion that imitates the pheromone that ant larvae emit to stimulate the brood-keeping behaviour of the adults. The beetle larvae also imitate the begging behaviour of ant larvae, which mechanically stimulates a broodkeeping adult ant to regurgitate a droplet of food.

GROUPS LIVING

Animals form groups to enhance. Their foraging success and gain better protection against predators; but groups living also exposes them to diseases, competition, and social interference. The cost and benefits of social living vary with the age, sex, experience, and physical condition of individuals. Social groups are maintained by chemical, visual, anditory and factile signals. But the animals do not always communicate their intentions clearly and accurately. Complex social systems have evolved from offspring remaining with parents to help near future broods and from co-operation among adults of the same generation. Many persons would regard any form of interactive group behaviour as social - a herd of deer, perhaps, or a winter roost of monarch butterflies. Students of vertebrates often consider parental care - for example, among song birds - as social behaviour. As we saw in the preceding chapter, therc are many examples of parental care among insects that are usually regarded as "solitary." In some cases, the mother even feeds the offspring progressively, resulting in much mother-offspring contact. In instances of communal nesting, several females share a nest, each preparing and provisioning her own cells. But all of these are examples of what entomologists call *presocial behaviour*. The highest level 'of cooperative behaviour, termed *eusocial behaviour* (literally, "truly social") is found in only four groups: termites, ants, and some bees and wasps. Eusocial insects have the following attributes in common:

1. Brood care is cooperative; that is, individuals often feed offspring that are not their own.

2. There is *a caste system* involving a reproductive division of labour, such that many colony members are sterile.

3. There is an overlap of generations some offspring assisting the parental generation in the rearing of further offspring.

The question of how this unique form of behaviour may have evolved is a topic of much lively discussion among entomologists. The diversity of lifestyles among presocial insects suggests that there have been several routes to eusociality. In this chapter we shall be concerned with types of behaviour especially characteristic of eusocial insects, but we shall also take occasion to consider the advantages of presocial and of eusocial behaviour and to ask why (considering the success of ants, termites and the like) not all insects have evolved eusociality.

SOCIAL COMMUNICATION

The behaviour of the many individual in the colonies of social insects must be integrated in such a way that there is cooperation in defense, building, foraging, brood rearing, and the production of reproductive individuals at appropriate times. This can only be accomplished by broadcasting messages throughout the colony. Since visual signals would be difficult to transmit within the darkness and complexities of the nest, social signals are more often acoustic, tactile, gustatory, or especially olfactory. We present here on outline of the types of messages conveyed with a few examples of the mechanisms that have evolved in the various groups of wasps, bees and ants (Hymenoptera) and termites (Dictyoptera). The nests of social insects present a rich source of food for vertebrate predators (such as skunks or bears) and for arthropod predators (such as other social insects). Not only are *they* often filled with thousands of larvae and pupae, but there may be large amounts of food in storage. All social insects have evolved methods of dealing with predators, either by attacking en masse or by fleeing to a place of safety. But first a message must be transmitted quickly throughout the colony concerning the danger. Such*alarm signals* are often highly volatile pheromones, which fade quickly unless renewed. Rapid movements within the colony, with much tactile stimulation, may also convey alarm. Termites, when alarmed, vibrate their bodies against the substrate, producing a sound audible to humans, and some ants are able to stridulate by rubbing together specialized ridges on parts of the abdomen. Alarm usually mobilizes defense, but in some cases the alarm signals themselves may also serve a defense function.

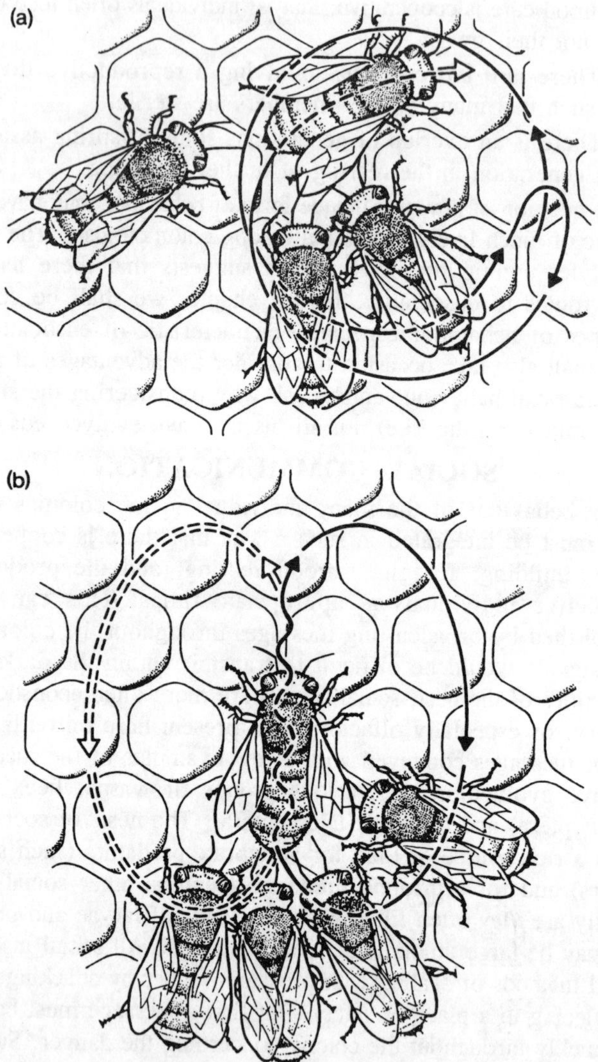

Fig. 5.1. A queen honey bee surrounded by a retinue of workers.

Attractants also play a major role in social life, especially with respect to the queen. In most social insects the queen rarely if ever leaves the nest and must be fed and groomed by the workers. In a honey bee hive, for example, the queen is usually accompanied by a circle of attending workers. Indeed, the term *queen* was first suggested by the retinue surrounding the mother of the colony, who of course "reigns" only in the sense that she produces chemical signals causing workers to forego reproduction and to attend to the queen. In the honey bee the signal is the continued production of ketodecenoic acid (often called *"queen substance")* from her mandibular glands.

The most prevalent attractants are the subtle combinations of odors usually called "nest odor" - apparently compounded of phero-mones on the cuticle of individuals; volatile pheromones in the colony; and the odor of the brood, food, substrate, and other unknown odor sources. Individual ants, termites, and other social insects crient toward these odors when close to the nest and are able to identify their own nest among others of the same species. Individ:.als also recognize one another as members of the same colony by these same cues, which may be said to be not only attractants but also *recognition signals*.

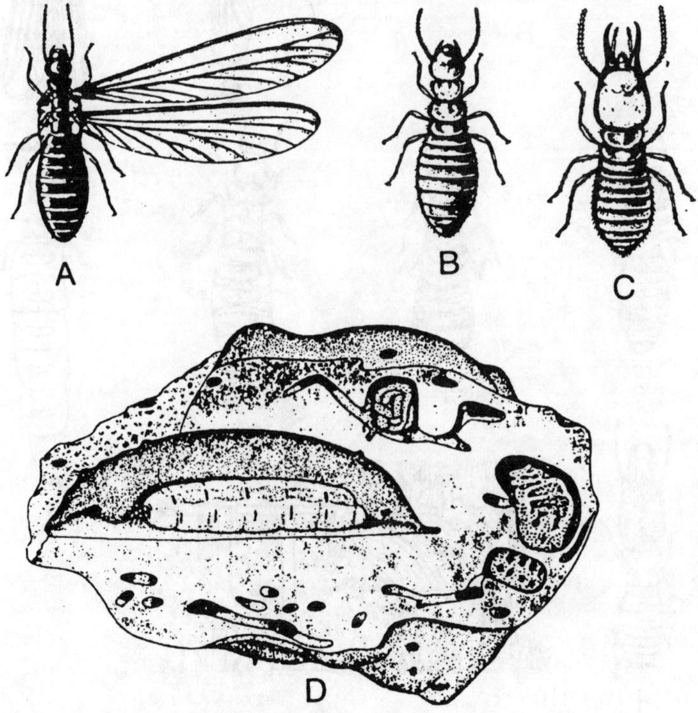

Fig. 5.2. Castes of termites.

Another major group of social signals serves in *recruitment* to food sources or new nest sites. One of the simplest forms of recruit ment is shown by ants of the genus *Leptothorax*. When a foraging worker is successful, she returns to the nest and regurgitates food to nestmates. She then raises her abdomen, extrudes her sting, and discharges a droplet of fluid. This serves to attract other workers, one of whom touches the abdomen or hind legs with her antennae and proceeds to follow the forager to the food source. The leader then lowers her abdomen, but if the follower becomes lost, the leader once again elevates her abdomen and initiates calling behaviour. *Tandem*

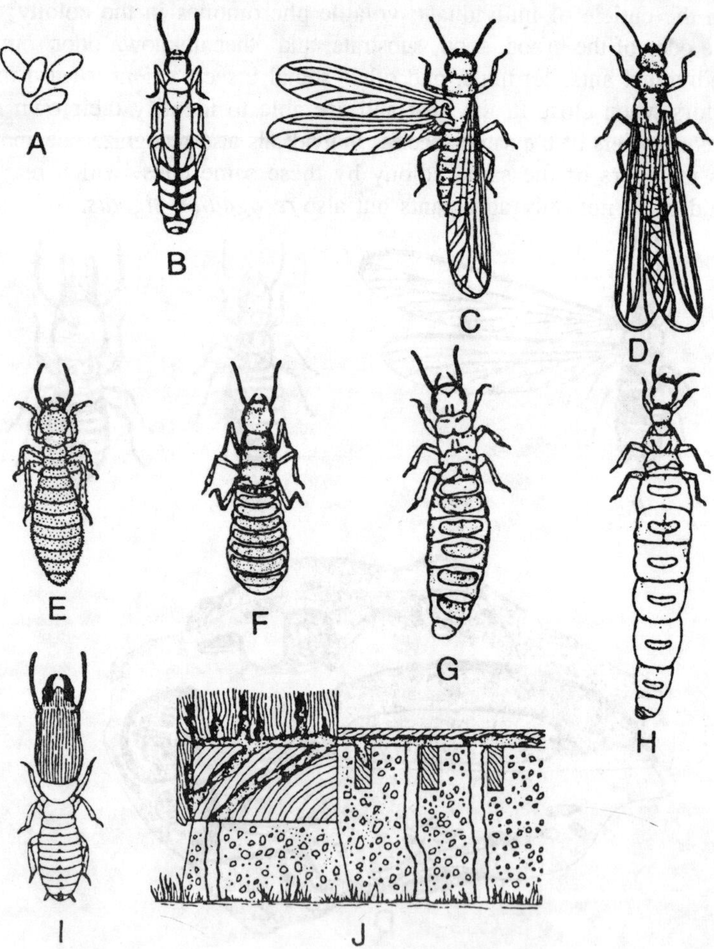

Fig, 5.3. Polymorphism in Reticulitermes. (A) Eggs, (B) Nymph, (C) Female winged form, (D) Male winged form, (E) Workers, (F) King, (G) Secondary reproductive (female), (H) Queen (abdomen distended with enlarged ovgaries), (I) Soldiers, and (J) Earthn tubes from soil across surface of concrete foundation to wooden sturucture.

running, as this is called, involving only two or at most a very few individuals, appears an inefficient system for recruitment to a food source, but it is interesting as an apparent evolutionary precursor of the more common and efficient method of laying *odor trails*. As E.O. Wilson has shown when a fire ant worker locates a source of food, she returns to her nest with her abdomen lowered, dragging her sting lightly over the substrate and depositing small quantities of a trail-marking pheromone. When she arrives at the nest and regurgitates to some of the workers, they are able to follow the trail to the food source, reinforcing it on the way back as long as the food lasts.

Termites also lay odor trails from abdominal glands a remark-able case of evolutionary convergence, since ants and termites belong to quite unrelated orders of insects. In more primitive termites, odor trails are used in recruiting workers to breaches in the nest wall. In more advanced termites, which forage outside the nest, odor trails serve in recruitment to food sources, much as they do in ants. In groups in which the workers are winged (wasps and bees), recruitment is accomplished quite differently. Some tropical social wasps as well as some stingless bees (tropical relatives of the honey bee) deposit pheromone on twigs, stones, and other objects between the food source and the nest or between a potential new nesting site and the old nest. The amounts of pheromone deposited are much larger than in the case of trail-laying ants and termites, and in some cases the odor can be detected by human observers. Workers are able to detect the odor from a distance of a few meters and are able to proceed along the trail by flying from odor spot to odor spot, even high into the trees in some cases.

Honey Bee Communication

Finally, a word must be said about the unique recruitment behaviour of the honey bee, the so-called dances described many years ago by Karl von Frisch. A worker bee, returning to the hive after having found a rich source of nectar, conveys information to other bees concerning both the direction and the distance of the food source. If she is standing on a horizontal surface (as would rarely occur in nature), direction is indicated by pointing the straight run of the dance directly toward the food source. Only the vertical surface of a comb, in the dark of the hive, direction is indicated by pointing the straight run to conform to the angle of flight in relation to the sun, as if the sun were directly above, thus substituting gravity for a visual cue.

These statements apply to the *waggle dance,* which is performed if the food source is more than 35 to 80 meters away (different races of the honey bee differ in this regard). In this dance more precise information on *distance is* indicated by the duration of the straight run: The greater the distance, the greater the duration of the straight run. If the food source is close to the hive, however, a different dance having no information on direction or distance is performed, the so-called *round dance*. This consists of a circle, at the end of which the worker turns around and repeats the circle facing in the other direction. Workers reading this message fly out in all directions near the hive and search for odors like those carried on the body of the dancing bee. Odors of the food source are also important in the waggle dance, which in itself serves only as an approximation of distance and direction. The dances are decoded within the hive by other bees, using tactile, olfactory and acoustic cues. Bees cluster about the dancer; contact her with their antennae; and having read the message, fly to the vicinity of the food source. At times there may be several workers dancing on behalf of several food sources. In this case the most persistent dancers tend to recruit the most workers. These same dances are also used for recruitment to new nesting sites at the time of swarming.

In recent years, there have been a number of criticisms of von Frisch's research possibly he underestimated the importance of odor of the food source clinging to the body of the dancers and the information in the wing sounds they produce; and it is true that different races of honey bees have different "dialects." But recent novel experiments have tended to confirm von Frisch's findings. James Gould, of Princeton University, established two feeding stations equidistant from the hive but in opposite directions, both similarly scented or unscented. In one the concentration of sugar was twice that in the other. Most of the foragers danced to the direction and distance of the station with the highest concentration of sugar, and nearly all recruitment was to that station. Factors such as site-specific odors, wind direction, and so forth were controlled, and it was also shown that in the absence of dancing almost no bees found the food sources. In a later experiment Gould developed a sophisticated design in which some of the bees responded to the information in the dances even though these were performed by bees coming from a different food source than that specified in. the dance. That is, the recruits responded to distance and direction cues in the dances rather than to odors conveyed by the dancers.

The communication signals of social insects are parsimonious in that the same signal is often used in different contexts to transmit different messages. "Queen substance" of the honey bee inhibits worker ovarian development and the initiation of queen cells, stimu-lates grooming and feeding of the queen by the workers, maintains colony cohesion during swarming, and attracts males during the queen's nuptial flight-a single substance conveying different information in different circumstances. This by no means exhausts the subject of social communication. For example, larvae of paper wasps may indicate hunger by hitting their heads against the cell walls, producing an audible

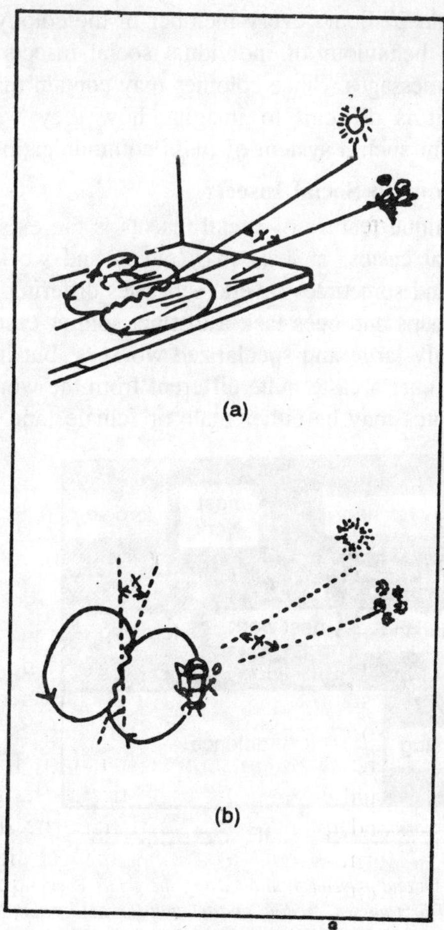

Fig 5.4. Waggle dance of the honey bee. On a horizontal surface (a) the straight part of the dance points directly toward a food source, but on the vertical surface of a comb (b) the straight part points to an angle with the sun as if the sun were directly above.

sound, queens on the nests of these same wasps may signal their dominance by tail wagging and other visual signals. interchange of food and secretions between adults and between adults and larvae conveys many messages on conditions within the colony. for example, the proper balance between the castes may be maintained by the amount of caste-specific pheromone being circulated in the colony. Studies using radioactive tracers have shown that in *Formica* ants substances imbibed every by a single worker are rapidly spread throughout the colony, and within 27 hours every member of the colony has received some of it. The behaviour of individual social insects is intimately guided by these messages. Since colonies may contain many thousands of individuals, it is difficult to imagine how they would function coherently without such a system of mass communication.

Division of Labour in Social Insects

The most unique feature of social insects is the existence in each species of several castes: at least two (queen and workers), often a third (soldiers), and sometimes several subcastes differing in appearance and function. Wasps and bees lack a distinct soldier caste; in the ants soldiers are simply large and specialized workers; but in the termites the soldiers constitute a caste quite different from the workers. Worker and soldier termites may be either male or female, and workers may

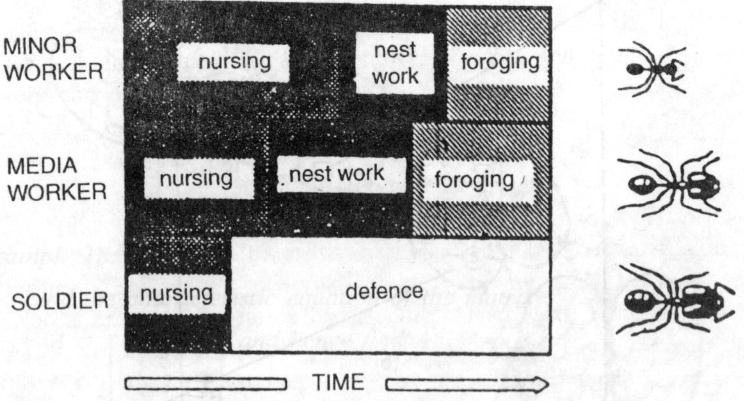

Fig. 5.5. Polymorphism and polyethism in an ant of the genus Pheidok. *Smallest workers, called minors, are at first nurses, feeding and tending larvae: later they do other kinds of work within the nest: and finally they may leave the nest to forage for a period, Larger work ers, or medias, spend less time as nurses and more in other activities. The largest workers, called majors, may also be termed soldiers, since a major part of their time is spend in colony defense. The increasingly disproportionate size of the head is a result of allometric growth: larger workers have received more food as larvae.*

be either immatures or adults. In contrast, worker Hymenoptera are always adult females. Workers and soldiers do not mate; they represent the worker force and defense of the colony, and reproduction becomes the sole function of the queen and males. In termites, a male reproductive *("king")* is a permanent attendant of the queen, but in Hymenoptera males die soon after mating.

Members of different castes of one species often differ radically in appearance, a striking case of *polymorphism* that has, for the most part, an environmental rather than a genetic basis. Members of different, castes and subcastes also exhibit very different behaviour, a phenomenon called *polyethism.* A soldier termite is a specialist in defense and often cannot even feed itself. But in other cases polyethism has a temporal element, as in the subcastes of worker ants. In the case of the honey bee, division of labour among the workers is wholly temporal. There is no polymorphism within the worker caste, but workers perform different tasks depending on their age.

How can all these diverse behaviour patterns be built into one individual? And how is one species able to produce several kinds of individuals that differ so much in appearance and in behaviour? If workers and soldiers do not reproduce, how are their genes conveyed to the next generation? If nature selection favours those individuals that produce the most surviving offspring, how does one account for the existence of sterile castes? Obviously the social insects present a host of questions that cannot easily be answered. Perhaps some will seem less intractable if we look briefly at certain species that seem not to be "fully eusoc ial" that is, that appear to be on the verge of acquiring a worker caste.

Determination of Caste in "Primitively Eusocial" Hymenoptera

Charles D. Michener and his students at the University of Kansas have for some years been studying a small ground-nesting bee called *Dialictus zephyrus*. These bees form aggregations in earthen banks, provisioning their nests with pollen and nectar gathered from flowers in the vicinity. In midsummer, nests contain several cooperating females, all superficially alike. But closer inspection reveals that a division of labour does occur. One of the females proves to be the major egg layer, while the others act as guards or foragers. The major egg layer ("queen") nudges the other females periodically, causing them to move into guarding positions, or she leads them down into the burrow where there are stimuli for building or provisioning. When the subordinates lay eggs, as they do occasionally, the queen eats them and replaces them with her own. If the queen is removed, one of the subordinates assumes her role. Ovarian development in the subordinates is believed to be retarded as a result of the queen's behaviour, but all the workers have the potential to mate and become queens (males are present throughout the summer).

A somewhat different situation prevails among bumble bees, which live in small colonies in cavities in the soil. Inseminated females overwinter and start colonies in the spring, and the workers and the new crop of males and queens are all the foundress's offspring. The queen dominates the workers by pheromones transmitted on contact, aided by aggressive behaviour, and the workers come to assume various roles in the colony, the smaller ones mostly as nurses, the larger ones mostly as forgers, although they may change their role as a result of age or the needs of the colony. If the queen is removed, of one of the larger workers will assume her role. Workers tend to be larger late in the season, and eventually a new crop of large females destined to be queens is produced (as well as males). Late in the season there are more workers present in the colony in relation to the number of larvae. The increase in size of individuals may simply be the result of the increasing worker: larva ratio; larvae receive more food and become larger adults.

Determination of Caste in Advanced Eusocial Insects

In the honey bee, behavioural dominance by the queen has been replaced by secretion of a pheromone (queen substance) that prevents development of the ovaries in the workers. Queens are reared in especially large cells and receive not only more food but food enriched by the contents of hypopharyngeal glands in the heads of the workers ("royal jelly"). In most of the more advanced social insects, the role of queen is sustained by pheromones. In colonies containing thousands of individuals, control by behavioural interactions between queen and workers would scarcely be practicable.

By and large, polymorphism in social Hymenoptera has a *trophogenic* basis; that is it is the result of differential feeding of the larvae or of different-sized eggs. Larvae receiving a minimal amount of food develop into small, sterile workers, a phenomenon sometimes called "nutritional castration." Better-fed larvae tend to produce larger individuals. In the ants these may have disproportionately large heads and mandibles, the result of allomevic growth, and may serve as soldiers. Allometric growth is a genetically determined tendency for certain body parts to grow at a more rapid rate than other parts and thus to be larger in the adult stage. Reproductives—the queens of the next

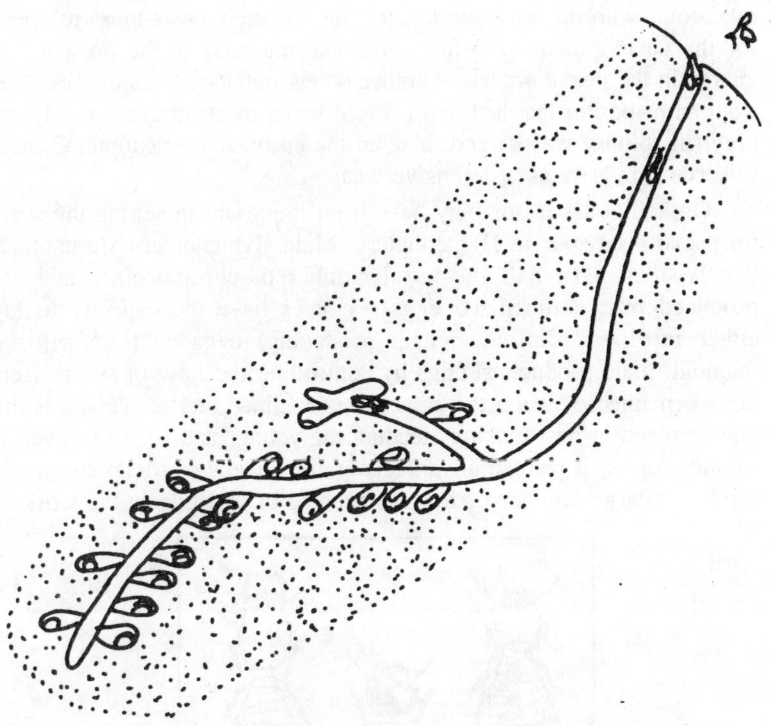

Figure 5.6. A nest of the sweat bee Dilic us zephynts *in a soil bank, in early summer. Four females are present; the queen is deepest in the nest near a cell being provisioned, the guard is at the entrance, and a forager is returning with pollen and nectar.*

generation and their mates are produced from larvae that are abundantly fed an sometime provided with food of different quality. Often they are reared in larger cells, the combination of large cells and a high worker: larva ratio ensuring a crop of reproductives.

Hymenoptera appear especially well suited for the development of social behaviour, as reflected in the fact that eusociality has evolved several times independently in the ants, in the wasps, and several time sin the bees; but only one other group of insects, the termites, has evolved eusociality. The Hymenoptera appear to have several features that together render them likely to become eusocial. These insects must have evolved fail-safe homing abilities as well as the ability to protect the larvae from predation, desiccation, and so forth. Limitation in sites suitable for nesting may cause them to aggregate in certain places and to produce more permanent, many-celled nests. Aggregated nests may improve the opportunities for parasites and predators, who do not have to look far for their hosts-thus, the need for the development of defense mechanisms such as the presence of guards in the nest entrance. Another potent defense, the sting, evolved from an ovipositor that had first evolved into a mechanism for paralyzing prey (in solitary wasps) and then, in the eusocial Hymenoptera, came to serve primarily as a defensive weapon.

On additional factor may have been important in setting the stage for social behaviour in Hymenoptera. Male Hymenoptera are haploid; that is, they have half the usual number of chromosomes and are produced from unfertilized eggs. Females have the capacity to lay either fertilized (diploid, female-producing) eggs or , unfertilized (haploid, male-producing) eggs by controlling the flow of sperm from the spermathecae when the eggs are laid. Since the female sex is the one involved in nest making, feeding the young, and so forth, even in solitary forms, it proved advantageous for queens of social species to produce a large number of females capable of assisting in the work of

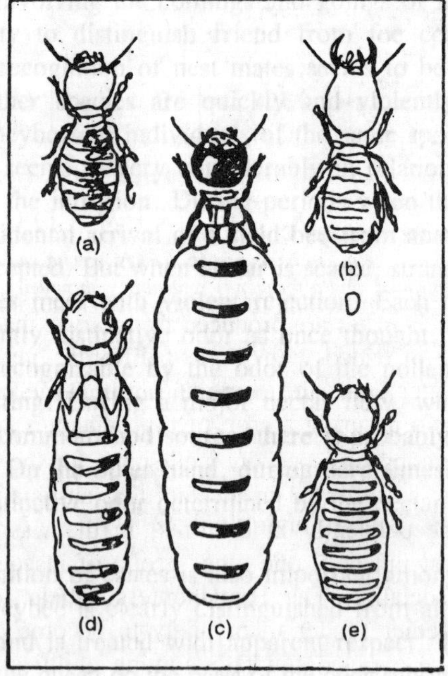

Fig. 5.7. The castes of termites. In these insects, in contrast to Hymenoptera, the "king" (not shown here is a permanent member of the colony. The queen (c) may ultimately become very large. The termites in (d) and (e) are supplementary queens: the one in (a) is a worker, in (b), a soldier. The worker is about 5 mm long in the species figured.

the colony, delaying male production until time of production of a new brood of potential queens. The ability to produce progeny of the desired sex, as needed, is one that we humans may envy.

Termites

Most of these remarks do not apply to termites, which are believed to have evolved from the ancestors of cockroaches, which do not make nests and are diploid. Hence, they seem to lack the preadaptations of Hymenoptera. Nevertheless many do aggregate. The group of cockroach like insects that gave rise to the termites probably lived gregariously in logs and digested cellulose with the aid of intestinal r icroorganisms as some species of cockroaches still do. Since these symbionts are cast off with each molt and must be reacquuired from others, and newly emerged individuals must obtain them from their elders, isolated individuals would soon starve. Both woodfeeding cockroaches and termites frequently feed at the anus of other individuals, thereby obtaining intestinal symbionts needed for digesting their food. It is apparently this factor that enhanced the development of eusocial behaviour in the Dictyoptera.

Caste determination in termites differs considerably from that in Hymenoptera. Since termites have gradual metamorphosis, the young are not helpless, and in fact by the third instar members of both sexes assist in work of the colony-an example of "child labour" unique in the insects. These immatures molt further and may in some cases develop into soldiers or reproductives, depending on a complex system of pheromones circulating in the colony. Soldier termites are typically wingless adults that differ greatly from the workers and reproductives. Termite colonies also contain "supplementary reproductives," which have wing pads and the capacity to become winged reproductives if the queen or king dies. Development of these various castes is mediated by the interaction of pheromones and hormones in ways that are far from fully understood. Presence of supplementary reproductives means that colonies are potentially immortal, and indeed the nests of termites sometimes persist for many years and result in structures of incredible size, considering the size of the builders. The nests of each species of termite are distinctively different, so that taxonomists sometimes find it easier to identify the species by the nest rather than by the termites themselves.

SOCIAL HOMEOSTASIS

Maintenance of a functional steady state in an organism or in a colony of organisms is termed *homeostasis*. The colonies of social insects have sometimes been compared to organisms; the individuals, to cells, sopte of which are specialized for reproduction, others for nutrition, others for protection. Colonies have a birth, a growth cycle, and an eventual death. As we have said, the nests are species specific, just as individuals can be recognized as members of different species. Thus, the term *superorganism* is sometimes applied to these colonies, though a little reflection will show that analogies between colonies and organisms are at best very rough and not overly instructive.

Nevertheless, the superorganism concept does help one to visualize the vast amount off coordination that must occur within the colony coordination that is achieved by complex systems of communication

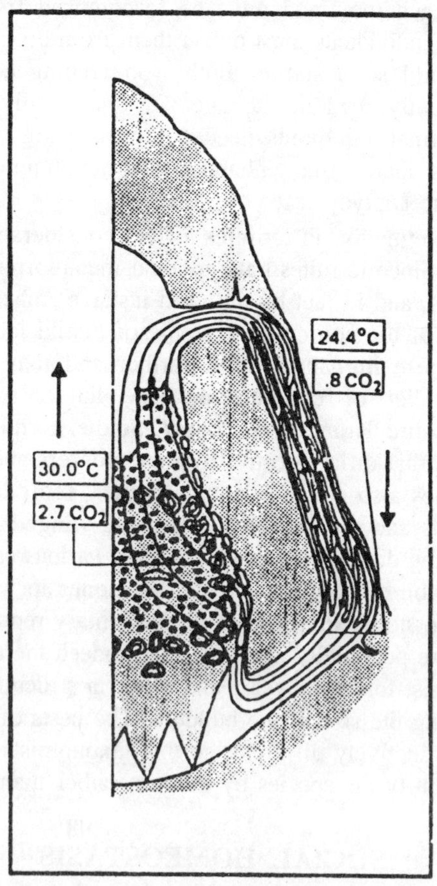

Fig. 5.8. Temperature regulation in the nest of an African termite. Only half of the nest is shown here.

operating with respoot to individuals that are diverse but limited the their responses and in their abilities to control other colony members. Integrity of the colony is maintained via nest structures that cannot easily be breached and via workersand soldiers prepared to respond to intruders with appropriate physical and chemical attacks.

In temperate climates, colonies of most species of bees and wasps are annual affairs, begun anew each spring by overwintered, inseminated females. Thus a nest of yellow jackets may contain only a few hundred or at most a few thousand individuals. Ant and termite colonies are, however, perennial, and in tropical climates colonies of some species reach enormous size. A single colony of army ants may sometimes contain over a million workers. Queens of certain termites are reported to lay as many as 30,000 eggs per day, or 10 million per year. Homeostatic mechanisms in colonies this size must be complex beyond belief.

Most social insects are able to control temperature and humidity of the nest at least to some extent. In temperate climates, many ants start to breed under stones in early spring, taking advantage.of the capacity of stones to absorb heat, then they move deeper into the soil in summer. Aerial nests of wasps are built in protected places, and those of hornets and yellow jackets are enclosed in protective paper sheaths. Fanning at the nest entrance and the carrying of water to the nest play a role in cooling the nest in hot weather for many species. Honey bees survive the winter by clustering in the hive. Clustering bees consume honey and move about within the cluster, generating enough heat so that the temperature of the cluster does not fall below about 20°C, even though the outside temperature may frequently be below 0°C. Similarly honey bees are able to maintain a hive temperature of about 35°C even on the hottest summer days, so long as water is available to them. Some of the most remarkable instances of "air conditioning" occur among some of the fungus-growing termites of Africa. Warm air generated in the core of the nest rises and passes into a series of small chambers in the nest walls, where it is cooled and where fresh oxygen is obtained; it then flows back into the core of the nest at the bottom, and a slow but continuous circulation is maintained.

SLAVERY IN ANTS

Before leaving the social insects, mention should be made of another unique phenomenon: slavery among ants. This behaviour is justly termed unique, since it differs from slavery among humans in usually, occurring between species; that is, members of one species enslave those of another, related species. It also differs in being a biological rather than a cultural phenomenon. Thus one could argue that it should not be called slavery at all, though the superficial resemblances so slavery in humans are striking. Slave-making species of ants are widely distributed, and most of the reported "battles" between ant colonies are actually slave raids. Certain reddish species of the genus *formica* undertake frequent raids on colonies of some of the common and rather docile black species of the same genus. Columns of workers approach and surround the nest to be plundered, causing alarm, attempts to escape, and often some combat among the workers. Eventually the more aggressive slave makers enter the nest, seize larvae and pupae, and carry them back to their own nest. When these develop into adult workers, they acquire the colony odor and perform their normal behaviour in the alien nest, effectively supplementing the worker force of the slave-making species.

Recent research by E.O. Wilson and his colleagues at Harvard University has shown that slave makers of at least some species have enlarged Dufour's glands in their abdomens. When they approach a nest of the slave species, they spray the contents of these glands onto the workers. The secretion consists of a mixture of acetates that causes the workers of the slave species to become alarmed and disorganized. Curiously the effect of the acetates on the slave makers is quite the reverse: They produce attraction and excitement as Wilson, says, "exactly the responses needed to conduct successful slave raids." By and large, colonies of most ant species defend themselves well against incursion by alien colonies, sometimes resorting to physical combat to maintain territorial boundaries. In honeypot ants of the deserts of the southwestern United States, territories are defended by ritualized displays in which workers of opposing colonies *"stilt wall,"* at first facing one another, then beginning to circle.and trying to push one another sideways. Such "tournaments," recently described by Bert Holldobler, of Harvard University, may go on for days. If one of the colonies is unable to recruit enough workers to the tournament area, it may be overrun by the stronger colony and the brood and other nest contents carried off. The surviving workers then become incorporated into the raider's nest. This is the only known example of slavery occurring within one species of ant.

SYMBIONTS IN SOCIAL INSECTS

In spite of the various behavioural and chemical defenses of the

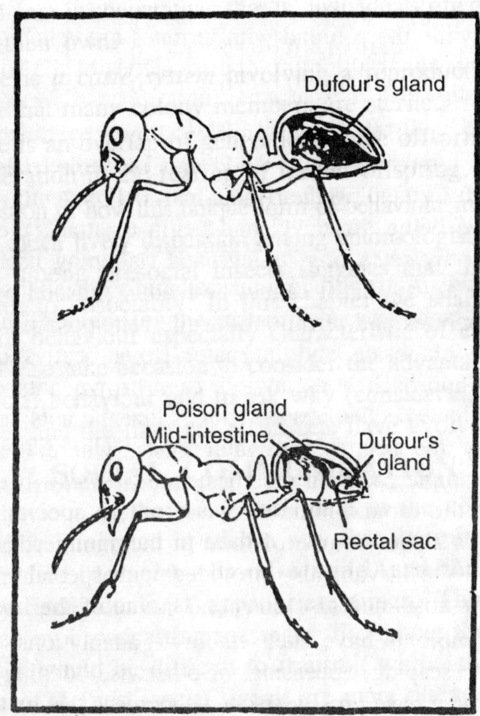

Fig. 5.9. The enlarged Dufour's gland of a slave-making ant (Formica subintegra) (above) as compared with that of a member of a slave species (Fonntca subsereceaa) (below).

colonies of social insects, quite a number of arthropods have evolved ways of breaching these defenses and taking advantage cf the security of the nest and the abundance of food provided. They do this by tapping into the communication codes-that is, by acquiring the ability to "speak the language" of their hosts. Many of them have glands that secrete substances attractive to their hosts, who "adopt" them as part of the colony. Altogether, according to E.O. Wilson, insects of at least 120 different families and 17 different orders have become "guests" of social insects, along with a variety of mites, millipedes, and other arthropods. As the noted student of social insects W. M. Wheeler put it many years ago: Were we to behave in an analogous manner we shouldd live in a truly Alice-in-Wonderland society. We should delight in keeping porcupines, alligators, lobsters, etc., in our homes, insist on their sitting down to table with us and feed them so solicitously with spoon victuals that our children would either perish of neglect or grow up as hopeless rachitics.

Symbionts associated with ants are termed *mynnecophiles* (literally, "*ant lovers*") while those found with termites are called *termitophiles.* Relatively few occur in the more open societies of the social bees and wasps.

One of the simplest associations is shown by the *"highwayman beetle,"* which intercepts black wood ants on their trails and solicits food from them by tapping their mouthparts. Frequently the ants soon realize they are being "tricked" and begin to attack the beetle. The beetle responds by retracting its legs and flattening itself against the ground in such a way that it cannot be readily grasped by the ants. In most myrmecophiles and termitophiles the relationship with the hosts is much more elaborate and intimate. Rove beetles of the genus *Atemeles* also approach ants, in this case brown ants of the genus *Myrmica,* but these beetles possess glands that the ants find attractive. The ants carry the beetles into their nests, where they spend the winter among ample food. In the spring *the Atemeles* beetles migrate to colonies of the mound-building wood ant, a species of *Formica,* which provide a richer source of food in the summer. Here they lay their eggs, and the larvae, also provided with special glands, solicit food from their hosts and also consume larvae of the host ants.

Not all symbionts have such elaborate adaptations, but all have some means of escaping, appeasing, or otherwise "duping" their hosts. Termitophiles often have grossly swollen abdomens that exude substances that are licked by the termites. In many cases we do not known precisely how the symbionts. "break the code" of their hosts or what they feed on in the nest. Although the large colonies of army ants and some of the tropical termites contain hundreds of *"guests"* of great variety, many of the symbionts appear quite rare. Evidently this is a precarious existence; as in espionage among humans, a slip may be fatal.

ADVANTAGES AND DISADVANTAGES

A great many insect species live essentially solitary lives, contacting other individuals chiefly at time of mating-and a few even dispense with this "inconvenience," reproducing parthenogenetically. Clearly a solitary way of life has advantages: Such individuals can more effectively hide from predators and avoid competition with similar lifestyles; they can also more effectively live in small spaces and exploit dispersed food sources. Group living also has obvious disadvantages: There are opportunities for the spread of disease and for the incursion of unwanted "guests" into large societies. Why then live in groups? One advantage might be that escape from predators is actually enhanced if, via communication resulting in alarm and defense behaviour i ha of the group, permits predator is driven off. Another might better exploitation of food sources that are strongly localized or so large and tough that one individual could not well exploit them, as seen in first-instar sawfly larvae feeding on pine needles or ants attacking a beetle. Still another factor might concern limitations in living space - that is, cockroaches may aggregate because only limited areas provide suitable conditions of warmth and moisture; or ground nesting bees or wasps, because soil of suitable consistency is patchily distributed.

Individuals of a species commonly compete severely for food and living space. For group living to succeed, individuals must survive and reproduce more successfully within the group than apart from it. This mcans that they must evolve a degree of tolerance, if not actual cooperative behaviour, with other members of that species. Clearly it will not pay an individual within a group to devote energies to competitive interactions; but it may very well pay to produce or respond to an alarm signal. Wherever, the advantages of group living outweigh its disadvantages, in terms of individual reproductive success, group living may evolve.

Social groups among insects (and among animals generally) usually consist of related individuals parents and offspring, siblings, or at least members of a local population having many genes in common. Often there are mechanisms for occasional outbreeding, such as dispersal at time of mating. Webs of a tent caterpillar commonly contain individuals from a single egg mass; lady beetles clustering for the winter are commonly the descendaatsof those that clustered there the previous winter. As we have seen, the colonies of eusocial insects are essentially "extended families," even when the queen has mated more than once or when there is more than one queen, there is genetic relatedness among colony members. Individual *Darwinian fitness* (that is, reproductive success) may in such cases be replaced by *inclusive fitness* (defined as net genetic representation in succeeding generations, including other relatives in addition to offspring). That is to say, an individual may devote energies to cooperative behaviour to the detriment of its own reproductive success to the extent that the individual it helps carries genes identical to its own.

The expenditure of energy in cooperative behaviour that might otherwise be spent in individual effort is often spoke of as *altniism,* and natural selection that involves inclusive fitness is often spoken of as *kin selection.* Whether or not unselfish behaviour among humans is a product of kin selection is a controversial topic we need not consider here; but in any case the word *altruism* as applied to insects does have this connotation and does not imply purposefulness on the part of the performers. Even with low degrees of relatedness among members of a colony, kin selection favours the evolution and maintenance of sterile castes if the benefit cost ratio is high enough. In this context it is much easier to understand the behaviour of a worker honey bee, for example, who leaves her sting in the body of a predator and dies thereafter: She is ensuring the survival of many thousands of individuals of very similar genetic constitution.

All of this is helpful in explaining the unique properties of eusociality. Workers and soldiers have lost all individual fitness (or most of it, since workers of Hymenoptera do in some cases lay viable, male-producing eggs). But the colony, as an extended family, may be enormously successful in survival and reproduction and may exploit and even modify the environment in ways no individual could do. A soldier termite guards a colony of thousands of individuals, and at much risk to its own life. But ultimately its genes (which are also those of the reproductive caste) will persist in succeeding generations via inclusive fitness. We have suggested reasons why eusocial behaviour may have evolved in termites and in Hymenoptera but not elsewhere. In Hymenoptera, eusociality has in fact evolved several times independently. In addition to permitting females to control the sex of their offspring, male haploidy, in this order, may result in an unusually close relationship among siblings. Since each male in the result of "virgin birth," every sperm he produces has all his genes, while each egg produced by a female has only half of hers (as in diploid species).

Because anY daughter of a male has a full set of his genes, sisters related through both parents are unusually closely related (by 3:4). On the other hand, daughters are related to their mother only 1 : 2. The assumption is that females are therefore more likely to evolve a tendenCY to cooperate with their sisters to rear more sisters than to start *then* own nest and produce daughters. How important this factor is in enhancing altruism in colonies of ants, bees and wasps in a moot point, bait one that must be kept in mind.

EUSOCIAL BEHAVIOUR

Eusocial Wasps

All of the eusocial wasps belong to the family Vespidae. Among these, the *generapolistes* (paper wasps), *Vespa* (hornets), and *Vespula* (yellow jackets) are the best known. Each of these genera have three

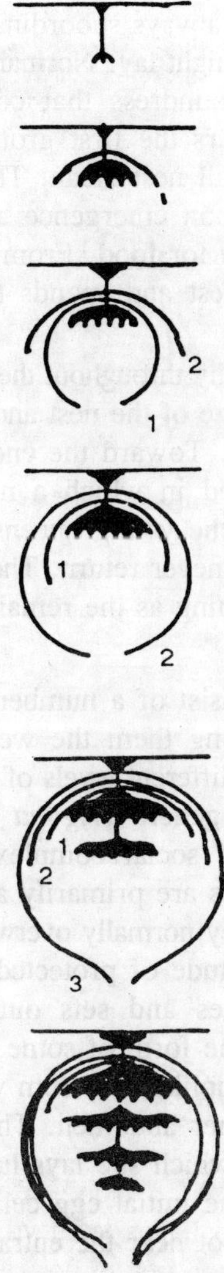

Fig. 5.10. The steps in the construction of a nest by a vespid wasp.

castes: *eeens* (fertile females), *workers* (nonfertile females), and *drones* (alts). In-temperate regions, wasp colonies are established each spry by overwintered queens and last but a single season. When a queen comes out of hibernation, she immediately begins the construction of a nest and rears the first small group of daughters. In the genus *Polistes,* a founding queen may be joined by other overwintered queens, but these auxiliary queens are always subordinate to the foundress, which eats any eggs her helpers might lay. Normally, however, wasp colonies are started by a single foundress that constructs an initial tier of hexagonal paper cells, rears the first group of larvae on macerated insects, and keeps the small nest clean. The first group of offspring are all workers, which upon emergence add new cells to the nest, tend the queen, and forage for food. From this time on, the founding queen rarely leaves the nest and spends the rest of her life laying eggs.

The colony grows rapidly throughout the summer as each generation of workers increases the size of the nest and the number of young that can be reared at one time. Toward the end of summer, some larger brood cells are constructed in which a number of males and new queens are reared. When the young queens and drones emerge, they leave the nest to mate and never return. The founding queen dies, and the colony declines to nothing as the remaining workers expire.

Eusocial Bees

The eusocial bees consist of a number of species with a variety of social life styles. Among them the well-known bumblebees and honeybees represent quite different levels of social complexity, whereas the stingless bees of the genera *Trigona* and *Malipona* display an interesting combination of social complexity and primitive nesting behaviour. The bumblebees are primarily adapted to cooler climates. Like the eusocial wasps, they normally overwinter as queens that survive the cold moths in the solitude of protected hibernations sites. In the spring, the queen emerges and sets out in search of a suitable subterranean nest site in the form of some preexisting cavity. Within the nest the constructs a cuplike cell from wax that is secreted by the intersegmental glands of her abdomen. The cup is then provisioned with a ball of pollen, on which she lays her first batch of eggs, and the cell is sealed. After the initial egg cell has been completed, the queen constructs a honeypot near the entrance to the nest and fills it with nectar. The first group of offspring are all workers that upon emergence assist the queen in producing more larval cells and in feeding the new brood. The subsequent brood is either fed by the workers or is allowed to feed directly on a mass pollen store, depending on the species. By late summer, the colony consists of several hundred workers and produces males and new queens; the colony then abandons its nest. The virgin queens are met by waiting males, copulate, and then enter hibernation.

The tropical, stingless bees construct their wax and resin nests in hollow tree trunks or roots or in subterranean crevices. The nest is usually divided into a brood area and food storage area. The brood combs consist of horizontal tiers of cells that open upward and are constructed one above the other like an upside-down wasp nest. Each tier is begun with a central cell to which rings of peripheral cells are added until each comb reaches its full diameter. Unlike the wasps, stingless bees construct one cell at a time, provide it with an egg, then provision and seal it before the next cell is built. Unlike the honeybees, which use their combs over and over again, the stingless bees tear down their cells after the young emerge. The food storage area consists of a series of wax pots that are filled with honey and pollen. Stingless be colonies expand to thousands of individuals and, unlike those of bumblebees, persist from year to year. As with the honeybees, stingless bees produce maiden queens and drones, from time to time, and the number of colonies in increased and dispersed by swarming. Unlike honeybee swarms, however, stingless bee swarms consist of a cluster of workers and a maiden queen rather than the old queen.

The honeybee originated in the tropics or subtropics but seems to have been preadapted, through its ability to regulate its nest temperature, to expand its range into regions of colder climate and still maintain perennial colonies. Entire colonies, instead of just fecund queens as in the wasps and bumble bees, overwinter. This not only permits the colonies to become much larger but permits and requires other changes as well. Because honeybee queens do not initiate new colonies each year by their own labour, they do not require any of the capabilities of their worker caste. Consequently, they have become much more differentiated from the workers morphologically and serve solely the functions of reproduction. New colonies are founded through the process of colony division by swarming, as in the stingless bees. The swarming process usually begins when a colony is strong and crowded. In response to some unknown stimulus, the queen reduces the level of queen substance the produces, and the workers respond by constructing a small number of queen cells. The larvae that hatch from the eggs"taid in these larger cells are fed exclusively on royal jelly and complete their development in about two thirds of the time it takes workers and drones to develop.

When virgin queens are developing within the colony the resident queen's egg production declines, and she is treated less hospitably until more or less forced to leave with a large retinue of older workers. Swarms containing the old queen are called prime swarms and may be followed a short time later by one or more afterswarms, each containing a new queen produced within the hive and already mated.

Swarms usually settle in a temporary cluster while a permanent nesting site is located. Once scout bees have found an communicated the location of a suitable nesting place, the temporary cluster breaks up and moves to the new site. The workers immediately begin to construct vertical sheets of hexagonal wax cells suspended from the roof of the nest site. The wax combs are constructed a precise distance apart and consist mainly of regular, well-fitted worker cells. The size and shape of the cells determine the kind of egg the queen lays therein and how each cell is provisioned. Worker cells receive diploid eggs and are provisioned with royal jelly for a few days, followed by a mixture of pollen and honey called bee bread. When a queen encounters an irregular, enlarged cell, she will lay a haploid egg, which becomes a drone. When an egg is laid in a cuplike cell, the workers will feed the larvae that develops only on royal jelly and thereby produce maiden queens. Thus the structural details of the wax comb play an integral part in the social organization of the colony. Since the queen that

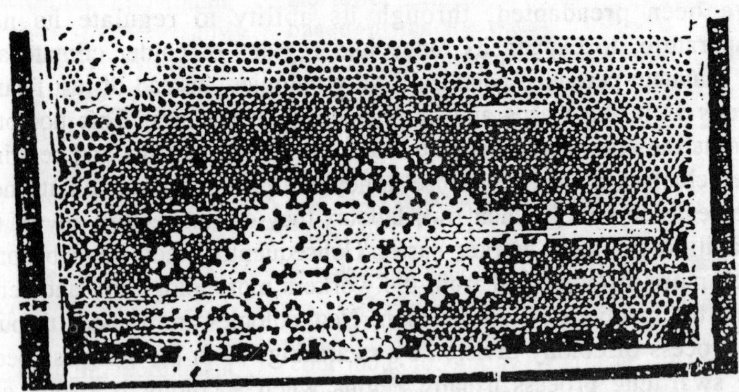

Fig. 5.11. A frame of honey comb from a commercial hive showing worker cells, drone cells, queen cells, and some capped brood.

accompanies a primary swarm is mated and the workers can immediately begin constructing a brood comb, the queen can soon proceed with egg laying, and the new colony grows very quickly. Meanwhile, the virgin queen left with the original colony must go on one or more nuptial flights to obtain enough sperm to last the 5 to 7 years that she might live. The original colony also grows rapidly, since the brood left by the departed queen emerges and gradually takes over the hive chores from the again workers that remained after the swarm.

Drones are produced throughout the more favourable part of the year. They are usually most abundant when the colonies are reproducing by swarming and therefore contain virgin queens that must be inseminated. Drones contribute absolutely no labour to the colony but are tolerated by the workers until late in the summer. As the supply of food in the field begins to decline in the fall, the workers become intolerant of the drones, driving them from the hive and not permitting them to reenter.

In respect to brood rearing and overwintering, the ability to regulate nest temperature is highly beneficial. The precision with which honeybee colonies do this is truly remarkable, but it would not be possible if it were not for the type of nest site selected and the way it is modified and utilized. The actual thermoregulatory process, however, is accomplished by the bees themselves rather than physically, as with the termites. During the months when a brood is being reared, the brood chamber is maintained at a temperature of 34.5 to 35.5°C, even though the outside air temperature may reach more than 60°C. In the winter, the cluster temperature ranges from 20 to 30°C and is never permitted to drop below 17°C, regardless of the outside temperature. When the outside temperature drops, the temperature in the hive is maintained by the metabolic heat generated by the workers, whose behaviour changes as the temperature declines. At first, the workers form a loose cluster toward the center of the hive. As the temperature drops, the cluster tightens. The workers at the center consume small amounts of honey and generate heat by vibrating their muscles; those forming the outer layers of the cluster act as an insulating blanket. As time passes, the outer bees move toward the center of the cluster, while those near the center move into the outer layers. During hot weather, the temperature of the brood area is maintained by a circulation of air in the hive created by workers that fan with their wings at the hive entrance. When this activity proves to be inadequate, other workers carry water into the hive and distribute it over the brood cells, which are then cooled as the water evaporates.

Ants

All ants are eusocial. The lack of presocial behaviour of the kinds found among the wasps and bees can be explained by the fact that the ants probably evolved from a group of presocial wasps. The variety of life styles displayed by the ants has long been of fascination to naturalists, perhaps because so many aspects of their social behaviour seemingly parallel our own. All living species of ants have a caste system that generally parallels that of the eusocial wasps and bees and clearly reveals a division of labour. The principal casts consist of males, ·queens, and workers the latter group being subdivided into different types in most species. Several genera also have castes intermediate between males and workers and between workers and queens, but these are generally less important than the main castes. Typical males are winged reproductives that contribute absolutely nothing to the labour of the colony although they do groom other adults and are groomed in return. Queens are the colony founders and mothers. They are usually winged when they emerge but shed their wings after their nuptial flight. During the establishment of a new nest, the queen

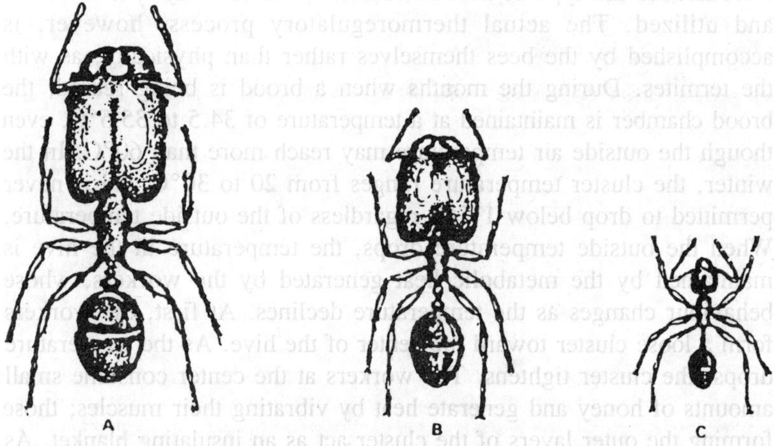

Fig. 5.12. Different forms of the worker cast of ants. (A) Major. (B) Media. (C) Minor.

performs all of the tasks later performed by the workers; but , once the first group of workers has emerged, the queen's activities are reduced to egg laying and grooming.

Workers are sterile females, and in the broad sense include both the labourers and defenders of the colony. There are often three subcastes of workers, based partially on size. The largest are the *majors* or *soldiers*, which are often considered to be a distinct caste because of the oversized (allometric) development of their heads and mandibles. The other workers are distinguished as being *media*, if of intermediate size, and *minors*, if small. The degree of workers polymorphism varies greatly from species to species, but, in species in which it is pronounced, a clear division of labour among the subcastes can be observed. The most unusual workers are the repletes of the honey ant *Myrmecocystus*. These individuals serve as casks for the storage of the honeydew brought to the nest by the foragers. When filled, the abdomen of a replete becomes a large swollen sac.

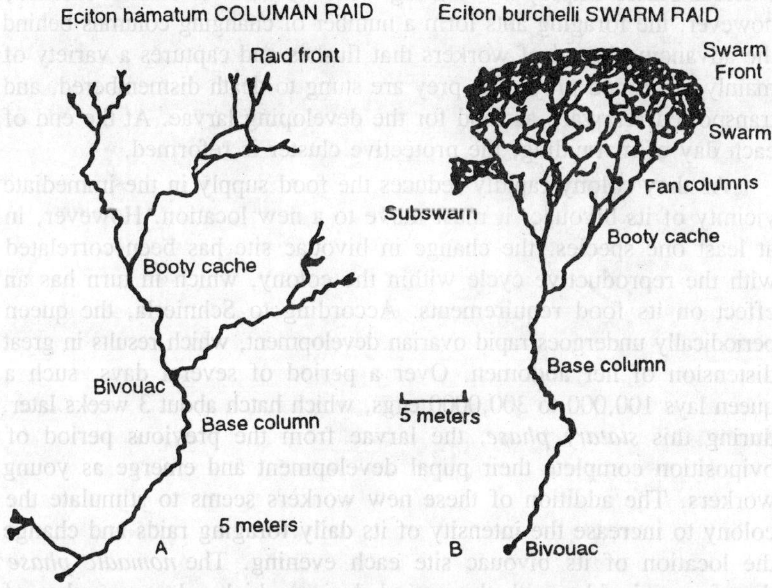

Fig. 5.13. Basic raiding patterns employed by army ants. (A) The column raid of Eaton hamatum *with an advancing front composed of several narrow columns of workers. (B) The swarming raid of* Eciton burchelli *composed of a mass of work ors advancing together.*

Ants are extremely numerous and ubiquitous. Their food habits are diverse, although most are omnivorous, and their social groups range in size from hundreds to perhaps millions. Certainly, the most spectacular of these groups are the legionary or army ants of the humid tropical forests. These ants do not construct nests but form temporary clusters called bivouacs in the shelter of a fallen tree trunk or other such partially exposed location. The workers form a solid mass up to a meter across, consisting of layer upon layer of individuals linked together by their tarsal claws. The queen, thousands of larvae and pupae, and, at certain times of the year, up to 1000 males and a few virgin queens, are located near the center of the ball of up to a half million workers.

The night is passed in a tight cluster, but, at first light, the chains of workers become detached and a hoard of individuals begins to move away from the bivouac site in all directions. Soon, one or more raiding columns form and move out in search of food. The workers lay a pheromone trail to guide those that follow, while the soldiers guard the column's flanks. Some species engage in column raids, whereas others employ a swarming tactic. Regardless of their method, however, the foraging ants form a number of changing columns behind the advancing hoard of workers that flushes and captures a variety of mainly orthropod prey. The prey are stung to death dismembered, and transported rearward as food for the developing larvae. At the end of each day of marauding, the protective cluster is reformed.

As they colony rapidly reduces the food supply in the immediate vicinity of its bivouac, it must move to a new location. However, in at least one species, the change in bivouac site has been correlated with the reproductive cycle within the colony, which in turn has an effect on its food requirements. According to Schnierla, the queen periodically undergoes rapid ovarian development, which results in great distension of her abdomen. Over a period of several days, such a queen lays 100,000 to 300,0000 eggs, which hatch about 3 weeks later. during this *statary phase,* the larvae from the previous period of oviposition complete their pupal development and emerge as young workers. The addition of these new workers seems to stimulate the colony to increase the intensity of its daily foraging raids and change the location of its bivouac site each evening. The *nomadic phase* therefore coincides with the period during which a large number of larvae must be fed. Once these larvae complete their development and pupate, the nomadic behaviour declines, and the colony enters another reproductive period, during which a single bivouac site is utilized.

People living in the temperate zone most familiar with the nest building ants, such as members of the genus *Mynnica,* which usually nest in the ground under a large stone, or the genus *Formica,* which construct the familiar mounds of twigs and other plant debris. These ants are characterized by the production of winged reproductives during the summer and early fall. In some species the emergence of the reproductives produces quite spectacular swarms, during which mating occurs. The nuptial flight results in the ubiquitous spread of potential foundresses of new colonies. After a short time, the newly mated queen sheds her wings and excavates the beginning of a new nest into which she seals herself. In the spring, she lays a small group of eggs and tends the larvae until they attain adulthood and become the colony's initial group of workers. These first offspring may take more than a year to complete their development, but the queen never leaves, relying on her internal food reserves and flight muscles for her own sustenance as well as that of her young.

Over the succeeding years, the colony grows very slowly until enough workers are present for it to enter a period of accelerated growth. In areas characterized by cold winters, the colonies enter hibernation for several months, and no eggs are laid until warmer conditions prevail in the spring. In most species, several years pass before winged males and females are produced to leave and establish

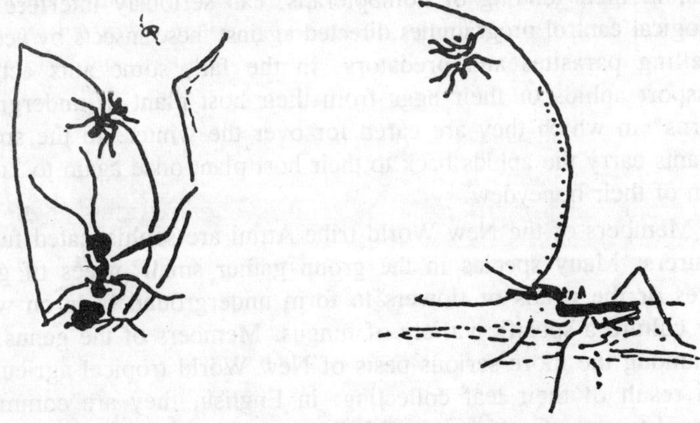

Fig. 5.14. Media worker of the fungus-growing ant, Aaa cephalotes, *cxutting and carrying a portion of leaf while being protected against attack from a phorid fly by a minor worker.*

new colonies in their turn. Colonies of many species contain only a few hundred individuals, whereas some contain many thousands; most nests contain only one queen, but some *Formica* nests have hundreds of active queens. In spite of the general similarities displayed by the nest-building ants, as far as the establishment and growth of new colonies is concerned, they show extensive adaptive radiation in other aspects of their behaviour. Most display a high level of variability in their choice of prey. Like the army ant, they forage widely for almost any kind of small animals, especially arthropods, that are available. A single nest of the European red ant, *Formica polyctena, is* said to gather up to a kilogram of such food in the course of single day. Chauvin concluded that the estimated population of 300 million red ants, which inhabit the Italian Alps, would be capable of destroying 15,000 tons of insects a year. But not all ants have the catholic tasii of F. *Polyctena*. Smme feed specifically on certain kinds of arthropods of their eggs. Others, often called "harvester" or "agricultural" ants, subsist entirely on seeds, and thereby become pests in some grain and grass-growing regions. When protein-rich foods are not needed for the rearing of larvae, many ants feed upon the nectar of flowers.

A number of ant species feed exclusively on the anal excretion of aphids, scale insects, and other homopterans. The so-called "honey-dew" is rich in sugars and free amino acids and forms an inexhaustible source of nutrient throughout the time when the producing insects are actively feeding. Some species of ants can be seen to stroke the cornicles of aphids to induce the flow of honeydew from the anus. Ants, in their tending of homopterans, can seriously interfere with biological cantrol programmes directed against these insects by actively repelling parasites and predators. In the fall, some ants actually transport aphids or their eggs from their host plant to underground "barns" in which they are cared for over the winter. In the spring, the ants carry the aphids back to their host plant once again to "milk" them of their honeydew.

Members of the New World tribe Attini are sophisticated fungus culturers. Many species in the group gather small pieces of green leaves or the petals of flowers to form underground beds on which they culture a specific variety of fungus. Members of the genus *Atta* are among the more serious pests of New World tropical agriculture as a result of their leaf collecting; in English, they are commonly referred to as leaf-cutting ants. Media workers carry the plant material piece by piece deep into their nests, where it is licked, cut into small piece, wet with an anal secretion, and formed into beds of moist pulp. The newly formed beds are then "planted" with fungal mycelia collected from established bed$. The fungus grows rapidly and soon produces on the tips of the hypae small spheres, which are fed to the ant larvae. The fungus beds are tended and harvested by smaller workers (minora) that never engage in the collection of leaf fragments. However, in the case of *Atta cephalotes,* these smaller workers may accompany the larger leaf-gatherers; they do not assist with the leaf cutting but ride back to the nest on the leaf portion, apparently warding off parasitic phorid flies with their mandibles and hind legs.

One of the more fascinating aspects of the fungus culture is how the ants are able to maintain a monoculture of their specific fungus; abandoned beds are rapidly overgrown by alien fungi of various species. Weber discovered that the worker ants tending the fungus beds "weed" them of alien hypae with their mandibles. It has also been postulated,

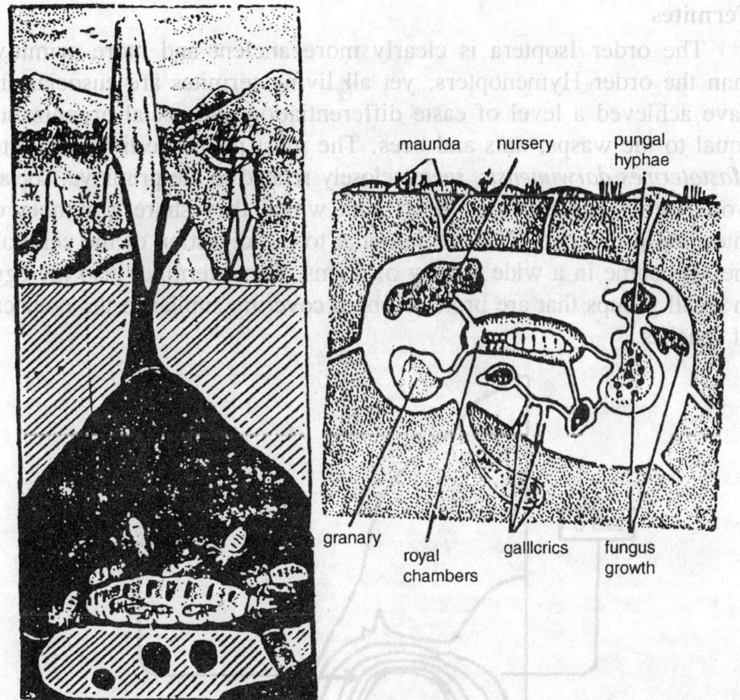

Fig 5.15. Mound nests of some Akustralian termites. (A and B) North-south and east west aspects of mounds of Anutennens meridionalt (C) Nest of Nasudwmes uiodiae. (D) Nest of Nasadtames walkai. (E) Nest of Amitennes vitiosus.

but not proved, that the ants employ fungicidal and bacteriocidal substances secreted by their salivary or anal glands. The cultured fungus is carried to each new nest by the foundress. Before departing on her nuptial flight, the virgin queen packs a small wad of mycelia into a cavity near the base of her labium. The wad is then deposited in the nest she excavates. The queen tends the initial fungus garden but does not consume any of the culture herself. However, the first workers to emerge feed upon it and fertilize it with their fecal material. Not all ants are as industrious as the aphid herders and fungus gardeners. The Amazon slaver ant, *Polyergus lucidus,* and the red ant, *Formica sanguinea,* are common species that make raids on other ant species to capture slaves. The raiders carry larvae and pupae back to their nests, where they are raised to assume the duties of nest maintenance. *Polyergus lucidus is* an obligatory slave keeper, as the workers cannot feed themselver. *F. sanguinea,* on the other hand, is a facultative slaver.

Termites

The order Isoptera is clearly more ancient and more primitive than the order Hymenopters, yet all living termites are eusocial and have achieved a level of caste differentiation and social organization equal to the wasps, ants and bees. The most primitive living termite, *Mastotermes darwiniensis,* seems closely related to the primitive, social, wood-eating roach *Crytocercus,* with which they share a number of intestinal protozoans that are essential to the digestion of the cellulose they consume in a wide variety of forms. Some termites also lay eggs in small groups that are protected by a covering similar to the oothecae of roaches.

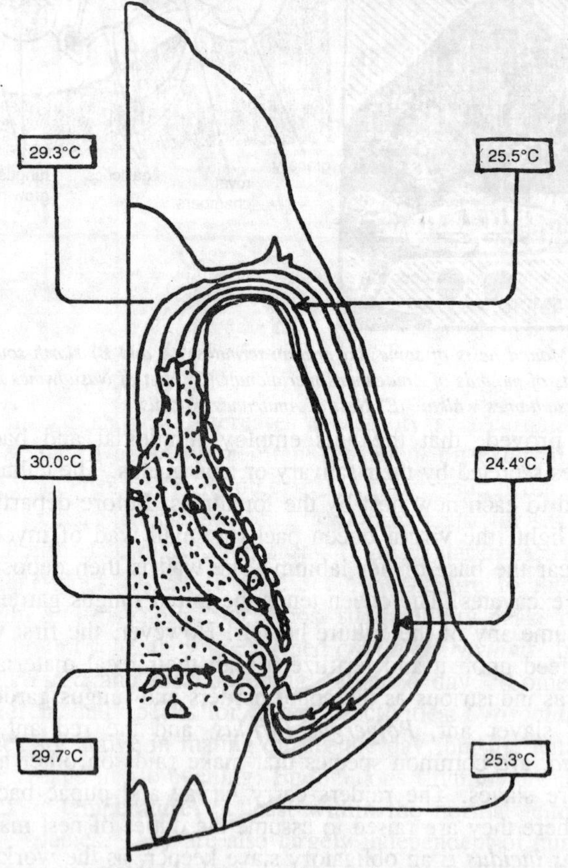

Fig. 5.16. Section through the mound nest of the African termite Macrotermes natalensis showing the basic design of the air conditioning runnels.

Termites lack cellulose-digesting enzymes and rely on their intestinal fauna of mutualistic flagellate protozoans, which must be passed continuously between individuals, to aid in the breakdown of their food. The passage of gut symbionts from old to young individuals. seems to have set the stage for the development of more advanced social behaviour. It has been postulated, therefore, that the social order of termites began with trophallaxis and led to the addition of brood care, rather than the reverse, as in the social hymenoptera.

The natural history of termites is quite varible. The so-called dry wood termites that frequently cause damage to the dry, seasoned wood of buildings usually live in colonies consisting of only a few hundred individuals. Winged reproductives are produced seasonally, usually during the warmer months, leave the nest soon after emergence, and spread rather ubiquitously. When a female completes her flight, she divests herself of her wings and runs about in an excited fashion until joined by a male. After pairing, the king and queen engage in a behaviour called tandem running, in which the king closely follows his queen in search of a nest site. Whenn the pair locate a suitable place to begin a nest, they take turns excavating an initial tunnel with a small chamber at the boottom. The king and queen seal themselves in by plugging the tunnel with chewed wood, and the queen proceeds to produce a small batch of eggs. When the young nymphs emerge, they are fed regurgitated food until they are able to feed upon the surrounding wood and thereby enlarge the nest. As the colony grows in the ensuing years, soldiers are produced that provide the colony with defense. When the colony is several years old, more alates are produced, which found new colonies. The foundress of a colony may live for more than 10 years, but if her egg production declines or she is killed, her duties may be assumed by secondary queens.

Most of the more highly evolved termites are soil dwellers that construct conspicuous mound nests. Alate reproductives are agian produced seasonally and often emerge from their nests at the beginn-ing of the rainy season. After a short, feeble flight, the reproductives shed their wings and engage in nest founding behaviour similar to that already described. The first brood consists of workers, but soldiers are produced later. In addition to workers, soldiers, and huge physo-gastric females, some colonies contain secondary and tertiary queens. As the number of individuals in the colony grows from year to year, the size of the mound is increased by the addition of layers of soil and excrement to form the most elaborate insect-built structures. The mound-building termites have adapted to virtually every form of food with a high cellulose content. The food is gathered by the workers, which forage throughout a large area surrounding the nest by way of a system of subterranean tunnels or covered pathways; some even forage on the surface over well-trodden trails marked with pheromones. Termites of the subfamily Macrotermitinae culture fungus on comblike structures built from their excrement. As in the ant genus *Atta,* the fungus beds of occupied nests are a pure culture. Instead of cropping the fungus in the manner of ants, termites consume the entire mass, including the excrement substratum. The colonies of fungus growing termites may contain as many as 2 million individuals. The primary queen is capable of laying up to 30,000 eggs a day; in a life span of up to 10 years, a single queen may produce tens of millions of offspring.

The gigantic mounds of tropical termites often have distinctive forms that are characteristic of particular species. In addition to providing protection, termite nests are often constructed in such a way as to provide a well-regulated interior microclimate. *Amitermes* orient their nests in such a way as to maximize sloar warming in the morning and evening. Microclimatic control is most highly developed in the fungus-growing genus *Macrotennes*. Its members construct a series of passageways, through which air flows according to its own density, so that temperature and carbon dioxide conditions favourable to the growth of fungus are maintained in the culture chamber.

The evolution of the termites is far removed phylogenetically from that of the Hymenoptera; yet, two grops have, by quite different routes, arrived at a complex level of social organization. There are some striking similarities in the social biology these distinct ordres display, but there are some fundamental differences as well. The most important differences markedly affect the make-up of the colonies. In the case of the termites, the queen cannot control the sex of her offspring, so the workers are both males and females (genetically). Furthermore, after the first few instars, the termite7474 immatures engage in work for the good of the colony. In the social Hymenoptera, the workers are all female, and the queen can regulate the production of males; the larvae are, in a sense, parasitic and contribute nothing to the well-being of the colony.

Protective Behaviour

The subject of defensive behaviour among insects is a complex one encompassing structural, physiological, biochemical, and behavioural adaptations. However, a consideration of defense belongs in a book such as this because virtually all of the morphological and biochemical mechanisms that have developed have been accompanied by the evolution of appropriate patterns of behaviour that make them effective. For instance, the protective colouration of an insect would be of little value if the animal's behaviour did not bring it to rest on an appropriately coloured background. .

At least to people unfamiliar with their ways, insects often seem to be more on the offensive than the defensive, especially when the observer comes under attack. There is no doubt that some insects, like blackflies and horseflies, are so aggressive in their attempts to acquire a blood meal that their hosts would view them as offensive; the same seems true of attacks by bees or wasps attempting to defend a nest that has been disturbed. However, neither of these displays of aggressive behaviour constitute offense, and the latter example is clearly one of defense. In fact, among the insects there are relatively few conflicts among members of the same species; and those that occur between species are, usually of a predator-prey, nature. In those species such as dragonflies, crickets and sphecid wasps, in which the males defend territories or battle over mates, the fighting is more ritualistic than injurious.

Self-defense against parasites and predators is a basic biological problem faced by all species. It is a particularly significant problem for insects because their success as a group stems to a considerable extent from their great mobility—a factor that exposes them to attack

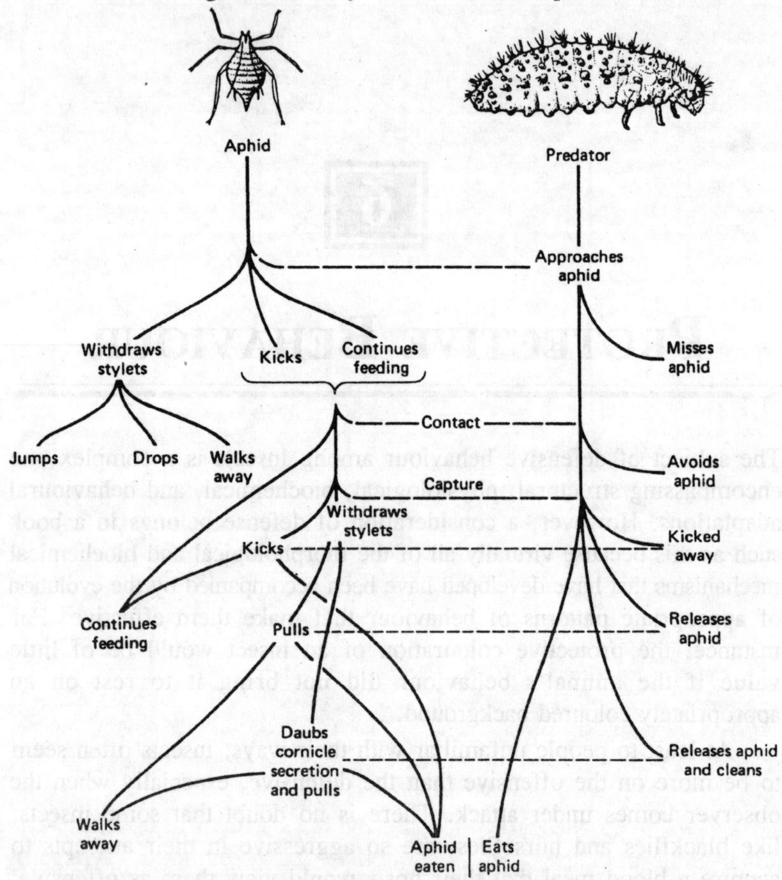

Fig. 6.1. The possible interactions resulting from an encounter between a predator and its aphid prey.

by a variety of other organisms. Consequently, the defensive strategies that have been evolved by insects are both diverse and remarkable. The fantastic attention to detail that nature has paid in the evolution of defensive traits provides ample evidence of both the intensity and the variety of selective pressures that the insects have been subjected to. The major mechanisms employed in self-defense can be classified mainly as behavioural, structural, chemical, and colourational. However, such a classification is justifiable on no other basis than that it provides an organized framework for discussion. Although there are some examples of purely behavioural defense that involve no other components, almost all defensive strategies have a behavioural component. Furthermore, many insects employ more than one defensive tactic, either in sequence or in combination, and there is often a great deal of behavioural integration involved. I hope that the following organization of this subject will not mask these characteristics. Systemic defensive mechanisms such as phagocytosis, encapsulation, immunity, and so forth, will not be considered.

INSECTS AS FOOD FOR VERTEBRATE ANIMALS

Vertebrate animals are commonly classified as herbivores, omnivores, or carnivores. Since strict herbivores are themselves primary consumers, their main associations with insects are as competitors or as hosts (for example, cattle grubs). Many omnivores and carnivores consume insects at least some of the time, and some are mainly or wholly entomophagous (or insectivorous) (for example, bats, swallows). Many freshwater fish depend heavily on insects, not only those occurring in the water but those that fall in or fly low over the surface. This is, of course, well-known to fly fishermen, who pride themselves on designing flies that resemble certain types of insects and on striking the surface film at the right time and place with the appropriate fly. Fish will commonly continue to feed for a time on a type of prey that is abundant, for example, a flight of newly emerged caddisflies. Trout tend to take food both at the surface and from the bottom, mayflies, caddisflies, and midge larvae being major items in the diet. The productivity of lakes and streams, in terms of energy made available by producers and primary consumers, is a major concern of fisheries biologists. Mosquito fish *(Gambusia)* have been introduced into many parts of the world for control of mosquito larvae, often with much success. To turn to another group, the Amphibia, the giant toad has been widely used in warmer parts of the globe to control ground-dwelling insects. Insects make up a considerable portion of the diet of many amphibians and reptiles.

Many mammals also subsist on insects. Even large carnivores such as the coyote consume a great many grasshoppers and beetles. Two whole orders, the Chiroptera (bats) and Insectivora (moles and shrews), are largely insectivorous. Studies in central New York by W.J. Hamilton, Jr., of Cornell University, showed that short- tailed shrews consume food equivalent to 50% of their own weight each day, and about 75% of their diet consists of insects. Surprisingly, deer mice, rodents one commonly thinks of an plant-feeders, also consume about as high a proportion of insects during the summer. In Canada, shrews and voles are major predators an a major forest pest, the larch sawfly. In some areas 37% to 98% of the cocoons are eaten by these mammals, and a portion of the surviving adults and their larvae are eaten by birds.

It is, of course, birds that have attracted the most attention and predators on insects. Several books have been written on the values of birds, often without regard for the fact that they consume many species that are beneficial to man. Being active fliers, birds do, however, have the capacity to congregate in areas of insect outbreaks, as evidenced by starlings flocking to grub-infested lawns, or warblers concentrating on trees infested with caterpillars. Perhaps the bestknown instance of birds destroying noxious insects relates to gulls and the Mormon cricket. Great swarms of these crickets descended on Mormon settlements near Great Salt Lake, destroying most of their crops and threatening the settlers with starvation. Gulls appeared by the tens of thousands and devoured most of the crickets, an historical event of such importance that a statue to the gulls was later erected in Salt Lake City. Although many birds are rather generalized feeders, most have some degree of specialization. Warblers and vireos, for example, forage for small insects among the leaves and small branches of trees, while blackbirds and thrushes forage mainly on or close to the ground. Flycatchers take flying insects they snatch in quick flights from their perches, while woodpeckers drill for the larvae of bark beetles and other wood-infesting insects. It is not always appreciated that many seed-feeders such as finches) consume large numbers of insects during the summer season.

The numbers of insects consumed by individual birds are very large indeed. Most birds fill their crops with food about twice a day. There is one record a flicker stomach containing over 5000 ants, another of a captive robin consuming 165 cutworms in one day, nearly twice its own weight. Nestlings commonly consume more than their own weight in a day, the food in many cases being a high-protein diet of soft-bodied insects. Studies of a nesting pair of blue tits, in England, showed that the 11 nestlings were fed from 25 to 42 times an hour, from early in the morning to late evening, for a total of 400 to 650 visits per day. The number or weight of insects required to sustain an individual bird through its lifespan would be difficult to calculate, but the figure would obviously by very high. It should be kept in mind that, as a general rule, the feeding behaviour of vertebrate animals differs considerably from that of insects. Insects tend to be programmed to respond to only a few of the innumerable potential stitauh in the world around them, for example, *Nasonia wasps* to fly puparia, horse bots to the legs and flanks of horses. Vertebrates are more broadly responsive and may sample a variety of foods before selecting those they prefer and learning where to find and how to catch those that suit them best. Many birds are known to develop a search image; that they discover a particularly edible item, remember its appearance aad where to find it, and hunt in such a way that others of the same Kind are quickly discovered. Experiments have shown that birds will concentrate on one type of prey to the point that its numbers have bene reduced far below those of other, equally palatable species, which have been overlooked. At a certain point a new search image *A* of course, be formed. Birds also become conditioned to avoid *prey* that sting, taste bad, or make them ill. It is not surprising that insects have developed a variety of adaptations that take advantage of these characteristics of vertebrate predators.

PRIMARY DEFENSES

It is convenient to recognize two major types of defuse mechanisms. ***Primary defenses*** operate before a predator initiates an attack, and in fact regardless of whether or not a predator is present- They may also be thought of as *passive defenses,* in the sense that the insect is, by its appearance and actions, merely bearing a message to potential predators. ***Secondary defenses*** are employed at the time of an encounter with a predator; they are *active* in that the insect has to behave in some way vis-a-vis its attacker. An insect may have both primary and secondary defenses. So diverse are these mechanisms that we can do no more than mention a few well-studied examples here.

CRYPSIS

Crypsis is a widespread phenomenon among sects. Although often called *"camouflage"* or *`protective colouration,'' in* fact it implies more than that. To be cryptic (which literally means *"hidden"*), an insect must not only resemble its substrate, but it must also behave appropriately, for example, by resting immobile or in an appropriate posture. *Generalized crypsis* implies an overall resemblance to the background, for example, by a speckled grasshopper resting on a pebbly surface. *Special resemblance* implies similarity to a specific object, such as a twig or a leaf. An insect may resemble its biotic environment, as in the case of the grasshopper cited above. Or resemblance may be to the biotic environment, usually some part of a plant, and may vary from the simple green colour of a caterpillar in one's salad to bizarre body forms copying lichens, spines, or even flowers.

Some insects are able to undergo an enhancement of crypsis by assuming more than one colour or by altering the environment to render themselves less easy to detect. Some mantids and grasshoppers undergo colour changer, when they molt, and in some cases, these are induced by humidity. High humidity may cause changes to green colours, low humidity to brown. This is highly adaptive in areas where there are marked wet and dry seasons, since grasses change colour similarly. The pupae of some butterflies may be either green or brown, depending on the colour of the immediate environment. This is believed to be a direct effect of light reflected from the substrate.

Examples of insects that modify their environment are provided by the larvae of certain leaf beetles, which cover their backs with cast skins, fecal pellets, and bits of debris, thus resembling from above nothing more than masses of detritus. Cryptic insects must have behavioural responses that function to orient them suitably. Bark-dwelling moths with longitudinal stripes on their wings must orient up and down on striped bark, while those with transverse stripes must position themselves sideways if the stripes are to blend with patterns in the bark. Certain caterpillars that infest pine needles are green with longitudinal white stripes, rendering them difficult to observe when resting on the needles. But at the last molt they become brown, flecked with black,, and from then on they rest not on the needles but on the brown twigs bearing the needles.

Crypsis does, of course, interfere with other life activities, such as feeding and mating. Thus, it is especially prevalent during the diurnal resting periods of insects that are mainly active at night, especially moths. Cryptic insects do not usually aggregate, for birds are frequently able to form search images for cryptic species, and by dispersing themselves these insects increase their chances that birds will find more rewarding prey. There are varying degrees of crypsis among species, and among individuals of any one species some are more successful than others in escaping detection. It is these betteradapted individuals that, on the average, survive to produce more offspring, thus providing the basis for the evolution of more perfect crypsis. At the same time a premium is placed on the keenest hunters among the predators. Thus, there is coevolution between predator and prey, resulting in improved abilities to find prey and more refined examples of crypsis.

Cryptic Effectiveness

It is true that examination of the stomach contents of various birds, lizards, and mammals often reveals the presence of cryptic species. However, there is now much experimental evidence that increasing degrees of crypsis result in increasing success in escaping detection by predators. For example, laboratory studies using chameleons as predators have been conducted with a species of grasshopper having two colour forms, green and yellow. Appreciable fewer green than yellow grasshoppers were eaten when placed on a green background, and *vice versa*.

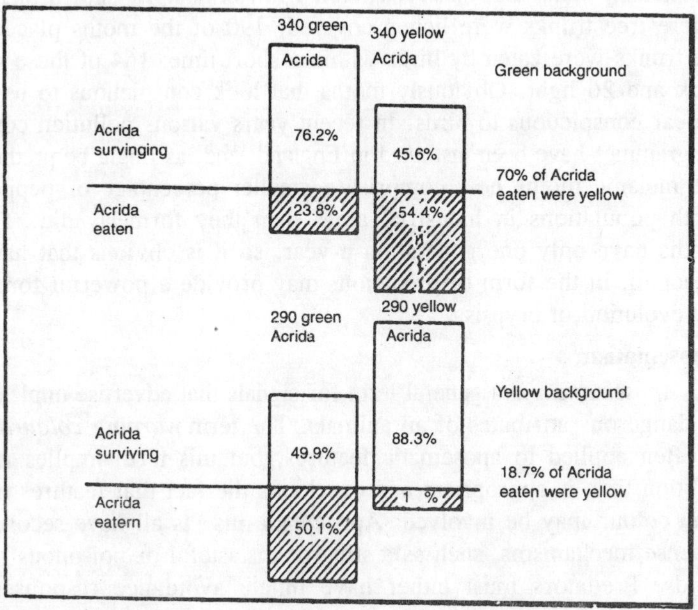

Fig. 6.2. Predation by a chameleon on green and yellow grasshoppers of the same species (Acrida turrita) on a green background (above) and on a yellow background (below).

Perhaps the best-known studies are those of H.B.D. Kettlewell, of Oxford University, concerning a common British insect, the peppered moth. These moths are whitish, with irregular black spots acid stripes, and blend beautifully with lichen-covered bark. Before the industrial revolution, one occasionally found black (melanic) individuals that were conspicuous against the lichens. But by 1895, around industrial centers in England, the melanics had become much more abundant than the "normal" form. By this time tree trunks in these areas had become blackened with soot and the lichens killed off; thus, the melanics blended best with the background. Kettlewell hypothesized that birds preyed more heavily on the whitish forms in industrial areas and thus had produced rapid selection toward melanism (known to be controlled by a single dominant gene). In order to demonstrate this, Kettlewell reared large numbers of normal and-melanic moths in the laboratory, marked them with coloured spots, and released them in both industrial and rural areas. These were then recaptured in light traps or traps baited with pheromone. In industrial areas, many more of the melanics than normal moths were recovered, and in rural, unpolluted areas the reverse was true. He also placed moths of both types on tree trunks in selected areas and observed them from blinds. In one rural area, where tree trunks were lichen covered, 190 of the moths placed on the trunks were eaten by birds within a short time; 164 of these were dark and 26 light. Obviously moths that look conspicuous to us also appear conspicuous to birds. In recent years various pollution control programmes have been instituted in England, and, as might be predicted, the melanic moths now comprise a smaller percentage or peppered moth populations in industrial areas than they formerly did. These moths have only one generation a year, so it is obvious that natural selection, in the form of predation, may provide a powerful force in the evolution of crypsis.

Aposematism

Aposematism is a general term for signals that advertise unpleasant or dangerous attributes of an animals. The term *warning colouration is* often applied to aposematic features, but this term implies more volition than is appropriate and overlooks the fact that features other than colour may be involved. Aposematic insects all have secondary defense mechanisms, such as a sting or distasteful or poisonous body fluids. Predators must either have innate avoidance responses to aposematic patterns or must learn these patterns by sampling prey. In the latter (probably much more common) instance, some individuals of each generation of an aposematic insect are likely to be sacrificed. However, some species have evolved though bodies that cannot easily be damaged or "deflection marks" that induce the predator to bite in some nonvital part of the body.

One of the best-known aposematic patterns consists of alternating bands of black and yellow, the pattern of yellow jackets and many other stinging Hymenoptera. These bright, alternating bands are conspicuous to colour-blind persons, and one assumes also to colour-blind animals (such as many mammals). A second common aposematic pattern consists of orange or red bands or patches, which are especially effective signals to organism with good colour vision (which is why hunters and highway crews wear orange jackets). Birds, in general, have colour vision similar to ours, and it is probable that these patterns evolved primarily as signals to birds. One example that quickly comes to mind is the monarch butterfly, the larvae of which feeds on milkweed. Most milk weeds contain cardiac glycosides that are retained in the bodies of caterpillars, the pupae, and on into the adult butterflies: when a bird easts a monarch it becomes ill and retches.

Another example is provided by wingless female mutillid wasps *("velvet ants")*. These insects spend much time walking over the ground in search of their hosts. Although a few species are cryptic, and coloured like the sand, the majority advertise their presence with bands of brilliant orange and red. With their long, venom laden stings and though integument, it is not likely that many are actually sacrificed in the learning process of predators. It should be remembered that colour vision in insects differs somewhat from that of humans and higher vertebrates, being extended on the blue end of the spectrum into the ultraviolet and not extended appreciably into the oranges and reds. It is true that some insects use bright colours in nuptial displays (damselflies, for instance), but the colours employed are usually blues (even ultraviolet in the case of some butterflies). It is no coincidence that flowers requiring insect pollination are usually blue or yellow, or have ultraviolet nectar guides; or that flowers that rely on hummingbirds for pollination (such as scarlet gilia) are primarily red. Insects displaying orange or red markings almost without exception have secondary defense mechanisms and are advertising this fact to potential vertebrate predators -or they are mimics of such insects. Still a third aposematic pattern consists of paired eye spots, for example, those on the hind wings of many moths. Since these are often associated with displays in the presence of a predator, we shall defer discussion of them to a later section (under of *"Secondary Defense Mechanisms"*). Large eye spots presumably imply the presence of an owl, a hawk, or a large mammal, and there is experimental evidence that eye spots do in fact deter predation by small birds.

Before leaving the subject of aposematism, it should be noted that it is common for many insets in a given area to have similar aposematic patterns. In temperate regions a great many different kinds of stinging Hymenoptera, for example, have "*yellow jacket*" patterns. In the tropics there are often literally dozens of butterflies in the same area having similar orange wing patterns; many of these feed on poisonous or bitter-tasting plants and are themselves unpalatable. This phenomenon was first noted in Brazil by the German biologist Fritz Muller and has since been termed Mullerian mimicry, although we prefer the term *mutual aposematism.* Muller pointed out that it is advantageous for distasteful species occurring together to evolve similar patterns, since in this way predators have fewer patterns to learn and exploratory predation is spread over several species. In contrast to cryptic species, those displaying aposematic patterns tend to occur in exposed situations and are often gregarious. Larvae of the mourning cloak butterfly provide a good example of gregarious feeders, covered as they are with long spines and streaked with red; but the chrysalids are cryptic, and prior to pupation the caterpillars crawl off in different directions, crypsis being enhanced by dispersal.

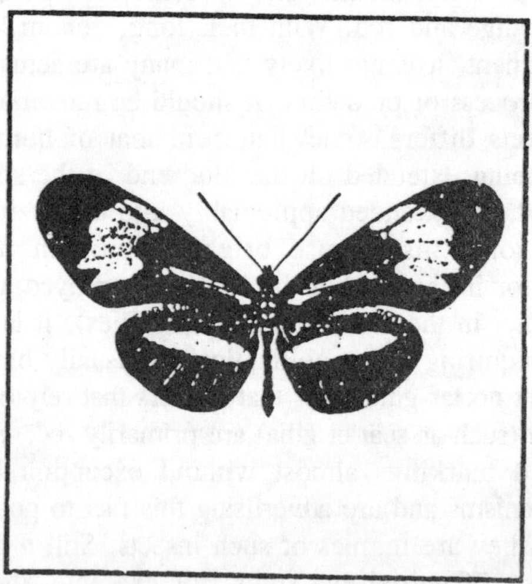

Fig 6.3. Heliconius erato, a tropical American butterfly considered highly unpalatable. The front wings have a bright red band, the hind wings a yellow streak.

Evidence of Aposemation

There is now much evidence that aposematism "works." In a pioneering study, the British ento- mologist G.D.H. Carpenter offered a variety of insects to monkeys and found that 73% of the cryptic insects were eaten but only 20% of those with bright colours. Lady beetles, with their characteristic red and black patterns, are known to be avoided by many kinds of birds and mammals. The British entomologists. J.F.D. Frazer and Miriam Rothschild "screened" a great number of insects for palatability, using caged animals, including diverse birds and mammals, lizards and toads. Lady beetles fell in the highest (most unacceptable) category. Equally unacceptable was the cinnabar, a lepidopteran that has been widely used in biological control of ragwort. The caterpillars of this species are gregarious and are striped with black and yellow, while the adults have red and black wings. The blood of the cinnabar contains considerable quantities of histamine as well as certain alkaloids. In nature, cinnabar caterpillars are preyed on extensively by ground beetles and are parasitized by braconid wasps, but shrews and voles will not accept them.

One of the best-known field studies on the adaptive value of aposematism was conducted by W.W. Benson, for the University of Washington. His studies were conducted in Costa Rica on a wellknown, unpalatable butterfly, *Heliconius erato,* having a bright red band on the black fore wing. Benson captured butterflies in their gregarious, nocturnal roosts and painted out the red bands with black; in the controls

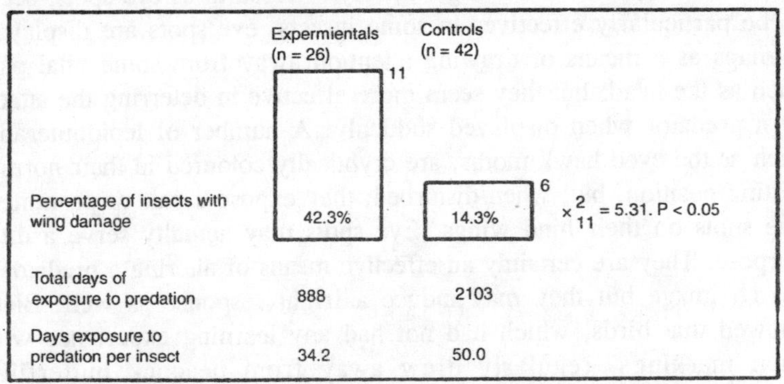

Fig. 6.4. Wing damage to Heliconius erato *experimentals (red painteQ,over with black) and controls (black painted over previously black areas). Controls also survived much longer, thus were exposed to predation for significantly longer periods.*

he merely painted black over black, to check against any effect the paint itself might have. By recording the return of these butterflies to the roost, he found that the experimentals survived an average of 32 days, the controls an average of 52 days. Furthermore, a much higher percentage of the experimentals had wing damage resulting from predation by birds, even though they were exposed for a shorter period, on the average, than the controls. It should be added that several other butterflies have much the same pattern as *Heliconius erato,* one of many examples of mutual aposematism in the American tropics.

Flash Patterns

Even the best camouflage does not fool all of the predators all of the time so many species have evolved a second line of colourational defense, referred to as flash patterns. The basis of the effectiveness of flash patterns is to induce a rapid change of the search image of the pursuing species. This is accomplished by quickly changing from cryptic to conspicuous and back again. The efficacy of the flash pattern strategy is amply demonstrated by grasshoppers with brightly coloured hind wings. When resting among the vegetation, many grasshoppers are well camouflaged but may be found with a little careful searching. As you approach close enough to make a capture, your quarry will often take flight, during which the colourful hind wings are exposed. This changes your search image, and, by the time you have made a mental adjustment, the grasshopper drops out of light among the vegetation, once again relying on its cryptic colouration for concealment.

Some flash patterns are apparently more effective than others. Concentric light and dark rings, usually referred to as eye spots, seem to be particularly effective. In some insects, eye spots are displayed perhaps as a means of drawing attention away from some vital part such as the head, but they seem more effective in deterring the attack of a predator when displayed suddenly. A number of lepidopterans, such as the eyed hawk moths, are cryptically coloured in their normal resting position, but, when disturbed, they expose a pair of prominent eye spots on their hind wings. Eye spots may actually serve a dual purpose. They are certainly an effective means of altering a predator's search image but they may induce a fright response as well. Blest showed that birds, which had not had any learning experience with such markings, regularly drew away from peacock butterflies (Nymphalidae) that suddenly displayed their eye spots. The fact that the birds in Blest's experiment drew away suggests that they were at least startled by the sudden appearance of an ominous pair of eyes. Blest also showed that the birds in his experiment withdrew when other shapes, such as a pair of crosses or a pair of single rings, were exposed suddenly. This suggests that eye spots could have evolved in a series of steps from more simple markings.

MIMICRY

The concept of mimicry was first proposed more than 100 years ago by the English naturalist Henry W. Bates. On the basis of observations he made on an expedition to the Amazon basin, Bates proposed that species with overlapping ranges *(sympatric)* could evolve a resemblance if the common colour pattern was beneficial to both species. Bates had observed that some palatable species and similar colour patterns to sympatric unpalatable species. He concluded that the unpalatable species (the *models)* were employing warning colouration, and the palatable species (the *mimics)* derive benefit from the fact that they are not attacked by predators that have learned the association between the colour and bad taste.

The preceding concept is known as *Batesian mimicry* and has been the subject of controversy ever since it was proposed. It seems to rule out the possibility that species come to resemble each other as a result of parallelism. However, it does not seem necessary to consider every case of resemblance as a case of mimicry. The predominance of black and red patterns in the wings of, South American butterflies, compared to a predominance of black and green patterns among African and black and blue patterns among Indian species is wellknown. We might expect, therefore, to encounter more similarity in the appearance of groups of species within each of these geographic regions than between them.

Opponents of the concept of mimicry argue that the gradual accumulation of traits that seems to function suitably in the development of crypsis could not have operated effectively in the development of mimicry. Although a mimic survives because it looks like a model that predators have learned to reject, it is questionable whether a species could gain sufficient protection from early minor changes for such changes to be selected. We must remember, however, that many mimetic patterns function while the species are in motion, so perhaps they do not need to be as highly refined as patterns employed in crypsis; camouflage must withstand the careful search of a predator, often very close at hand. It can be counter argued that such changes occurred as the result of major mutations or had their beginning in convergence. No matter which side of the argument one chooses to take, it is a matte of fact that there are many pairs of species that look alike in which one is well-defended and the other is defenseless. There are also a number of species that retain their original colour pattern in some parts of their range but in other areas are clearly similar in appearance to unpalatable species with which they overlap. Finally, there seem to be just too many examples of mimicry in which details of the resemblance are extraordinary and result in some obvious benefit to the mimic to pass it all off as an accident of parallelism or convergence.

For *Batesian mimicry* to remain effective, it is obvious that there must be a numerical balance between the model and the mimic such that a predator does not have more experiences with palatable than with unpalatable prey of the same appearance. For a mimetic pattern to evolve, a palatable species must be considerably less abundant than

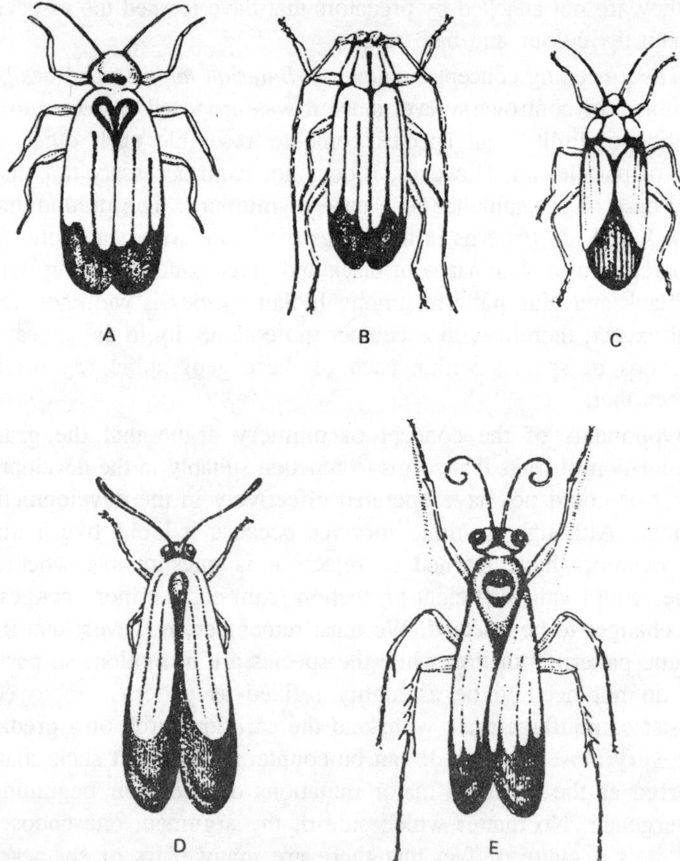

Fig. 6.5. A mimicry-ring consisting of (A) the distasteful soft-shelled beetle Lycus rosaatus (B) a cerambycid beetle, (C) a lygaeid bug, (D) a butterfly, and (E) a pompilid wasp.

the model, and it must remain so in order to benefit from the similarity. This raises an interesting question as to how the development of a mimetic pattern by a palatable species affects the level of predation on the unpalatable species. Certainly, the learning of young predators would be slowed by encounters with palatable prey. This could increase the predation pressure on the model and lead to the selection of divergent colour patterns. Viewed in this way, the gradual development of mimicry seems completely possible, as both model and mimic could evolve together rather than only the mimic having to undergo a large-scale change.

The naturalist Miller noticed that in some groups of mimetic species all of the individuals are unpalatable. Consequently, when two or more unpalatable sympatric species have a similar appearance, we call it *Mitllerian mimicry*. At least in theory, it would seem to be beneficial for a group of species to adopt a common warning signal rather than different signals. A predator would have to learn to recognize only one pattern instead of several separately. Assuming that the predator requires a number of bad experiences to learn the appearance of an inedible prey, a group of inedible species could share the number of individuals that must be sacrificed to educate the predator.

Various workers have argued that closely related species may look alike because of a common ancestry. For example, two genera of black and yellow striped wasps probably inherited the pattern from a similarly coloured ancestor. In such a case, we cannot consider one to be the model and the other the mimic, since, in a strict sense, there is no mimicry at all. However, this technicality does not seem as important as the more fundamental question as to whether Miillerian mimicry is effective, which it apparently is. For example, in South America there is a group of Mnllerian mimic, consisting of four different families. In addition to the Miillerian species, there are two species of edible Batesian mimics, and all of them are avoided by predators. Mimicry is commonly though of as similarity in colour patterns because of the influence of the early workers who mainly studied butterflies. However, it is obvious that colour similarity alone would not be as effective as similarity in over-all appearance there are in fact many examples of insects from different orders that resemble each other in both form and colour. One of the most diverse groups that forms a so-called mimicry ring involves a cerambycid beetle, a hemipteran, a butterfly and a spider-wasp; all bear a rather striking similarity to a highly unpalatable soft-shelled beetle.

There are also many examples of mimicry that rely mainly on form in that both model and mimic are monochromic. In some cases, the benefit that befalls the mimic is obvious, as in the case of the defenseless longhorn beetles (Cerambycidae) that closely resemble foul-smelling tenebrionids. In other cases, as with many ant mimics, the significance of the resemblance is obscure. In spite of their chemical

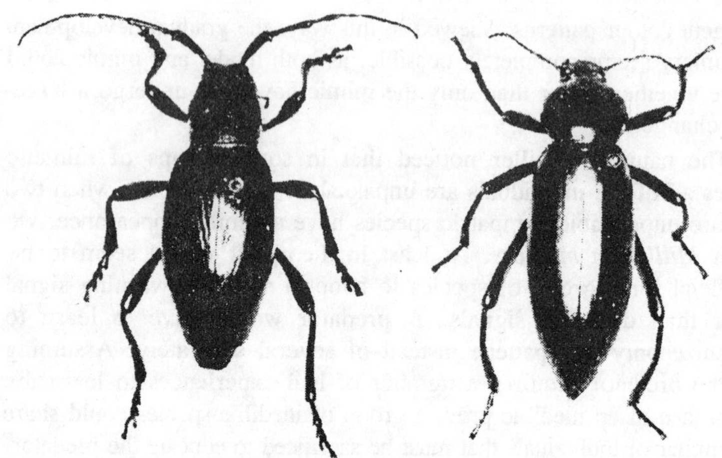

Fig. 6.6. A defenseless, monochromatic ceramycid beetle (left) that mimics a foul-smelling tenebrionid beetle (right) with which it is sympatric.

Fig. 6.7. An example of ant mimicry. (A) Small black ant from southern California and (B) a small, ground-living, myrid but found in the same area. Note the elbowed antennae, constricted waist, and pediclelike wings of the hug that improve its antlike appearance.

The Evolution of Mimicry

defense, ants are eaten by birds, reptiles, amphibians, and mammals, so it seems unlikely that ant mimics would gain much protection against predation simply through resemblance. It may help some species to mix with ants and thereby remain unnoticed, even to the extent of becoming permanent residents in their nests, but there are many successful ant guests that do not look like their hosts. Perhaps the answer lies in the fact that because ants are generally numerous, a few individuals of another species could move among them without being conspicuous and thereby enjoy an improved chance of survival. Whatever, the basis for it, the similarity between ants and totally unrelated insects can be truly remarkable.

Many similar experiments have now been performed with diverse mimics and predators, with generally similar results. Some of the most interesting ones have confronted of the major criticisms of mimicry theory: how can one account for the evolution of (for example) a viceroy from a black and white ancestral species without invoking a sudden saltation or total genetic reorganization? In other words, how can mimicry evolve when being "jut a little bit mimetic" would seem to have no possible advantage? Lincoln Brower and his associates at Amherst College have addressed this problem, *using Heliconius erato,* mentioned above in another context. They found that birds trained to avoid this butterfly also refused to take uniformly black butterflies of similar shape as well as red- banded butterflies of a different shape. In further studies, they varied the unpalatability of the model and found that the more unpalatable it was, the more the birds tended to extend their rejection to species only rather remotely resembling the model. *Stimulus generalization* such as these experiments imply means that under certain conditions even a slight resemblance to an unacceptable model may have value in terms of natural selection. If in each generation individuals with most resemblance to the model leave even a slightly greater number of progeny than average, in time a more "*perfect*" mimic may evolve.

It should be noted that in many butterflies only the female sex is mimetic, the male having the "normal" colour of its group. In at least some cases, colours of the male play a role in courtship and mating, and it is advantageous for males to retain patterns that release sexual behaviour in the females. The tiger swallowtail of the eastern United States provides a particularly interesting case. The females of this butterfly are dimorphic, having either mainly black or yellow and black "tiger' colouration. Males always have the tiger pattern and are most successful in mating with females coloured like themselves. But in the southeastern states there is a mostly black butterfly that has been shown to be highly distasteful to birds: the pipevine swallowtail.

In the Southeast, tiger swallowtail females that are black mimics of this species survive longer, on the average, but yellow and black individuals have greater mating success. Thus *a balanced polymorphism is* retained. But in the North, where the pipevine swallowtail does not occur, all females are "tigers," since here there is no selective advantage in being black.

The diana fritillary, of the southeastern states, exhibits similar *sex-limited mimicry,* the females copying the pattern of the pipevine swallowtail, the males retaining the usual speckled pattern of fritillaries. In this case, there is no polymorphism; but cases are known, especially among African swallowtails and relatives of the monarch, in which there are not two but several different female morphs, each having a colour pattern like that of a different distasteful model. In situations involving polymorphism, the mimetic species may achieve a population size greater than that of its model, since each morphs has a different model. In general, it is disadvantageous for mimics to become more plentiful than their models, since birds will encounter more mimics than models and learn much more slowly to associate distastefulness with a particular pattern. Before leaving this subject, it should be mentioned that mimics must also behave like their models to be effective, just as a cryptic insect must "behave like a piece of bark," or whatever it resembles. Cases are known in which mimicry is primarily behavioural. For example, certain species of darkling beetles have glands at the tip of their abdomen from which they are able to spray repellent benzo-quinones. When approached by a predator, these beetle assume a characteristic stance, with the abdomen high in the air, ready to discharge their secretions. Black, ground-dwelling beetles of at least two other groups also assume this stance when approached by a predator, even though they lack these glands.

Aggressive Resemblance

Since insects so readily evolve one or more of several cryptic, aposematic, or mimetic patterns, it is not surprising that some predatory insects have evolved colouration or behaviour like that of their host or have evolved crypsis serving primarily to gain access to a host. Such behavior hardly qualifies as "defense"; rather it is offense. We discuss it briefly here because it has often been termed *"aggressive mimicry,"* though it represents quite a different phenomenon from true mimicry, not only as to function but as to the nature of the signals: for these are, of course, directed toward other insects and not toward vertebrate animals. Some of the best examples of aggressive resemblance occur among the many thousands of inquilines in the nests of ants and termites. Many of these, beetles especially, are remarkably antlike in form, and some produce secretions that are eagerly sought by their hosts and may resemble pheromones of their hosts. Many termitophiles and myrmecophiles produce or acquire cuticular odors that copy those of their hosts. These inquilines commonly feed on foodstuffs in the nest and some actually feed on immature ants or termites. A most remarkable instance of aggressive resemblance occurs among fireflies and has been described by James Lloyd, of the University of Florida. Male fireflies produce a pattern of flashes characteristic of their species, and it is answered at a specific interval by females of their species on the ground. Females of certain species have evolved the ability to respond to flashes of males of alien species. These males fly down to the females and are promptly consumed.

SECONDARY DEFENSE MECHANISMS

Many insects have structures or behaviour effective at close quarters with a predator. This applies not only to aposematic species, all of which are assumed to have undesirable qualities, but to many palatable insects. In its simplest form, it may simply involve a butterfly dishing away from a pursuing bird, or a caterpillar thrashing violently when seized by a predator. Some of the more specialized defenses are striking indeed, and we shall be more particularly concerned with these.

Flight Patterns

For small, flying insects the best defense may be escape. Probabilities of escape may be increased by swift or evasive flight or by an abrupt colour change on settling. Band-winged grasshoppers show brilliant colours of the hind wings while in flight, but when they land, these are covered by the cryptically coloured front wings, causing the insect to "disappear" suddenly. Many butterflies (anglewings, in particular) have the upper wing surfaces brightly coloured, but when they land only the lower surfaces are exposed, and these are commonly coloured like bark or dead leaves. It is believed that *flash colours* such as these promote escape from pursuing birds.

Bats are major predators on night-flying moths. Several groups of moths have evolved receptors tuned to the ultrasonic cries that bats use in the manner of sonar in locating prey. These receptors have only two sensory neurons each, one for low-intensity sounds and one for high-intensity (closer) sounds, and since they are bilateral, the moth has means of perceiving both distance and direction. Moths respond

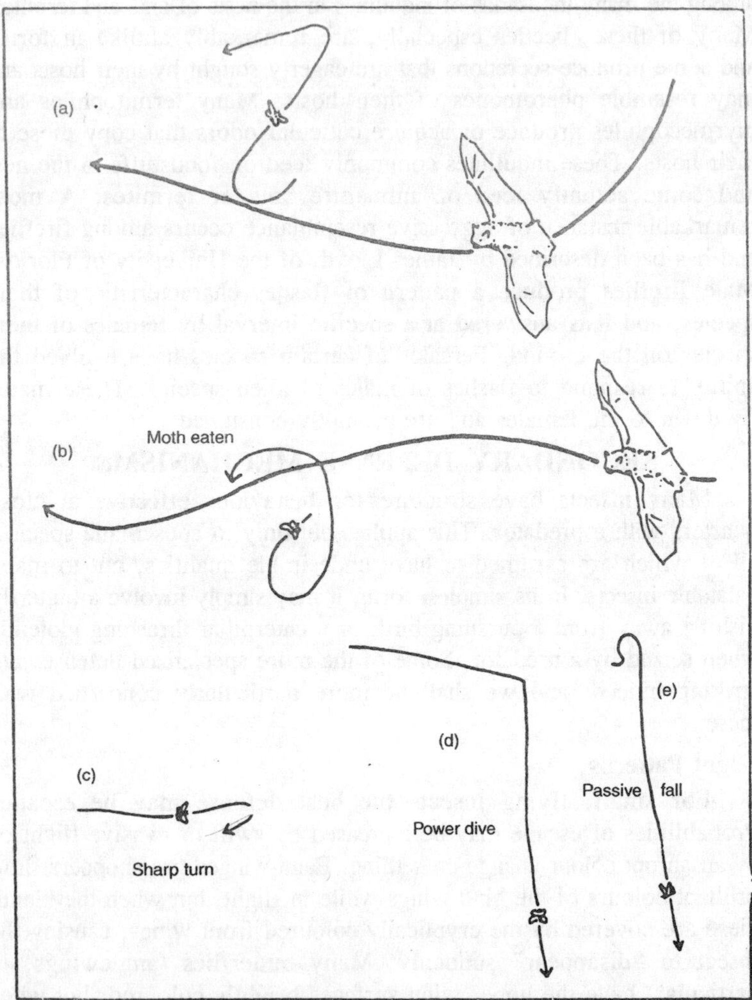

Fig. 6.8. Escape tactics of moths being pursued by bats. Erratic flight paths (a and b) are sometimes, but not invariably, successful. Other escape tactics are shown in c-e.

to bats at some distance by flying swiftly away, but at close quarters they undertake erratic flight patterns or sudden power dives. One group of moths, the tiger moths, has gone one step further and evolved sound-producing organs that advertise to the bat their distasteful qualities. These moths respond to the approach of a bat by producing a series of clicks,' and it has been demonstrated that bats veer away from clicking moths.

Death Feigning

Since many predators are attracted to moving prey and reject dead insects, it is not surprising that many relatively defenseless insects become inert when. approached. Leaf beetles and weevils are especially prone to death feigning. This is easily observed by home gardeners who control Colorado potato beetles by hand-picking; for as soon as disturbed, these beetles drawn their legs beneath them and drop to the ground. As soon as the disturbance is over, they climb back onto the plant and resume their feeding.

Spines, Poisonous Hairs and Stings

Many caterpillars are hairy, and some are covered with stiff, branched spines. In some cases, the tips of the hairs or spines break off easily and are capable of causing momentary irritation or a rash. This is true, for example, of the densely spiny larva of the io moth. The sting of Hymenoptera is believed to have evolved primarily as a means of paralyzing the prey, but in bees, many ants, and social wasps it has lost this function and serves in defense. The nature of the venom of social species differs considerably from that of solitary forms, consisting of a mixture of pain-producing substances. In a few species (such as the honey bee) the sting is barbed and remains imbedded in the skin, causing the death of the worker and releasing a pheromone that may bring other workers to the attack. It is interesting that the males of several groups of solitary wasps (which lack an ovipositor and therefore a sting) have the last abdominal segment prolonged into a stout spine, which is wielded much like a sting and can sometimes pierce the skin, though there are no poison glands. It is probable that such a "pseudosting" is nearly as effective as a true string in deterring predators, especially since male wasps commonly have aposematic patterns similar to those of the females.

Detachable Body Parts

Many insects have integumentary outgrowths that readily become detached, without seriously harming the insect. These include the waxy or powdery coverings of certain aphids and whiteflies, the hairs of caddisflies, and the scales of brisle-tails and of moths and butterflies. Thomas Eisner and his colleagues at Cornell University have shown that moths and caddisflies are often held only momentarily spider webs, since the scales or hairs stick to the adhesive strands and become detached from the body, permitting the insects to escape with minor damage. To what extent deciduous outgrowths play a role in escape from vertebrate predators in uncertain, but it is known that moths shed clouds of scales when pecked by birds. It is probable that scales first evolved as an escape mechanism and only later, in many Lepidoptera, assumed a role in conveying messages via colour patterns. That is, an originally secondary defense may have become also a primary defense, reducing the frequency of predator attacks and at the same time retaining a role in escaping from such attacks.

Deflection of Attack

Many butterflies have small spots along the edge of the wing, and it is believed that these attract the attention of predators and cause them to bite at a nonessential part of the body. Butterfly collectors are aware that the wings of fritillaries and others having such deflection marks on the margin of the wing commonly have triangular beak marks at the margin. The "tails" of swallowtails may also serve a role in deflecting attack from the body, and as collectors are all too aware, these are commonly damaged unless the butterfly has recently emerged.

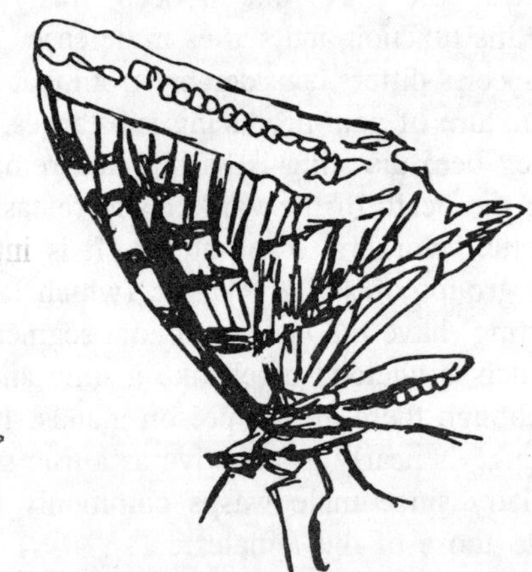

Fig. 6.9. A swallowtail butterfly with a large beak mark at the "tail" of the right wing. This butterfly is "mud- puddling," obtaining moisture and minerals from damp soil in the manner of many butterflies.

Hair-streaks have not only antenna-like filaments at the posterior margins of the wings, but usually a colour spot at the base of the filaments, simulating a head. Thus a perched hair-streak often seems to have its "head in the wrong place," causing a predator to seize only a piece of the wing.

Startle Displays

Some insects, when approached closely or attacked by a predator, suddenly undergo movements, produce sounds or scents, or display colours serving to "threaten" or "bluff" a predator. The usual effect is probably to startle or to cause a momentary indecision, permitting the insect to escape. There is evidence that birds and mammals remember encounters with displaying insects and to a certain extent avoid them. Both cryptic and aposematic insects may have startle displays as a "second line of defense" in the event of attack.

Walkingsticks, which one thinks of as the ultimate in crypsis, have a variety of displays. Many tropical species have short, brightly coloured hind wings that are suddenly erected, abruptly increasing their size; this sometimes may be accompanied by stridulation that is said to resemble the hissing of a snake. Michael Robinson, of the Smithsonian Tropical Research Institute, in Panama, has described a number of such cases, including one wingless species that flexes its abdomen up and down while stridulating, suggesting a scorpion or (more remotely) a snake about to strike. Some walking sticks have sharp spines capable of pricking an aggressor, and others have caustic secretions that can actually be aimed at an aggressor. A number of different insects produce squeaking sounds when seized, such as long horned beetles and mutillid wasps. Even the relatively inert, unprotected pupae of some Lepidoptera produce squeaks when handled. Some bright-coloured, distasteful tiger moths produce an odorous froth, from thoracic glands when disturbed. larvae of swallowtail butterflies have eversible, hornlike glands ; on the thorax called *osmeteria.* These produce a volatile substance smelling rather like rancid butter, and in fact its major component is butyric acid. Swallowtail caterpillars often have aposematic patterns, and many have eye spots that are dramatically displayed by elevating and inflating the thorax.

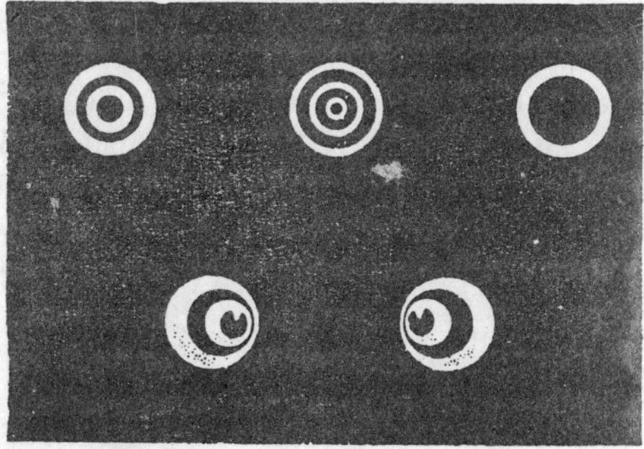

Fig. 6.10. Artificial eye spots used by David Blest in experiments with birds. The single circle (upper left) elicited the fewest escape responses; the shaded figures with eccentric rings (lower two), the most.

Eye spots deserve special mention, since they occur in a wide variety of insects and are usually associated with some type of display. We refer here not to the small, marginal deflection spots on butterfly wings, but to the large eye spots often found on the heads or thoraces of caterpillars or the hind wings of mantids, moths and other insects. Hawk moths provide a particularly fine example. Many species are cryptically coloured but have brightly coloured hind wings, each containing a large eye spot. When disturbed, the moth spreads its fore wings and undergoes quivering motions, presumably serving to further startle a predator. Some moths and butterflies have spots shaded in such a way as to have remarkable resemblance to the eyes of owls or snakes.

David Blest, of University College, London, has shown that the sudden appearance of any bright colour releases escape responses in certain birds. This proved to be particularly true of eye spots. Blest fed several species of birds with mealworms, using a box that would flash a light beneath, revealing a pattern on the floor of the box. The sudden flash of a pair of paralle lines or crosses caused some escape responses, but pairs of circles caused many more such responses. Eye spots shaded so as to appear three-dimensional were especially effective in *"frightening"* the birds. He concluded that many small birds respond innately to the sudden appearance of eyes that might represent those of a large predator. However, Blest showed that birds do sometimes habituate to butterflies with eye spots when these prove palatable. Thus eye spots are most effective if not too widespread in nature and when displayed only under certain conditions.

Chemical Defense

The ultimate form of defense is the use of one or more chemicals that are in some way repugnant to a predator. These may be obtained from the host plant (as in the case of the monarch butterfly) or synthesized by the insect. Defensive chemicals (called *allontones)* may be contained in the blood or may be produced by specialized exocrine glands. Many insects that exhibit chemical defense are aposematically coloured, and some are mimicked by insects lacking such defense, as we have seen.

Integrate Defense System

Many insects have not one but several defense mechanisms. In this way they may achieve protection against different predators or against the same predator at different levels of motivation of different stages in the learning process. Commonly larvae and adults are protected quite differently; for example, the larva of the viceroy butterfly resembles a bird dropping, while the pupa resembles a dried leaf, and the adult is a mimic of a distasteful species, the monarchy. In the same life stage, insects may have several *"line of defense."* Walkingsticks are cryptic, but it attacked they may have startle displays or discharge irritating chemicals at the intruder. Some tiger moths have cryptic fore wings and brilliantly coloured hind wings, which provide flash colours, but if actually attacked discharge noxious fluids from thoracic glands.

In a now classic study of 15 species of preying mantids on Trinidad, Jocelyn Crane, of the New York Zoological Society, found that all 15 were cryptic, some being sticklil e, others leaflike, some like bark or lichens. All 15 had escape mecha isms: dropping, dodging, or jumping. As a third line of defense, several species had startle displays, differing in dctails but usually invt ving body swaying, spreading the wings, and raising the forelegs and bdomen. As a least resort several species would actually strike the predator with the raptorial forelegs. Crane hypothesized that the elaborate displays evolved by ritualization of simultaneous tendencies to remain motionless and to escape.

Fig. 6.11. The startle display of a preying mantid. This mantid is cryptically coloured, but when disturbed it assumes an aggressive pose and threatens to strike, at the same time displaying bright colours on the hind wings.

Perhaps the most impressive integrated defenses occur in the colonies of social insects. Some tropical social wasps produce sounds by drumming on the carton of the nest; and if approached, they display by wagging their brightly coloured abdomens, or, as a last resort, stinging the intruder en mass. Yet their defense against army ants may be very different; they simply flee and found a new nest elsewhere. The nests of termites often have walls nearly as hard as stone, but if the walls are breached, a horde of specialists in chemical defense quickly arrives on the scene.

The question is often asked: if these things are true, why is it that some insects have several defense mechanisms, some have only one and some appear to have none at all? A partial answer is to be found in the reproductive capacities. Insects such as aphids or house flies, which have no spectacular defense strategies (but like most insects may have subtle ones), compensate by having unusually high reproductive rates. They are specialists in reproduction rather than survival. Every species may be said to maintain itself in nature by achieving some sort of balance between reproductive potential and survival capacity.

BEHAVIOURAL DEFENSE

As already indicated, behaviour is an important component of all forms of defense, but there are some insects that rely almost entirely on behaviour for protection. Perhaps the most straightforward approach to defense is to flee; this is extremely effective among the insects because of their small size and their ability to accelerate very rapidly. Many leafhoppers (Cicadellidae) move rapidly sideways to the opposite side of the branch they are on and simply attempt to stay out of sight. Taking flight is a particularly effective means of escape, as anyone who has attempted to capture a fly or a grasshoppers with bare hands

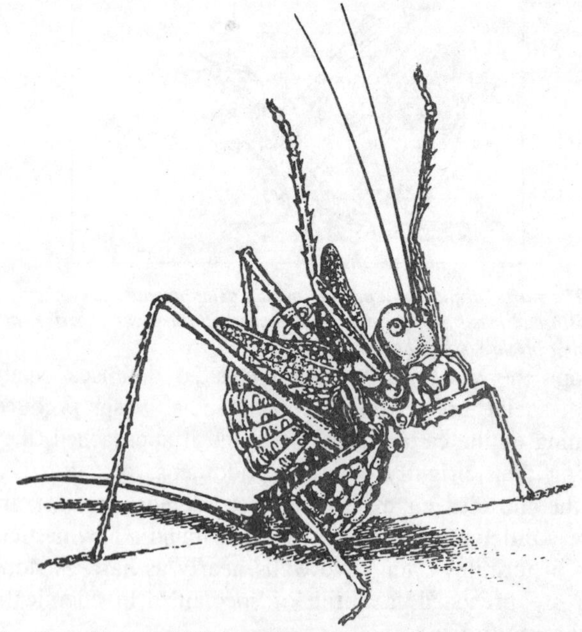

Fig. 6.12. The katydid Neobareuia spinosa *in its threatening posture.*

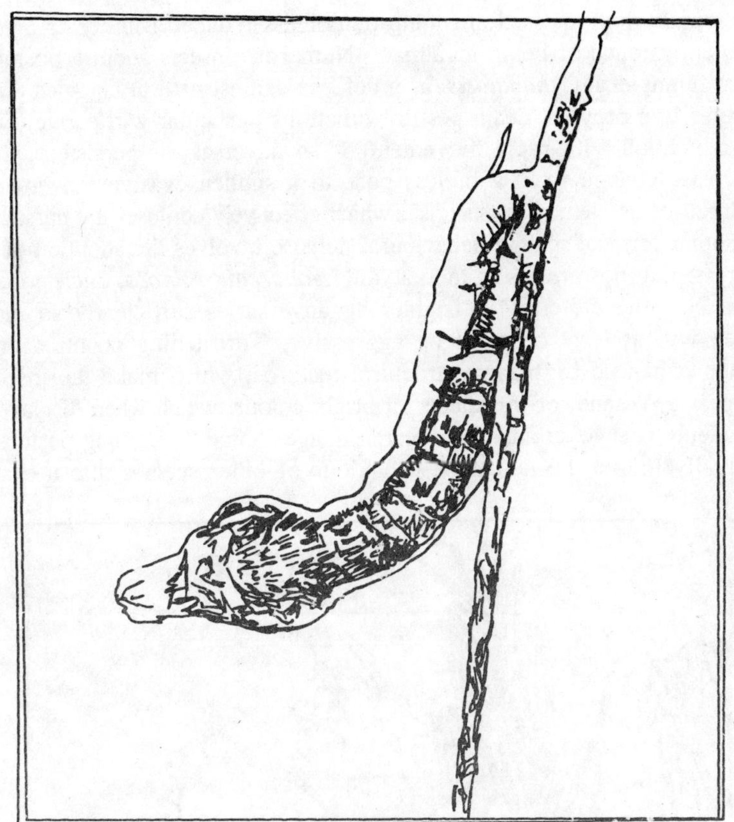

Fig. 6.13. The caterpillar of Leucorrhampha omata assuming its defensive posture in which it resembles a small snake.

will readily testify. In fact, the selective pressure of predation almost certainly played a major role in the evolution of the insect flight mechanism. Jumping is also an effective means of escape in both flying and flightless individuals. Wingless aphids successfully avoid predation by larval coccinellid beetles by jumping suddenly.

Reflex dropping is also an effective form of escape. Behaviour of this type is displayed by a number of kinds of beetles, especially weevils, and a variety of caterpillars. Geometrid larvae often drop from their food plant on a strand of silk when disturbed and the reel themselves back up when the danger has passed. Other caterpillars, like those of the California tussock moth, just drop freely to the underlying vegetation. The opposite of rapid movement is, obviously, to remain motionless. Remaining motionless reduce visibility or gives the appearance of being inanimate. Numerous insects adopt a posture that feigns death *(thanatosis)* as a defense against natural enemies that prefer live prey. A death posture functions particularly effectively in combination with rapid movement. If an adversary is persistent, the surprise change from a lifeless pose to a sudden evasive movement introduces an element of surprise, which effectively confuses the pursuer. Another form of mainly behavioural defense involves the adoption of a threatening posture, as in the katydid *Neobarettia spinosa.* Such poses can be quite effective in frightening adversaries sufficiently so that they will at least cease to be aggressive. Threatening postures are often enhanced by bizarre structural features, which make the insect appear grotesque, or by patches of bright colour, which when displayed suddenly change an attacker's search image. Some threatening postures actually mimic the defensive behaviour of other species that use an

Fig. 6.14. Typical frothy protective secretion produced by a spittle bug. Cercopidae: Homoptera.

additional mechanism as their first line of defense. This can be seen among non-stinging species that engage in the abdominal thrusting behaviour characteristic of stinging species. One of the most fascinating threatening postures is adopted by the larvae of the Brazilian sphingid, *Leucorrhampha,* which, at rest, blend well with their normal background. When disturbed, the larva twists its body to expose a pattern of scalelike markings and then sways back and forth in the manner of a small snake. A special kind of behavioural defense involves the construction of an individual protective shelter or the utilization of a wide variety of natural crevices and holes formed as a by-product of feeding. Boring insects, for example, create a protective place in which to live as they tunnel though the woody parts of plants. Others, such as the ambrosia beetles, excavate tunnels beneath the bark as a place in which to culture their fungus food and rear their young. Many species use plant parts or other materials to construct protective cases in which to rest or pupate. In the broadest sense a case can be considered as any extra covering intentionally formed by an insect, regardless of whether, it is composed of a body secretion or largely of foreign material. Thus, the frothy secretion of spittle bugs, the wax threads of woolly and the resinous shells of scale insects can, along with silken cocoons, be considered as extraorganismic protective devices.

The larval lepidopterans are the predominant group among the terrestrial case makers. Some fasten their cases to fixed objects: others construct portable cases that they carry about. Often the case of the last larval instar is sealed to serve as a pupation site. The coleophorids construct tubelike cases of silk, leaf material, and feces that cover their entire body with the exception of the head capsule. When feeding, the larva is attached to the plant by its mouth parts so that its case stands out from the plant surface. The bagworms (Psychidae) live in portable cases and move about freely, carrying their abodes wherever they go: when it is time to pupate, the case becomes a pupation site. Their cases are frequently made from twigs or leaf pieces bound together with silk in a species-specific fashion.

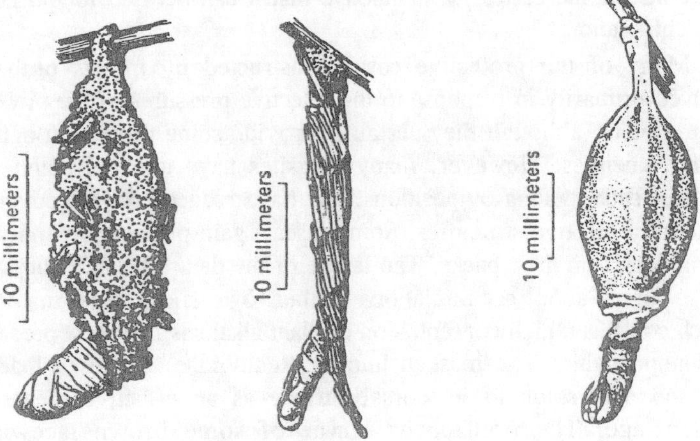

Fig. 6.15. Examples of the portable protective cases constructed by the larvae of psychid moths known as bagworms.

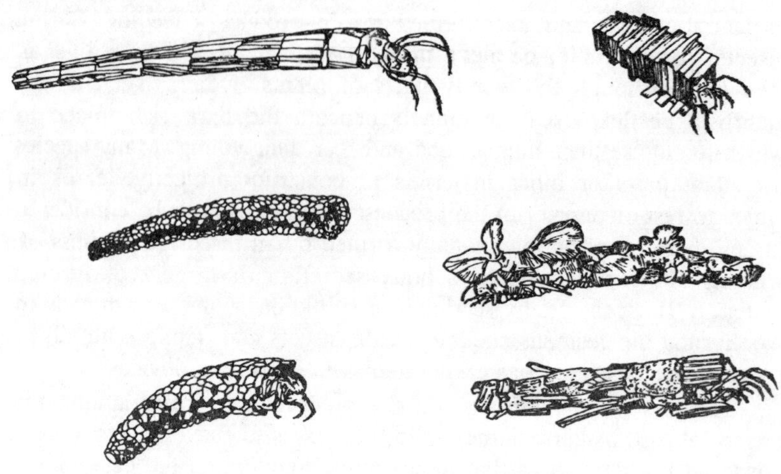

Fig. 6.16. Caves constructed of a variety of different materials by the larvae of caddisflies.

Among the aquatic insects, the caddisflies are by far the bestknown case builders. As in the related Lepidoptera, trichopterans construct both permanent and portable cases from a wide range of materials, including bits of leaves, twigs, sand grains, and pebbles that are bound together with silk into a tubular structure. When larval development is complete, the case is firmly secured and sealed for pupation. For many insects the case is so distinctive that it can be used for purposes of identification.

Many of the protective cases constructed by insects probably evolved primarily in response to the selective pressures of the physical environment, although they certainly provide some protection against natural enemies. However, many parasites have evolved countermeasures, such as long ovipositions, that have reduced the effectiveness of some protective structures. Some insects gain protection simply by piling debris on their backs. The larvae of the datura beetle (Chrysomelidae) carry about accumulations of their own sticky fecal material, which contains a high concentration of plant alkaloids that most predators find unpalatable. The masked hunter (Reduviidae) carries a load of lint and dust stuck to its dorsal surface as an effective means of camouflage. The predaceous larvae of some brown lacewings (Hemerobiidae) are called trash carriers because they pile the remains of their victims upon their backs.

STRUCTURAL DEFENSE

In some insects, the integument becomes so heavily sclerotized that it provides adequate protection against almost any form of natural attack, including the beaks of insectivorous birds. This is especially true of beetles, among which the ironclad beetles (Tene- brionidae) and some weevils (Curculionidae) are well-known by collectors because of the difficulty of penetrating them with mounting pins. In some ants, the front of the well-sclerotized head capsule of the soldier caste is flattened and can be used to plug temporary openings in the nest against intruders.

The mouthparts of insects are particularly useful in defense, as are the modified cerci that form the forceps at the tip of the abdomen of earwigs; the latter become proficient at picking up adversaries, such as ants, and throwing them to one side with a flick of the abdomen. Insects do, however, have a variety of specialized defensive structures, mainly in the form of spurs and modified setae. The leg spines of insects are primarily and aid to locomotion but become effective weapons when the legs are raked across a victim. Caterpillars belonging to several families have a cloak of hairlike setae that make them unpalatable to a variety of insectivores and increase the difficulty of oviposition upon them by parasites. Short fragments of these setae break off and readily enter the skin, causing irritation and festering similar to that caused by a bark sliver. There is no question as to the effectiveness of these hairs as a protection against predators. During outbreaks of the western tent caterpillar, *Malacosoma pluviale,* for example, birds of all kinds completely ignore, what would appear to be an abundance of food.

Chemical Defense

Arthropods in general and insects in particular display the widest diversity of chemical defenses of any group of terrestrial animals. Chemical defense among the insects can be divided broadly into the use of compounds referred to as *venoms,* injected by a skin-perforating apparatus, and the use of odoriferous or repugnatorial substances sequestered from their food or produced by special integumentary glands. Thus, the chemicals used for defense can be either manufactured within the insect *(endogenous)* or obtained from some outside source *(exogenous)*. Arthropod venoms were reviewed by Beard, whereas other forms of chemical defense were reviewed by Roth and Eisner and Eisner.

For the most part, endogenous defensive chemicals are produced by multicellular structures comprised of glandular epithelium and a saclike reservoir with a cuticular lining in which the secretion is stored. The defensive compound is usually discharged by muscular or hydrostatic compression of the reservoir or by its evagination. Several staphylinid beetles have tubular glands that, under pressure of the hemolymph, turn inside out like fingers of a glove.

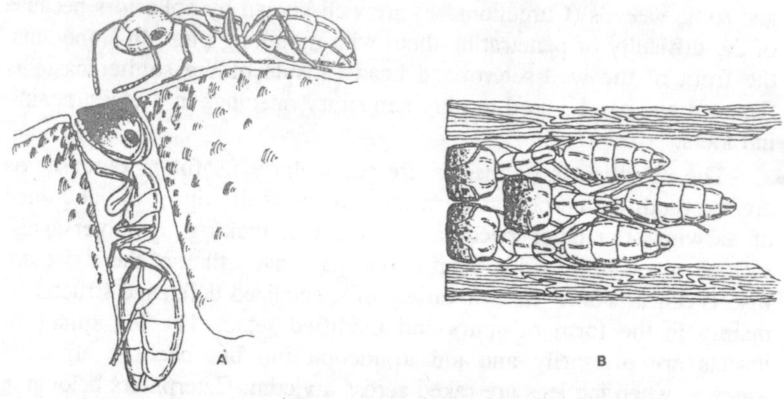

Fig. 6.17. Nest-guarding behaviour of soldiers of the European ant Camponotus truncates. (A) A long soldier blocking a small opening. (B) A group of soldiers blocking a large entrance hole.

Non-venomous defensive secretions are highly variable. Roth and Eisner and Eisner and Meinwald listed numerous defensive compounds that are used singly or in combination by arthropods. Not all such compounds are insect-made. Often they are simply special chemical constituents of the diet that, when sequestered by an insect, render it unpalatable. Probably the best-known example is the sequestration of the cardiac glycocides of milkweed plants by the larvae and adults of the monarch butterfly. Other insects, lepidopterans in particular, are rendered undesirable as prey by various other plant-derived compounds that become incorporated into their tissues. Obviously, the potential predators of such insects have no way of knowing that these prey are unpalatable unless they try them and learn that they should be avoided. Apparently, the learning of predators is enhanced if distastefulness is associated with a specific visual image. In the course of these predator-prey relationships, many unpalatable species have evolved patterns of bright-colored markings, often referred to as *warning* or *aposernatic colouration*. This will be discussed briefly under colourational defense later in this chapter.

In some species, the distasteful components of an insect's food are actually concentrated for release against an adversary before it takes a trial taste. The larvae of some swallowtail butterflies have a thoracic pouchlike structure called an *osmeterium,* where odiferous plant components accumulate and from which they are expelled when the pouch is everted in response to a disturbance. One well-known

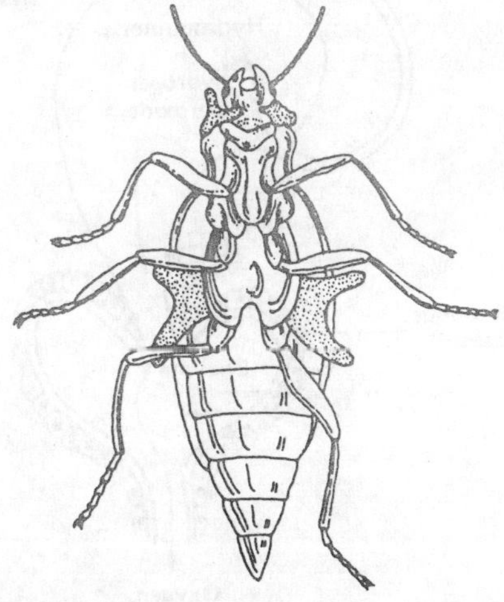

Fig. 6.18. Ventral view of the staphylinid beetle, Malachius bipustulatus, showing evertible defensive glands.

example is the larva of the anis swallowtail, which upon disturbance everts a bright orange-red osmeterium and its contents of volatile anis oil. Recently, Roth and Eisner discovered that a man-made herbicide known to be repellent to ants is sequestered by a species of grasshopper when it feeds on sprayed foliage; the herbicide is incorporated into the froth the grasshoppers release for defense. Defensive chemicals that are not injected can be separated broadly as being odoriferous or repugnatorial. Numerous insects, including roaches, earnings, several families of beetles, and several families of bugs, have rather characteristic odors that our own sense organs readily detect as undesirable. Many of these compounds are not released merely in the presence of danger but are released constantly to the surface of the integument from the epithelial glands that produce them. Any one who has handled the large black "stink beetles" (Tenebrionidae) or whirligig beetles (Gyrinidae) knows how long these odors can linger. Indeed, they may cause an entire insect in collection to smell for months after the specimens have been pinned and dried. One species of ant produces *citral,* a compound closely related to citronella, commonly used incommercial insect repellents.

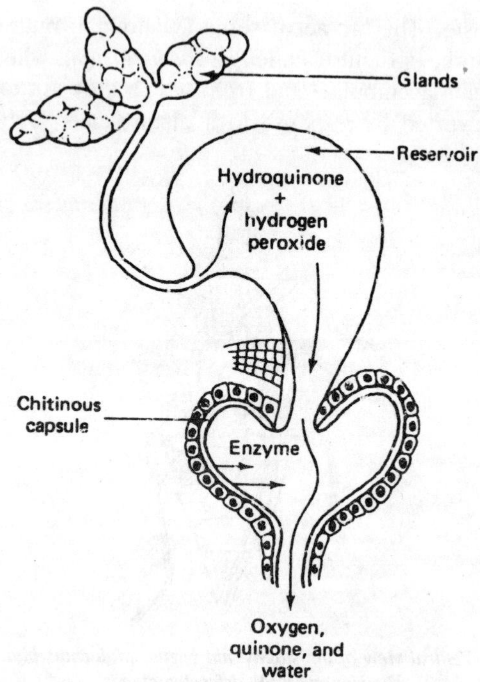

Fig. 6.19. Defensive system of the bombardier beetle Brachinus.

Most of the chemicals used in insect defense function largely as repellents that deter attackers, but in higher concentrations some of these substances are highly toxic. Some chemicals, however, seem to be primarily toxic. The meloids are often referred to as-blister beetles because a compound called *cantharidin* in their integument is a powerful mucous membrane irritant and vesicant, which was once thought to be useful as a human aphrodisiac. Another compound, *pederin,* produced by staphylinid beetles of the genus *Paederus,* produces a dermatitis. *A saponin* compound that is extract from a beetle and used by Kalahari bushmen to coat their arrows is a powerful paralytic. The formicine ants derive their name from the fact that they are stingless and rely on *formic acid* secretions in their attack on other organisms and in colony defense. The formic acid is applied topically as a spray that these ants can propel up to 30 cm, or subcutaneously through wounds caused by their mandibles.

Perhaps the most often described example of chemical defense encountered among the insects is that of the famous bombardier beetles of the carabid genus *Brachinus*. These small black beetles derive their name from the audible report that accompanies the explosive emission of their defensive secretion. By raising and rotating the tip of its abdomen, a bombardier beetle can accurately aim its "cannon" at an adversary. The internal defensive apparatus consists of a reservoir into which hydroquinones and hydrogen peroxide are secreted by associated glands. The two compounds pass posteriorly into a cuticular chamber where they come in contact with a catalytic enzyme. The reaction that occurs when the three compounds are mixed together results in a sudden liberation of oxygen that expels a visible cloud of quinone at the enemy.

In the broad sense, venoms include all forms of toxic compounds that are injected. This definition would therefore encompass the chemicals produced by epithelial cells associated with setae, urticating hairs, and spines; salivary secretions injected by the mouth parts; plus the venoms of aculeate hymenopterans. Unlike nonvenomous compounds, venoms are usually ineffectual when applied topically. However, when injected into an organism, venoms induce their characteristic response. Some venoms, such as the salivary secretions of many predaceous insects, have a general toxicity because of their primary function as aids to digestion. These tend to degrade or liquify the surrounding tissue in an irreversible manner. In some blood-feeding species, such as mosquitoes, these secretions contain an anticoagulant that facilitates feeding by retarding clotting.

The venoms produced by the sting glands of aculeate hymenopterans may have evolved from the paralyzing venoms employed by the parasitic wasps. Some paralyzing venoms have a fairly widespreac effect, but others are specific to only a few host species. Such specificity appears to be attributable to the chemical nature of the compounds rather than to the host preference of the parasite. Furthermore, many venoms are unstable and produce only a temporary paralysis that accommodates oviposition, whereas others produce permanent paralysis. The venoms of social bees, wasps, and ants are used mainly for the defense of the colony. The chemical nature of insect venoms is highly variable, and only a few have been adequately studied from a biochemical standpoint. The social insects often enhance their defensive capability through coordinated group behaviour. Angered bees and wasps will often respond to danger with a rush of defenders from the nest; group stinging behaviour may then result in response to an alarm pheromone released in association with the venom. An alarm pheromone has also been found to occur among several species of aphid. When attacked by a predator, the prey aphid produces a droplet from its cornicles. A volatile component of the secretion repels other aphids within a distance of 1 to 3 centimeters. Ants also employ alarm pheromones that drawn

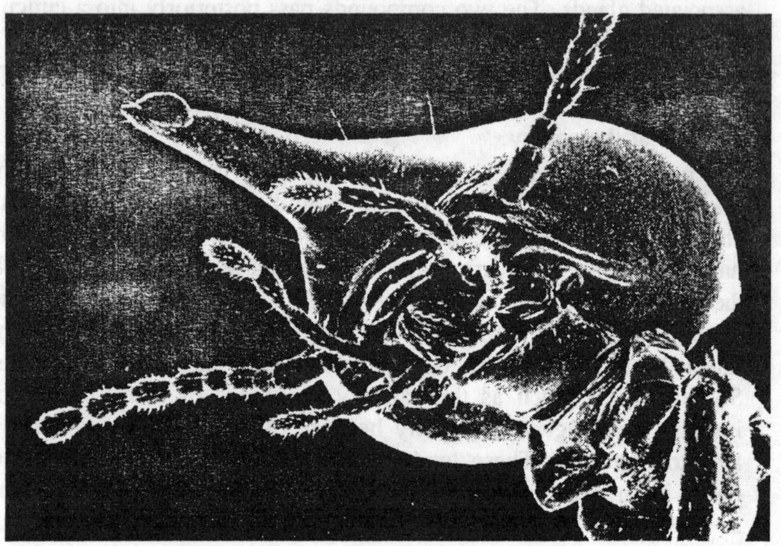

Fig. 6.20. Scanning electron micrograph of the head of termite nasute, Nasutitermes exitiosus. viewed from below. Note the droplet of defensive secretion of the tip of the snout.

workers to a disturbance in the vicinity of the nest. Other ants will encircle a portion of food and discharge a defensive secretion outward to repel the foragers of other species. Workers of the weaver ant, *Oecophylla longinoda,* mark, and in a sense defend, their territories against invasions by alien workers.

In some termite species, specialized soldiers known as nasuti eject a sticky frontal gland secretion from a projection of the head that resembles a nozzle. When workers are traveling back and forth over exposed trails, the nasuti line up along the sides of the pathways with their snouts pointing outward to provide protection to the foragers. A group of nasuti in a cooperative effort will also encircle an adversary and discharge the secretion, which hardens into a sticky thread. By swinging their heads from side to side, they can throw loops into the threads and quickly entangle an enemy much larger than themselves.

METACHROMATIC

Defensive or, more correctly, protective colour patterns can be grouped under four categories: cryptic colouration, flash patterns, warning signals and mimicry.

Cryptic Colouration

Cryptic coloration is simply camouflage. Crypsis can result from either blending into a featureless background or looking like a particular object that forms a common component of the environment. The success of this form of protection is highly dependent on the closeness of the match between the colour and pattern of a species and that of its habitat background, but it also depends on the existence of appropriate behavioural mechanisms. A cryptic individual must select a suitable background on which to rest and must either remain motionless or move in an appropriate fashion, such as the gentile swaying motion displayed by some leaflike species. For example, the mottled colour pattern of the grasshopper genus *Philippiaeris,* from the rocky desert areas of central Chile, ranges from a light sandy beige to a dark green. Certainly, one of the truly fascinating aspects of protective colouration in general, and of cryptic patterns in particular, is the level of perfection that has evolved in so many species, as some of the following examples will demonstrate. The long evolutionary history of insect has provided ample opportunityp for a high degree of refinement in their protective colour patterns.

Protective colouration also provides numerous examples of similar patterns having evolved in totally unrelated groups that occupy similar habitats where they are subjected to the same kind of selective pressures. The structural similarity between caterpillars and the larvae of sawflies is quite remarkable, but the similarity in the colour patterns of these groups is truly amazing. Members of both groups, which feed on the needles of coniferous trees, are often the green colour, of the needles and bear similar longitudinal, light-green stripes that resemble the midrib and characteristic lighting patterns of these elongate leaves.

Several basic colour patterns are employed that help insects to blend well into featureless backgrounds. Disruptive colouration tends to break up the outline of the body, with light and dark markings that suit a mottled background or create the impression of a random pattern of sunlight and shadow. No matter how well an organism's colour matches its background, the insect will reveal its position readily if it casts a shadow. Shadow elimination by compressing the body and wings tightly against the substrate therefore becomes an important behavioural aspect of camouflage. Even when an organism is coloured to match its background, predators with stereo-scopic vision can detect the presence of a prey as the result of the three-dimensional image created by differential lighting. This is overcome quite well by patterns of countershading. A solidcoloured caterpillar, for instance, would be highly visible on a leaf of similar colour because of the higher level of light reflectance from its dorsal surface compared to that of its lateral surfaces. If an individual is more darkly coloured along the middorsal line and there is a gradation to lighter colour along the sides, it has the effect of flattening out the visual image perceived by a predator.

Only a few insects are capable of adaptive colour change such as that displayed by chameleons and a few fishes. Some locusts can vary their colour from nearly white through yellow and brown to almost black and thereby match the colour of their backgrounds. The change is not as rapid as in some vertebrates but comes about gradually, supposedly in response to the light intensity reflected from the background. Similarly, the colour patterns developed by the pupae of certain lepidopterans are determined in advance by the background colour perceived in the larval stage. Several genera of stick insects, however, display a chromatic rhythm, being paler by day than by night. This change is the result of the movement of pigment granules in the epithelial cells, which is under the control of hormones. Not all insects live in habitats with a generally featureless background into which they can blend. In habitats characterized by open space, where an individual might frequently form a silhouette against a rather uniform colour field such as the sky, better protection is afforded by resemblance to a commonly occurring object. This similarity to inanimate objects is usually referred to as *horn morphism* (shape), *homochromism* (colour), or *homotypism* (form and colour), whereas mimicry is more properly reserved for the resemblance to another animal.

A common kind of homotypism displayed by insects involves the resemblance to leaves, twigs and floral parts. Leaf look-alikes, including katydids, stick insects, and butterflies, present a wide variety of examples that illustrate the incredible perfection evolution can produce. In this regard, one of the interesting aspects of leaf resemblance emerges in the examination of a series of species with activity periods that span the passage of the seasons. In accordance with the changing condition of the leaves among which they hide, the wing veins as well as markings on the wing surface of these insects simulate the appropriate pattern of leaf venation and configuration. Insects that are active during the spring, when the leaves are fresh and unmarred, are green and look like perfect new leaves. Those that are active later in the year may resemble tattered older leaves, discoloured and damaged through the course of time. These patterns are achieved with irregular wing margins and clear areas that resemble perforations, combined with blotches of colour that resemble physical damage or splashes of bird droppings.

Larval stages also resemble inanimate objects. The caterpillars of some sphingid moths have countershading and diagonal markings, which make the individual look like a rolled-up leaf, complete with a stalk provided by a thick terminal spine. Geometrid moth larvae, or loopers, often resemble twigs, complete with budlike swellings and appropriate bark markings. One cannot examine the cryptic colouration and behaviour of insects without wondering how it is possible for such perfect copies of non-insect objects to have evolved and how much protection they afford the species that have evolved them. If they do not occur by chance, why are all species not protected in this manner? Crypsis is just one of a number of defensive strategies, and it is best suited for those species that are sedentary, diurnal, and live in well-lighted habitats. Furthermore, as perfect as camouflage may be, it can never provide complete Protection. For example, some birds pick up certain kindly of objects at random, and, as long as they encounter a reasonable number of prey items for their effort, they are likely to continue and even concentrate on those objects that their prey resembles most closely.

Obviously, if the prey becomes more difficult to see, a predacious species must improve its search ability in order to survive. If we recognize a coevolution between the hunter and the hunted, the members of the latter group that most perfectly blend into their surroundings will always have the best chance to survive predation and will consequently leave proportionately more offspring than the variants that are more easily seen. There is a sizable body of experimental evidence that illustrates the protective value of a slight resemblance to a non-insect object, even under cage conditions where the search effort of a predator is greatly reduced. Since some apparently poor crypsis reduces predation at least a little, we can see how there would be enough selection to drive evolution toward better and better crypsis. Thus, after countless generations, we see an accumulation of inherited characteristics, which in some cases border on cryptic perfection. The fact that some of the details cannot be seen clearly without the aid of a magnifying glass is a concern that stems from an anthropocentric view of the natural world.

GROUP DEFENSE

Group defense is well-known as an important behavioural adaptation of eusocial insects. Termite workers are summoned to block openings and repair the damage to their nest, and nasuti function in groups to encircle an attacker and entangle it in strands of sticky frontal gland secretion. Bees, wasps and ants are all known for their group stinging behaviour in defense of their nests, and the specialized soldier caste of ants acts in groups to defend columns of foraging workers. However, group defensive behaviour is not restricted to eusocial species. Good experimental evidence for the effectiveness of such behavior among the more generalized hymenopterans known as sawflies has been published. Careful study of other gregarious and colonial species may reveal that group defense is actually quite common.

Larval sawflies of several species of *Neodiprion* and *Diprion* exhibit group defensive displays comdprised of synchronous jerking motions of their anterior and posterior ends, and may also extrude a sticky resinous material from their mouthparts. Prop found that this behaviour discouraged both parasites and avian predators. Tostowaryk found that when *Neodiprion* larvae were dispersed, the pentatomid bug, *Podisus modestus,* could attack an individual larva and retreat with it without disturbing neighbouring larvae. However, when the sawfly larvae were in a compact group, the struggle associated with the predator's attack of an individual stimulated a group defensive response by the remaining members of the colony. Even if the predator's attack was successful, it became smeared with the larval exudate, which slowed subsequent attacks. The end results of the group defensive behaviour were an increase in the number of unsuccessful attacks by *P. modestus* and fewer attack attempts per unit of time.

7

DIETARY BEHAVIOUR

Insect feed on almost every form of organic material, living and dead, coal and natural gas being the two notable exceptions. Some species, often referred to as generalists, feed on a very wide range of foods - the roaches are a good example. Many species of scavengers are also rather omnivorous, in that the decaying material on which they feed is comprised of both animal and plant matter from numerous sources. Most insects, however, are more specific in their food relationships and restrict themselves to some particular kind of food (plant tissue, sap, nectar, animal flesh, blood and so forth.) Often, within the food type, a limited number of species serve as hosts.

Several terms commonly used to describe the food range of animals are polyphagous, oligophagous and monophagous. *Polyphagous* species feed on a wide range of foods normally representing several families of plants or animals, whereas *oligophagous* species feed on a narrower range of foods, often from within a single family. However, the separation of polyphagy from oligophagy is at best arbitrary. *Monophagy* - feeding restricted to a single species - would seem to be more precise, although the interpretation of Dethier that insects attracted to a group of food species by a common chemical stimulus are monophagous seems logical. Monophagy in the narrow sense is fairly limited, but the opposite extreme, *pantophagy,* probably never occurs. When we view the over-all pattern of food preferences among the insects, there is a clear indication that some mechanisms exist that have divided the species among the food resources available. In the case of all insects that feed on other living species, one important mechanism is coevolution. Few multicellular, terrestrial, or freshwater species of plants and animals are immune to insect attack; the chinaberry tree, *Melia azedarack,* may be an exception. Conversely, there is probably no plant species attacked by all of the herbivorous insects that share its geographical distribution.

Insects and their hosts have been engaged in the process of food allocation by natural selection for a very long time. The host species disadvantaged by insect attack have had to evolve protective or defensive mechanisms in order to survive the attack and/or competition from other species. When a host species evolves some form of insect-feeding deterrent, the associated insect species, in essence, faces a reduction in its food supply. If it is to survive, the insect must also adjust and often does so by evolving a mechanism that, at least temporarily overcomes the host's defense. This ongoing scheme of attack and counterattack has played a major role in the evolution of insects and their hosts. One important outcome of this process has been the reduction in the number of general food relationships and an increase in some degree of food specificity or preference.

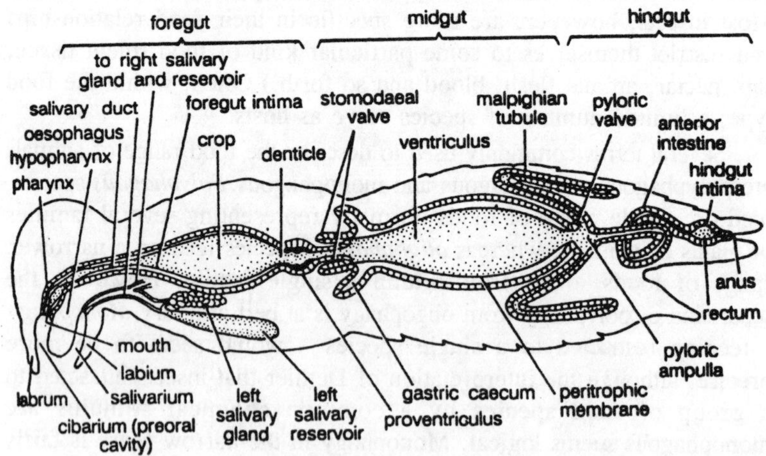

Fig. 7.1. Alimentary canal of a generalised insect.

The features of both the host species and its insect associated that bring about some change in their relationship must be inheritable so that these traits can be passed on from generation to generation and the degree of benefit they convey can be tested by natural selection. Often the changes are enzymatic or physiological, but behavioural adjustments also occur that reduce the chance of the insect's losing contact with its host during necessary periods of displacement. Coevolution and other ecological mechanisms such as competition, which affect the way various resources are apportioned among the species of an ecosystem, are generally the same for all types of food relationships. However, the details of the stimulus-response patterns involved in the selection of plants by herbivores, insect hosts and prey by parasites and predators, and vertebrate hosts by blood feeders are somewhat different.

The host selection behaviour of insects is complicated further by the fact that many species display some degree of adult-larval divergence in their food habits. In those species, such as the grasshoppers and many true bugs, the adults and their offspring feed side by side and display the same stimulus-response patterns in their plant hose preference. In many species, however, the adults feed on an entirely different kind of food than do the young. Such is the case of most biting flies, a variety of aquatic species, most lepidopterans, many hymenopterans (particularly the entomophagous parasites), and some beetles. For these species, either the adults and young must display different patterns of food-fording and recognition behaviour or the female must select the larval food as part of her oviposition behaviour. In the latter group, food location, at least for the larvae, is never a problem, since, if the female does her job, they are surrounded by food from the time they hatch. If the female errors in the deposition of her eggs, her larvae die of starvation and, in the process, weed out any aberrant genes that would be detrimental to the species established food relationship. Whether or not the surrounding food is satisfactory may still be ascertained by the larvae, however. In the case of the less discriminatory feeders, such as filter-feeding aquatic lavae, there is little or no problem. For some plant feeders, however, the larvae may have to select young foliage over old or locate a suitable feeding site.

Studies of the behaviour of insect groups with different trophic relationship have had a somewhat different focus, and our understanding of the host selection process has not advanced to the same point to each group. Therefore, phytophagous insects, entomphagous insects, and blood-feeders separately are considered.

Selection of Host Phytophagous Insects

Roughly one half of the specie of insects feed on plants. A relative few, like the electric buck moth, *Hemileuca electra,* which feeds exclusively on flat top buckwheat, *Eriogonum jasciculatum,* feed on a single plant species; probably none feed on all of the plant that occur within their range. Most feed upon the members of a single family or a few related families, as, for example the white cabbage butterflies (pieridae) that eat members of the mustard family. Some, like the gypsy moth, *Porthetria dispar,* which feeds on more than *200* species of plants from a wide range of families, have more catholic tastes, but may display some definite preferences. Insects use visual, chemical (olfactory and gustatory), and tactile cues in the location and recognition of the plants on which they feed. Whereas olfaction is an effective means of long distance communication among insects, most available evidence indicates that it functions most commonly over only short distance in host selection. Unfortunately most of the studies of olfactory preferences have been conducted under the unnatural conditions of still air in laboratory olfactometers of variable design.

There have been only a few reports of insects in the field flying considerable distances from downwind to host odor sources, but of course, the fact that visual cues and other orientation mechanisms might have been operating cannot be ruled out.

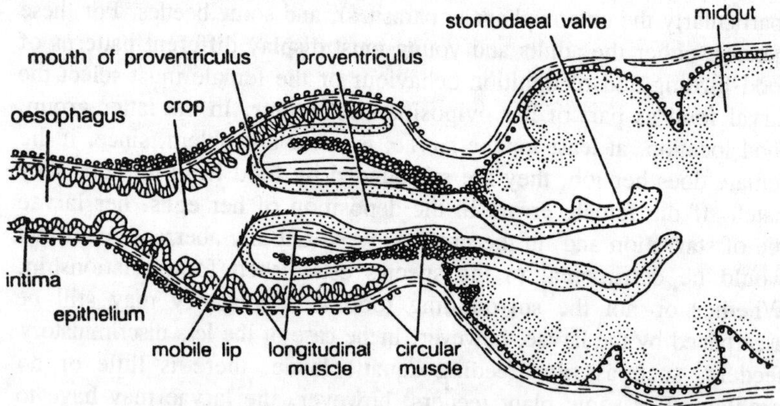

Fig. 7.2. Longitudinal section of the proventriculus of honey bee.

The response of phytophagous insects to the colour of vegetation seems to play an important part in food location but not in the discrimination of host species. As Thornsteinson suggested, the narrow spectrum of the light reflected from green plants would probably prohibit the decisive recognition of food plants by colour. A number of phytophagous insects including aphids, leafhoppers, and certain beetles are strongly attracted to yellow and yellow-green, and it seems likely that these pests can locate crops by the colour contrast between them and the surrounding native vegetation. The colour of flowers also attracts bees from a distance, although selection may be made at close range on the basis of fragrance; finally, visual cues provided by nectar guides may lead the bee to the location of the nectar. Visual form can also aid in plant host location and selection. Bumblebees orient to the form of inconspicuous flowers. Some bark beetles orient toward vertical silhouettes in preference to horizontal ones, and the white pine weevil, *Pissodes strobi,* shows a preference for the longer, larger-diameter terminal leaders in a pine forest.

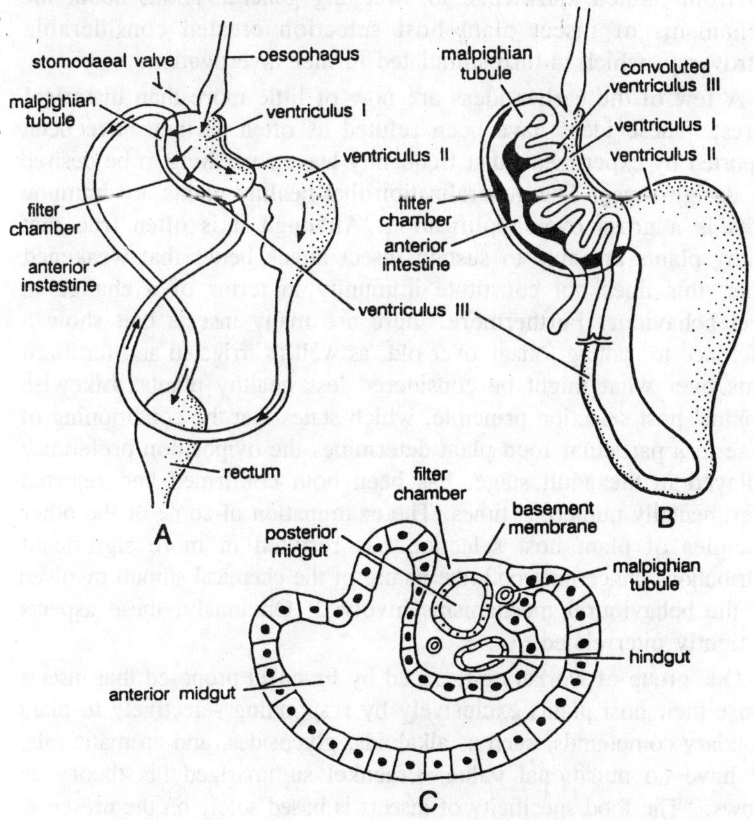

Fig. 7.3. Filter chambers of bugs. (A) Filter chamber with straight ventriculus, (B) Filter chamber with convoluted ventriculus, (C) T.S. filter chamber.

Tactile stimuli, in addition to contact chemoreception, also play a role in host selection, but probably to a lesser extent than visual and chemical cues. The surface characteristics of bark and foliage influence the choice of both feeding and oviposition sites. Bark and ambrosia beetles often display a preference for rough bark over smooth bark areas when initiating their brood galleries. The cereal leaf beetle prefers smooth-leafed wheats over varieties that are pubescent, and some leaf-edge-feeding caterpillars that do not normally feed on holly leaves will do so when the sharp points are removed. The role of chemical stimuli in the selection of plant hosts by insects has garnered most of the research attention, perhaps because the manipulation of odor cues would have greater practical application. The premature leap from limited knowledge to sweeping generalizations about the mechanisms of insect plant host selection created considerable controversy, which in turn stimulated further investigation.

A few of the earlier ideas are now of little more than historical interest. These ideas have been refuted as often as they have been supported by experiments that frequently leave something to be desired in a design sense. The generalization that healthy plants are immune plants is a gross oversimplification. Although it is often true that healthy plants are able to sustain insect attack better that weakened plants, this does not constitute immunity in terms of a change in insect behaviour. Furthermore, there are many insects that show a preference for young foliage over old, as well as irrigated and fertilized plants over what might be considered less healthy plants. Likewise Hopkins' host selection principle, which states that the conditioning of larvae to a particular food plant determines the oviposition preference displayed in the adult stage, has been both confirmed and rejected experimentally numerous times. The examination of some of the other principles of plant host selection has resulted in more significant contributions concerning both the nature of the chemical stimuli involved and the behavioural mechanisms involved. Obviously, these aspects are tightly interrelated.

One group of workers influenced by Fraenkel proposed that insects choose their host plants exclusively by responding selectively to plant secondary compounds, such as alkaloids, glycosides, and aromatic oils, that have no nutritional value. Fraenkel summarized his theory as follows: "The food specificity of insects is based solely on the presence or absence of these odd compounds in plants, which serve as repellents to insects in general and as attractants to those few which feed on each plant species." Fraenkel's theory would seem to fit well with the concept of the coevolution of insect herbivores and plants. It has been suggested that the feeding of herbivores was the selective pressure that led certain plants, particularly the angiosperms, to evolve chemical defenses in the form of metabolic by-products (odd substances). The herbivores would, in turn, have experienced a decline in their food supply, and some species are thought to have responded to this selective pressure by evolving some countermeasure; any species with a means of overcoming the plant's defensive mechanism would at least temporarily obtain an advantage over competing herbivores.

One might then envision that changes in the behaviour of the insect might not only have helped to overcome a plant's defensive strategy but also to exploit it by using the odd substances as a means of host recognition. In other words, an allomone would become a kairomone. Such a pattern of coevolution seems highly plausible, but Dethier cautions that the coevolution of plants and their herbivores is not a limited system. He suggests that the strength of selective pressures, such as competitors and the physical environment, might be changed by the feeding of herbivores. There is ample evidence that some insect exert a powerful selective pressure on their plant host, but most have a lesser impact. It would seem, therefore, that we should adopt the broader view of Dethier. If plants evolved odd substances as part of their defensive weaponry, several behavioural responses by insects are possible. The substances that may act as repellents, inhibitors, or oviposition of feeding deterrents to a range of herbivores might become chemical cues that attract and stimulate feeding by a few herbivores or have no effect at all. That is, if a herbivore was unable to detect a plant's odd substance(s), it would neither be repelled nor deterred.

Other workers have proposed that insects select their food plants on the basis of nutrient value and respond to feeding stimulants such as sugar, lipids, and amino acids. Since these compounds are widespread but not recognized readily except by contact chemoreception, questions have been raised concerning their role in host selection. Clearly, some compromise theory is needed: the dual discrimination theory of Kennedy and Booth, which suggests that selection is made on the basis of both odd substances and nutrients, seems more realistic. However, the wide-variety of insect-host relationships seems to preclude any generality. Some insects, like the aphids studied for many years by Kennedy, not only seem able to discriminate between host plants and even leaves within a species but are also bale to discriminate between alternate host species at different times of the year. Others, like the gypsy moth mentioned earlier, are able to feed on a wide range of host plants. However, this does not mean they are indiscriminate, and their more catholic taste would seen well adapted to their habit of dispersing as first instar larvae, or *vice versa*.

On the other hand, there are insects that seem bound to a limited number of plant hosts by the latter's odd substance. Several insect species, including -the cabbage butterflies, are attracted to the Cruciferae by the presence of mustard oil glycosides, but even her sapid nutrients are equally essential to food selection. Other species cited as examples of plant host specificity do not respond positively to any identifiable secondary compound. For example, the Colorado potato beetle, *Lepinotarsa decemlineata,* which feeds on the potato family (Solanaceae), apparently does not recognize or respond to the alkaloids that act as deterrents to other species; primary substances such as sugars and amino acids along with the secondary compounds seem to act synergistically in the initiation and sustaining of feeding by the beetle.

Dethier proposed that the diversity of feeding habits displayed by phytophagous insects might be expected on the basis of the fact that "Behavioural changes can be both rapid and reversible and. thus constitute a formidably effective response to whatever evolutionary innovations plants essay." He also proposes that the coevolution of insects and plants need not have resulted from a sequence of attacks and counterattacks, but rather from random mutations in both the neural systems of insects, and the chemical systems of plants. He suggests that this could account for the fact that some plants evolved deterrents to insect feeding before the phytophagous insects evolved, and might be the reason why some plants that could well serve as food for many insect species do not.

Selection of Host Blood-feeding Insects

The number of insects that feed on blood are few in comparison to those that feed on plants. Although there are a few blood feeders scattered throughout a number of orders (i.e., Thysanoptera, Mecoptera, Lepidoptera and Hymenoptera), the majority are true bugs (Hemiptera), sucking lice (Anoplura), biting flies (Diptera), and fleas (Siphonaptera). Members of these latter groups extract blood from a variety of invertebrates - particularly other insects -and vertebrates belongin, to all classes. The flightless sucking lice are mainly associated with birds, and spend their entire life cycle on their host or within the host's nest. The fleas, also flightless, are often closely associated with their host in a physical sense and tend to be fairly species-specific. Among the hemipterans and biting flies, there exists a wide rang in the degree of host specificity, as well as the dependence on blood as food. Most of the research attention, however, has been focused upon those species that have man as a principal host, namely, a few true bugs (especially *Rhodnius* and *Triatoma),* mosquitoes, black flies and tsetse flies.

In spite of the comparative lack of species diversity among blood feeding insects and the concerted effort to gain an understanding of the factors involved in the selection of individual human hosts, generalities seem to be as elusive here as in the area of plant host selection.

As in phytophagous insects, blood-feeding species seem to employ the full spectrum of their sensory capabilities in host location. If a generality can be made regarding differences in stimuli used by plant and blood feeders, it is that vision-particularly colour vision-is less important and thermoreception, is clearly more important, for the latter group. In the area of chemoreception, it is once again difficult to determine the relative importance of nonnutritive odd substances, phagostimulants and nutrients. Visual stimuli are most important among daytime active blood feeders, as one might expect. Tabanid flies seem more responsive to movement than to other visual characteristics, whereas blackflies, although responsive to movement, are attracted to dark silhouettes with a matte rather than glossy finish; the shape of solid geometric silhouettes did not seem to effect attraction although the flies did land most frequently near the corners or points of the targets.

Most blood-sucking flies do not display a high level of host specificity and frequently feed on nectar and water in addition to blood; the tendency of some insects to extract blood from commonly available hosts can be misleading. Humans are a suitable and sometimes favoured host of blood feeders, perhaps because of the readily available, naked feeding surface. The fact that insect bites cause considerable discomfort and often form the basis of disease transmission has stimulated a search for the factor or factors that make one host more or less desirable than another. One. often hears reports suggesting that some people are bitten by insects more frequently than others, and scientists have latched on to this fact and used it as the starting point of host selection research. Concerning host selection by mosquitoes, Hocking states: "Every imaginable part of the human body and its products must by now have been fractionated in every possible way in search for a specific chemical attractant. Although many compounds including amino acids, sex hormones, and some metabolic by-products have been found to be attractive to mosquitoes, none are as attractive as an intact individual. Brown found moisture to be the most powerful single attractant to mosquitoes, with warmth next in importance. Carbon dioxide seemed to be an important activator. Several estrogens and over half of 26 amino acids tested were also attractive. However, there is some uncertainty as to the role played by the latter group of substances, as they are not particularly volatile and do not occur naturally in a pure state.

The importance of thermal stimuli to host location by mosquitoes has been demonstrated by a number of investigators, but Brown and Hocking conclude that the evidence supports the detection of convection currents (which can be either warm or cool relative to the ambient air) over radiant heat. The attractiveness of convectional currents may be enhanced by the odors they carry, and *vice versa.* However, in the case of *Rhodnius, Triatoma,* and the bed bug *Cimex,* the thermal response is probably to a temperature gradient. In general, the location and selection of hosts by blood feeding insects seems no less complex than that of phytophagous species. There is a multiplicity of possible stimuli, many, of .which, like temperature and volatile chemicals, are fundamentally inseparable. For this reason laboratory experiments that examine responses to a single stimulus may produce spurious results.

Selection of Host Entomophagous Insects

The food habits of entomophagous predators an parasites (parasitoids) are highly variable. Generally, predators are less discriminatory than parasites, but there are some predators, such as the coccinellid

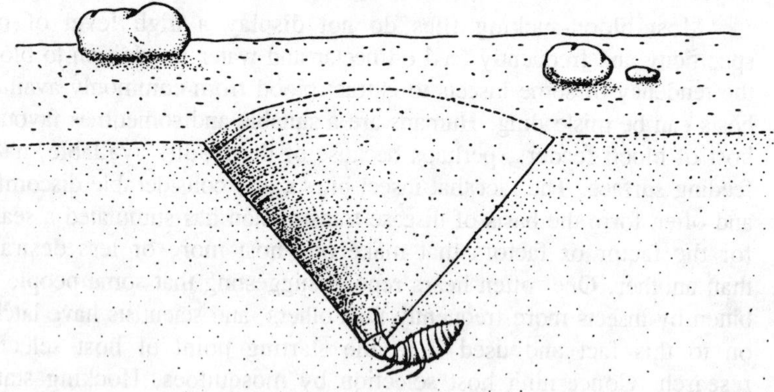

Fig. 7.4. Section through the pit trap constructed by the larva of an ant lion showing the position of the larva lying in wait for its prey.

beetle, *Vedalia cardinalis,* which preys almost exclusively on the cottony cushion scale, *Icerya purchasi,* which are prey-specific. Predators also tend to consume prey in both adult and larval stages, although various combinations occur. For example, syrphid fly adults are primarily nectar feeders, whereas the larvae of some species are active predators; some flies of other families are scavengers as larvae and predators as adults. Parasites, on the other hand, are more likely to display greater host specificity and adult-larval feeding divergence is common. Most of the parasitic hymenoptera, for example, are parasitic as larvae and nectar-pollen feeders as adults.

Predators tend to capture their prey by either sitting and waiting for them to come within reach or by active pursuit a few, like the larvae of antlions, construct taps. In many species vision plays a predominant role in prey capture. Ambushers, like preying mantids, respond to movement and will strike at any object of appropriate size when the stimulation of specific groups of omatidia (the fovea) indicate that it is within range. Pursuit-type predators will respond to most moving objects of appropriate size, although the more prey-specific species may sub, sequently select prey on the basis of tactile or chemical stimulation. The wasp *Philanthus will* pursue a variety of prey but will only capture bees or prey tainted with the odor of bees. Mechanical stimuli may also be important. Water striders, for example, locate prey trapped in the surface film by orienting to the ripples that radiate outward as the prey struggles to free itself. Aphideating coccinellids will search more or less at random by visually scanning their vicinity; once an aphid has been captured and consumed, the beetle will engage in a localized search involving frequent turning movements. This type of behaviour is particularly effective for predators that feed on gregarious and more or less sedentary prey.

Most entomophagous parasites are carnivorous only as larvae. Although a few species in several different orders have specialized, actively hunting, first instar larva that locates a host for itself, most depend on the capacity of the female to oviposit on or in a suitable host. How the female locates and selects her oviposition site is as variable and complex as host recognition by plant and blood feeding species.

In some species, the female does not search for the host but simply oviposits in the host's habitat. For instance, some tachinid fly parasites lay their eggs on the foliage of plants that serve as the food for their caterpillar hosts; the eggs are then ingested with the foliage. The human warble fly, *Cordylobia anthropophaga,* lays its eggs in sand tainted with urine; the larvae remain inactive until stimulated by the vibrations and rise in temperature associated with the visit to the site by another host. In the latter case, the urine probably provides an adequate chemical stimulus; however, in those parasites that must locate the plant habitat of their host, the clues used are poorly known; visual, chemical, tactile, and even sound stimuli are all possibilities. Laboratory experiments conducted by Cade indicate that the tachid fly, *Euphasiopteryx ocharacea,* locates its cricket hosts by orienting to the latter's song. Both parasites and predators of scolytids have been shown to be attracted to the odors (terpenes) given off by the bark beetle's host trees as well as the pheromones released by the beetles while the trees are under attack. Ullyett discovered that ichneumonid wasps, *Pimpla bicolor,* were attracted from a distance to a ruptured cocoon of its moth host.

Once a host has been located, female parasites often tap it a number of times with their antennae indicating that perhaps tactile, and contact chemical stimuli are involved in host recognition. The ovipositor of the hymenopterous parasites are also richly endowed with sensory receptors, apparently used to locate hosts feeding beneath a substrate, and perhaps in host recognition.

Food Acquisition

In spite of extensive research the results of which appear in an enormous body of entomological literature, our understanding of food finding and recognition by insects is far from complete. However, regardless of the basic food typa,,utilized, host selection is clearly a catenary process. The suggestioh of Dethier, that the behaviour of phytophagous insects consists of three component phases, seems equally applicable to blood feeders, parasites and others. Dethier's phases are (1) orientation to the food, (2) initial biting response, and (3) continued feeding. Thornsteinson recommends that dispersal be added ass a fourth phase that would complete a regenerating cycle, but whether or not that is valid depends on one's basic concept of what constitutes dispersal. The host selection behaviour of entomophagous insects has been divided into phases defined as (1) host habitat finding, (2) host finding, (3) host acceptance, and (4) host suitability, but the first two phases appear to be a subdivision of the first phase of Dethier while the remaining two phases in each case seem parallel. Each of the phases defined by Dethier is in turn made up of a sequence of responses, often to stimuli of various kinds (visual, chemical, tactile), that cannot be broken; that is, each response is dependent upon completion of the one that precedes it an in the response chains of Wigglesworth. One must realized however, that each response in the chain is not necessarily a reaction to a single isolated stimulus. Stimuli obviously interact, as when the convection currents generated by a warm-blooded organism carry olfactory cues perceived by biting flies. Furthermore, one kind of stimulus may prime an organism to respond to a different kind of stimulus as when a butterfly is primed to land on a piece of colured paper when the scent of a flower is added to the air.

One of the difficulties that has impeded our progress in gaining an understanding of host selection has been the inability to observe those links in the chain that result in orientation to the host from a distance. Host finding can involve two basic kinds of behaviour:

1. Non-directed behaviour (such as klinokineses) which results in a change in the frequency of random turns so that the probability of host contact is increased, and orthokineses, which arrest random search.

2. Directed behaviour (taxes), which results in orientation to a specific host stimulus or group of stimuli.

There seems to have been a preoccupation with host attraction and orientation to a source of stimulation, particularly chemical stimulation. Most laboratory experiments dealing- with these subjects have been conducted in restrictive arenas and with olfactometers that employ odorcarrying airstreams that do not allow the insects to maneuver normally. There is however, sufficient evidence amassed from field observations to suggest that both directed and non-directed behaviour is often involved. Insects with a variety of food relationships, as well as those that use pheromones for reproductive assembly, demonstrate what can be best described as an odor-released or odor-induced amenotaxis (response to an air current). This certainly seems to be the case in the mate-finding behaviour of males of the noctuid moth; *Tnchoplusia ni,* and probably fits the early stages of host searching by mosquitoes, some phytophagous species, and probably carrion feeders. Since the air is seldom still and even a small amount of turbulence caused by convection curents and objects in the environment would result in odor plumes rather than uninterrupted gradients, klinokineses can be expected to play an important role in host finding. The searching insect would simply fly upwind on a more or less straight course, as long as it was adequately stimulated by the appropriate chemical; however, once the scent was lost, it would begin to fly back and forth until the odor was detected again. The sequence of responses that results in actual acceptance of the host and sustained feeding is more readily observable. At close range, visual,s tactile, and contact chemical stimuli may all play a role in maintaining contact between an insect and its host, the initiation of probing or exploratory feeding, and finally sustained feeding. The termination of feeding if the insect remains undisturbed occurs in response to proprioreceptors associated with the digestive tract. The final stimulus that determines whether an insect will feed or not is most commonly of a chemical nature. Nutrients, frequently sugars, are strong feeding stimulants, but some of the odd nonnutritive substances discussed earlier are important to the feeding behaviour of certain species. For example, the cabbage aphid, *Brevicoryne brassicae,* requires sinigrin, common in the mustard family, as a feeding stimulus; when it is present, the aphid will feed on abnormal hosts.

The following partial description of feeding behaviour in the blow fly, *Phormia regina*, by Dethier is probably typical of the feeding response sequences of many insects: "Stimulation of chemoreceptors on the tarsi triggers proboscis extension; extension places the chemosensory aboral hairs of the lebellum in contact with the food; stimulation of the hairs results in spreading of the labellar lobes which places oral taste papillae in contact with the food; stimulation of the papillae triggers and drives ingestion..."

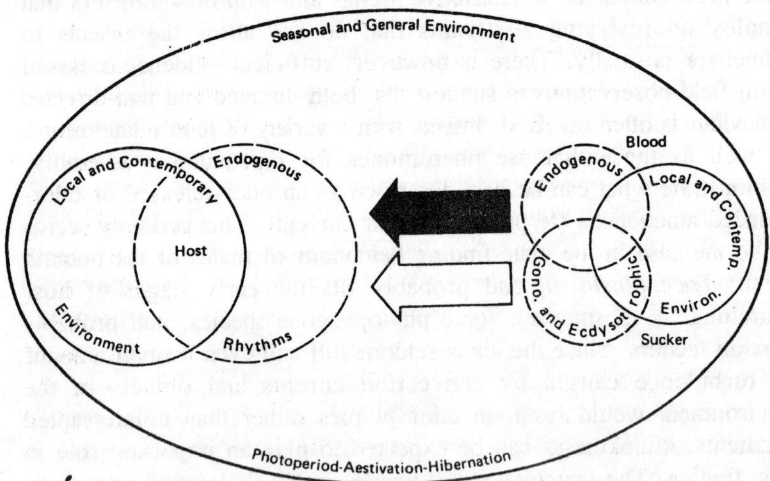

Fig. 7.5. Interacting cyclical changes that influence the attraction of blood-sucking insects to their hosts. Similar constraints regulate the feeding behaviour of herbivores and entomophagous species as well.

Finally, one must bear in mind that the feeding behaviour of any insect is regulated not only by its own endogenous rhythms and developmental physiology, but also by the life cycle and activity rhythm of its host species. Furthermore, most species function in relation to the constraints imposed by environmental factors such as photoperiod, temperature and so forth. Hocking presented a diagram showing the interaction of cyclical changes that influence the feeding behaviour of blood feeders, but a similar scheme should apply to any species regardless of its basic trophic relationship.

BREEDING BEHAVIOUR

Reproductive behaviour involves first the location of mate, followed by courtship and mating, oviposition, and sometimes brood care. Territoriality may arise out of competition for mates or food. Reproductive behaviour is typically complex and highy variable. The evolutionary role of this complexity and variability is, generally assumed to be reproductive isolation.

Mate Location

A wide variety of mechanisms function in bringing together the sexes. Initially, over relatively long distances, these mechanisms usually involve the visual, olfactory, and auditory modes of communication, singly or in combination. The visual stimuli associated with mate location and the responses they elicit vary in complexity. The simplest pattern, observed among water striders (Gerridae, Hemitpters), involves a male insect approaching any moving object of appropriate size that happens to enter its visual field. Other insects require more specific stimuli to induce approach. For example, male darnselflies in the family Lestidae (Odonata) approach any insect that has transparent wings and flies in a manner similar to that of damselfilies. Damselflies in the genus *Calopteryx* (Calopterygidae) require even more specific stimuli, the males of different species being able to recognize members of their own species by the amount of light allowed to pass through the wings.

More complex visual stimuli involved in mate location include the use of luminescent organs in signaling for a mate. This is best exemplified by the fireflies in the beetle family Lampyridae. In some species both the males and females produce light and have a very complicated signaling system; in other species only the males produce the light signals. In either case the light-signaling systems are species-specific. In fact, several species have been discovered through observation of differences in signaling systems. The mating behaviour of *Photinus pyralis, is* described in the following quote

At dusk the male and female emerge separatelty from the grass. The male flies about two feet above the ground and emits a single short flash at regular intervals. The female climbs some slight eminence, such as a blade of grass and waits. Ordinarily she does not fly at all, and she never flashes spontaneously. If a male flashes within three or four yards of her, she will usually wait a decorous interval, then flash a short response. At this the male turns in her direction and glows again. The female responds once more with a flash, and the exchange of signals is repeated-usualy not more than five or 10 times -until the male reaches the female, waithing in the grass, and the two mate.

In some tropical species of fireflies, several males congregate in a single tree and flash synchronously. McElroy *et al.* describe this phenomenon as follows

In Burma and Siam and other eastern countries, all the fireflies on one tree may flash simultaneously, while on another tree some distance away this same synchronous flashing would be apparent, but out of step with those of the first tree. Observers have been particularly impressed by the display, which is one of the interesting sights of the far East. In some cases visual markers in the environment may be involved in mate location. For example, among the true flies males may swarm or sit near a marker and wait until a female approaches the marker.

The use of olfactory cues in mate location is widespred among the insects. Sex pheromones are produced by specialized glands in males, females, or both sexes of a given species. Sex pheromones are very potent substances; "Detected by the insect in fantastically minute amounts, these attractants are undoubtedly among the most potent physiologically active substances known today." The sex pheromone *bombykol,* produced by the female silk moth, *Bombyx mori,* can elicit a response from a male in a concentration of 1000 molecules per cubic ccntimtcr. Elcctrophysiological studies of antennal receptors have revealed that a single molecule of bombykol can initiate a single nerve impulse. Most sex pheromones are apparently species-specific; however, there are several known examples of non-specificity.

The production by female insects of pheromones that attract males has been observed and described for several species in a num-ber of orders. The combined lists of Jacobson, and Jacobson are composed of 12 species of cockroaches (Orthoptera); 4 secies of true bugs (Hemiptera, Heteroptera); 4 species of homopterans (Hemiptera, Homoptera) 184 species of moths and butterflies (Lepidoptera); 34 species of beetles (Coleoptera; 31 species of bees, wasps, sawflies, and ants (Hymenoptera); 8 species of true flies (Diptera); and 3 termite species (Isoptera) in which the females are known to produce sex pheromones. Some examples follow. In the Gypsy moth, Lymantria dispar (Lymantriidae), virgin females produce a pheromone that is capable of luring males over a distance of 100 meters. The containers in which virgin females have been held apparently absorb some of the odorous substance since they remain attractive to males for 2 to 3 days following the removal of females. Virgin females of various species of silk moths (Saturniidae) "call" males by protruding posterior segments of the abdomen and exposing pheromone-secreting glands to the atmosphere. This *"calling"* posture only occurs at certain times of day or in response to certain stimuli and is controlled by the release of a *"calling"* hormone from neurosecretory cells in the corpora cardiaca. Female cockroaches produce a sex pheromone that stimulates male alertness, antennal movement, searching locomotion, and vigorous wing flutter. Filter paper that has been in contact with virgin females has the same effect.

As mentioned earlier, males in many species produce sex pheromones. The combined lists of Jacobson and Jacobson are composed of 5 species of cockroaches, 4 species of true bugs, 61 species of moths and butterflies, 11 species of beetles, 19 hymeno-pteran species, 12 species of true flies 4 species of scorpionflies (Mecoptera), and I neuropteran species in which males produce sex pheromones. The pheromones produced by the males of some of these species serve both as attractants and excitants or excitants alone. Two examples of male production of sex pheromones follow. Males of the greater wax moth, *Galleria mellonella,* secrete from glands on their wings an odorous substance that is very attractive to females: The odor is dispersed by the male vibratings its wings and dancing around.

Bumble bee *(Bombus terrestris)* males produce an attractant in their mandibular glands that lures females. This substance has been extracted from bumble bee mandibular glands with pentane and identiffied as farnesol, a substance present in the flower oils of many plants. These flower oils may be the bee's source of farnesol.

Three species of beetles in the genus *Dendroctonus* (Scolytidae) provide an interesting variation in the function of sex pheromones. In these species a substance that is attractive to both sexes is produced by sexually mature, unmated females feeding on fresh Douglas fir phloem. Since both sexes are attracted by this odorous substance, it serves to bring them together, which eventually leads to courtship and copulation. *Trypodendron lineatum,* an ambrosia beetle, produces a substance that has a similar affect. Such substances have been called assembling scents.

Acoustic signals serve to bring the sexes together for a large number of insects-many Orthoptera, Hemiptera-Homoptera and Diptera; a few Lepidoptera, Hemiptera-Heteroptera and Coleoptera. Calling songs may be quite elaborate and are usually species specific. In general, a response to one of these songs depends in part on the state of internal readiness for courtship and copulation. In the majority of cases, specialized structures are involved in the production of sounds, but several insects produce sounds as a direct result of wing movements in flight. Examples of sounds produced in this fashion that serve to bring the sexes together have been found in members of the Diptera, Hymenoptera and Orthoptera. For example, the flight sound of a mature female mosquito is very attractive to a male and elicits copulatory behaviour. The males react similarly when the frequency of the flight sound is produced by a tuning fork. In some insect groups the acoustical counterpart of the "assembling scent" has been found. For example, cicadas in the genus *Magicicada* sing an aggregating song in chorus that is responsible for assembling both males and females. In many cases, aggregation of males and females may occur in association with biological activities other than sex, for example, at emergence. oviposition or feeding sites. Such aggregation can sub-sequently lead to sexual activities. Once an insect has been induced to approach a possible mate, other stimuli are usually required to release further pursuit. These are generally olfactory, but they may also be a characteristic behaviour on the part of the pursued. An insect that recognizes a member of its own species may or may not be able to distinguish the sex of the individual it pursues. Males of *Pyrrhocoris* and *Gems* (Hemiptera-Heteroptera) and *Leptinotarsa* (Coleoptera Chrysomelidae) recognize members of their own species by specific odors but will attempt to copulate with either sex. On the other hand, some fruit flies are able to recognize the sex of an individual by its odor.

Courtship and Mating

Following mate location, variable and often elaborate behaviour is released which ultimately leads to copulation. Courtship displays function in species and sex identification the meeting of solitary individuals, and in the stimulation and maneuvering involved in copulation.

During courtship, escape and attack responses are usually inhibited, at least to the extent that copulation may occur. However, they may not be inhibited completely. For example, as mentioned earlier, the female praying mantid very often devours the head and part of the thorax of a male that is attempting to copulate. This is not as tragic as it seems since removal of the head, in particular the subesophageal ganglion, increases the vigor of the male's copulatory movements. Signals from the intact subesophageal ganglion are, thought to inhibit various endogenous nervous patterns in the rest of the body. Thus decapitation removes inhibitionn of copulatory move-ments. In addition to releasing vigorous copulatory movements, the female mantid also obtains a highly nutritious meal.

Many of the cues that serve in mate location act further as releasers of courtship and copulation. For example, the flight sound of the female mosquito not only attracts males but also releases copulatory behaviour. In many insects the sex pheromone produced by one of the sexes also serves as an excitant (aphrodisiac), stimulating courtship or attempts at copulation. For instance, the sex pheromone produced by female American cockroaches *(Periplaneta americana)* not only attracts males but induces a wing-raising display and attempts to copulate. In the absence of a female, males may attempt to copulate with one another if the female odor is present. This female sex pheromone is also capable of eliciting courtship behaviour in males of other *Periplaneta* species and males of *Blatta orientalis* (oriental cockroach). In some insects, the sexually excited male or the female may produce a substance that acts as an excitant for the opposite sex Such is the case in *Lethocerus indicus,* a giant water bug, and a family of beetles.

During sexual excitement the male is easily recognized by its odor, for its abdominal glands secrete a liquid with an odor remini-scent of cinnamon.... This substance, produced in two white tubules 4 cm long and 2-3 mm thick, occurs to the extent of approximately 0.02 ml per male and is used in southeast Asia as a spice for greasy foods.

The female does not secrete the substance, which is believed to act as an aphrodisiac to make her more receptive to the male. Males of Malachiidae, a family of tiny tropical beetles, entice females first with a tarty necter and then expose them to an aphrodisiac. The males possess tufts of fine hair growing out of their shells (in some species on the wing covers, in others on the head). These hairs are saturated with a glandular secretion that the females cannot resist. During the mating season, the male searches for a female; when he finds one he offers his tuft of hair, which the female then accepts and nibbles upon. In so doing, her antennae come in contact with microscopic pores in his shell, through which the aphrodisiac substance is excreted, thus putting her in a state of wild excitement.

Insects show a seemingly endless variety of sexual patterns. Some are simple, the male and female simply coming together and copulating with little or no courtship maneuvers. On the other hand, many have elaborate and sometimes bizarre patterns of courtship. Two examples will give you an idea of how elaborate some of these courtships are. The silverfish, *Lepisma saccharina,* guides the female to an externally deposited spermatophore by spinning a series of threads that restrict her movements to those which bring her closer and closer to making contact with the spermatophore. Jacobson cites the work of Bornemissza in the follwing description of cortship and copulation of two species of scorpionflies *(flarpobittacus,* Mecoptera.) : Males of both species hunt for the soft-bodied insects on which they feed; females have never been observed hunting, capturing, or killing prey in the field. When the male holds its prey and begins to feed, two reddish-brown vesicles are everted on the abdomen between tergites 6-7 and 7-8 and begin to expand and contract, discharging a musty scent perceptible to humans. This scent attracts females to the vicinity of the male, moving upwind in his direction. As soon as the female is within reach, the male retracts his vesicles and brings the prey to his mouthparts. The female attempts to get hold of the prey but is prevented by the male, whose abodomen seeks out the tip of the female's abodomen and copulation takes place. *Once* in copula, the male voluntarily passes the prey with his hind legs over to the female.

Rivalry and Territoriality

Rivalry between males may arise over the courtship of the same female and may result in direct physical aggression or displays. Reactions to members of the same species are different from those involved with escape or defense, which are stimulated by threats of danger. When a male grasshopper appproaches another male that is serenading a female with a courtship song, they face one another and sing a characteristic "rivalry" song. Eventually one of the males leaves, and the other continues the courtship. Male silverfish, *Lepisma* (Lipismatidae, Thysanura), will fight over a female.

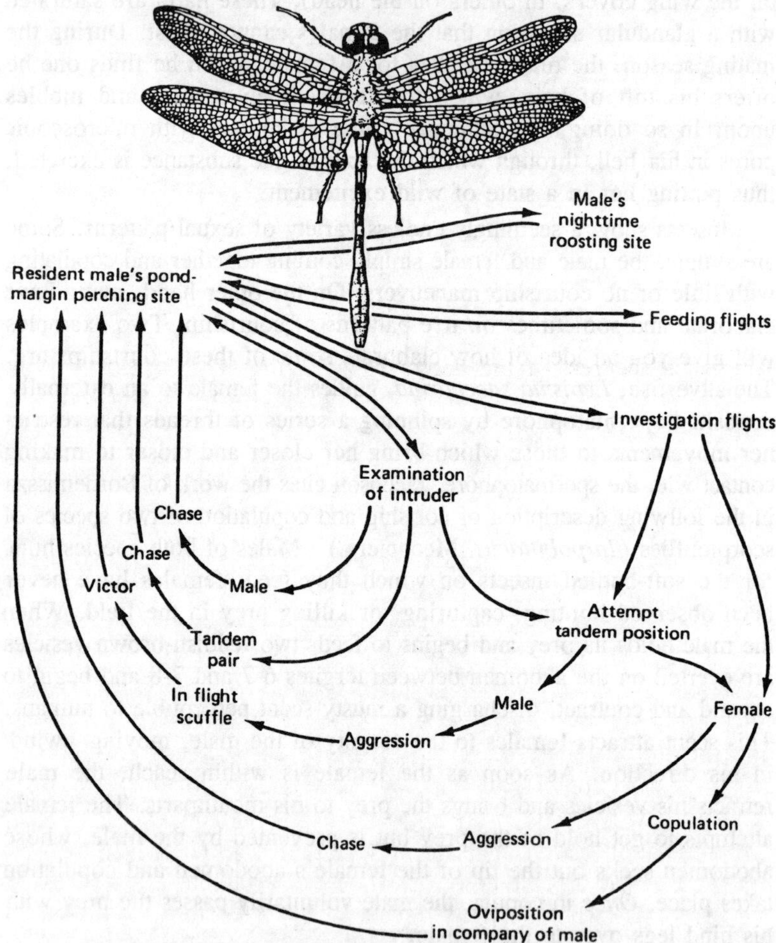

Fig. 8.1. Diagrammatic schema of territorial and reproductive behaviour of the dragonfly Libellula saturata (Uhler).

Territorial behaviour is not common among insects, but there are some very definite examples. Males of certain odonates in the genera *Calopteryx* (damselflies and *Pachydiplax* (dragonflies) defend territories against other males. A male entering another's territory is met with

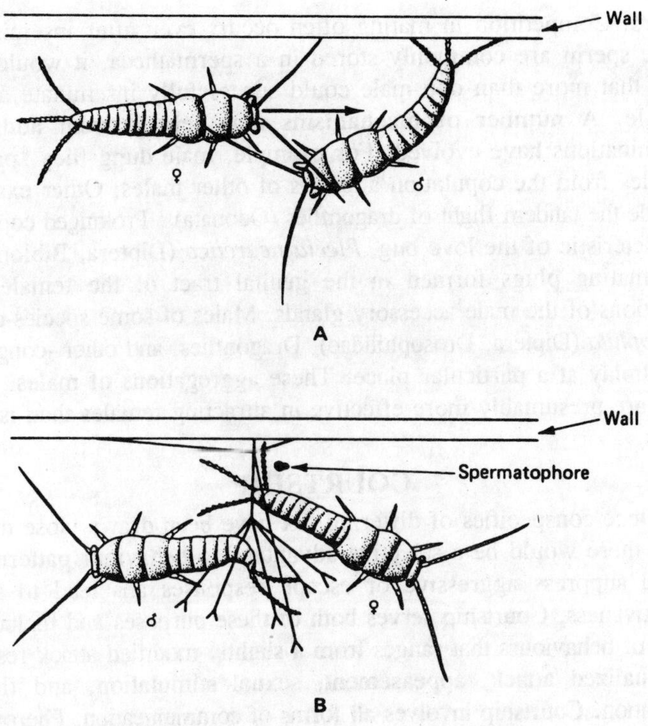

Fig. 8.2. Courtship in the silverfish, Lepisma saccharin A. Approach. B. Female is guided to the spermatophore by the threads.

an attack. Females are recognized by sight since there is distinct sexual dimorphism in these particular species. Instead of aggression, these females are met with attempts to copulate. In some other genera of dragonflies (e.g., *Aeshna* and *bibellula)*, when the sex of an approaching member of the same species is not recognized, males will attempt to copulate with males. The tendency for males to avoid such encounters results in their spreading out into individual territories. The suggestion has been made that such sexual encounters between males preceded the evolution of territorial behaviour. Male crickets are territorial : when one male enters another's territory, he is greeted by the "rival" song of the other. This is followed either by the exit of the intruder or holder of the territory or by fighting. A rank order may become established among males whose territories are in close proximity to one another. A female entering a male's territory is also greeted with the "rival' song, and will either leave or remain quietly. Price provides a list of examples of territoriality in several insect orders. Competition in mating often occurs even after insemination. Since sperm are commonly stored in a spermatheca, it would seem likly that more than one male could successfully inseminate a given female. A number of mechanisms that help prevent additional inseminations have evolved. For example, male dung flies "protect" females from the copulation attempts of other males. Other examples include the tandem flight of dragonflies (Odonata) ; Prolonged copulation characteristic of the love bug, *Plecia nearctica* (Diptera, Bibionidae); and mating plugs formed in the genital tract of the female from secretions of the male accessory glands. Males of some species-certain *Drosophila* (Diptera, Drosophilidae), Dragonflies, and other -congregate and diplay at a particular place. These aggregations of males, called *leks,* are presumably more effective in attracting females than isolated males.

COURTSHIP

Once conspecifics of differing sex have been drawn close to each other there would be a selective advantage to behaviour patterns that would suppress aggressive or escape responses ans lead to sexual receptiveness. Courtship serves both of these purposes and includes an array of behaviours that ranges from a slightly modified attack response to ritualized attack, appeasement, sexual stimulation, and finally, copulation. Courtship involves all forms of communication. Pheromones are used in numerous species for both recognition and sexual excitation. Males of some beetles will attempt to mate with a piece of paper treated with female sex pheromone, while ignoring an actual female held captive under glass nearby. During the courship of the grayling butterfly, *Eumenis semele,* the male spreads its wings and bows toward the female so that her antennae come in contact with scent patches on his forewings. Many grasshoppers move about the female in an excited manner while singing a courtship song prior to attempting copulation. Visual displays are also common and sometimes spectacular, as are the aerial displays of some butterflies and the bioluminescent flashing of fireflies. Tactile stimulation, though often no obvious, is also important and widespread. In some species the male offers the female and object or some food,'which apparently increases the female's receptiveness. The male of the seed-feeding bug, *Stilbcoris,* usually approaches the female with a seed impaled on his beak. If the female accepts the seed, she will insert her beak into it, at which time the male moves closer, grasps her, and begins copulation while she continues to feed; males without seeds are rejected. A variety of

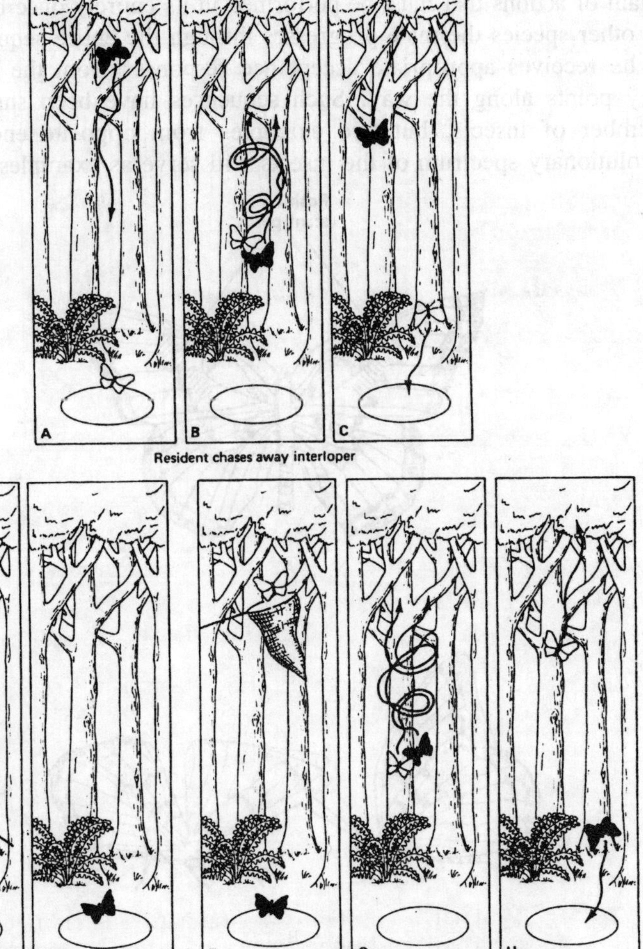

Fig. 8.3. Diagram of the ritualized combat over mating territories displayed by males of the speckled wood butterfly, Pararge aegena (A-C) *The usual pattern of behaviour displayed when an interloper (black) approaches a resident (white). (D-G) The experimental design used to demonstrate that the resident always retains control of the territory.*

insects, including cockroaches, scorpionflies, wasps and flies, regurgitate material that the female consumes prior to or during mating.

The courting of some species involves a long sequence of behavioural acts by the male to which the female may or may not respond. Sometimes the male's fixed action pattern consists of a long chain of actions that must be performed in its entirety once begun, but in other species the male progresses through the entire sequence only if he receives appropriate acceptance responses from the female at key points along the way. Such sequences have been studied in a number of insects, but two examples from opposite ends of the evolutionary spectrum of the insects will serve as examples.

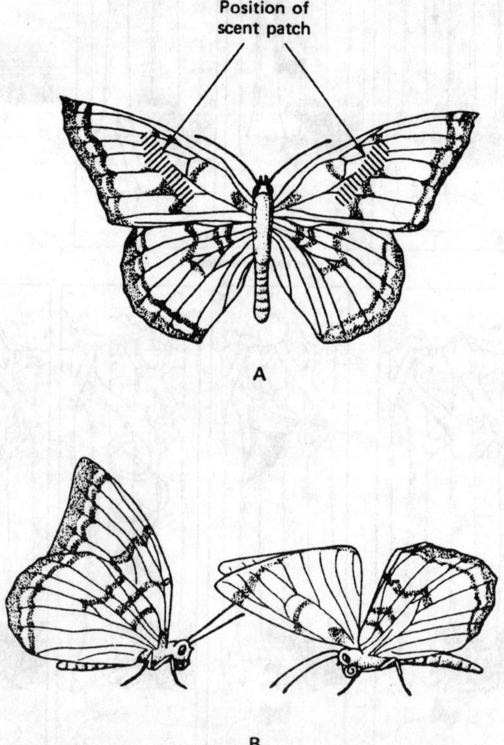

Fig. 8.4. Chemical communication in the grayling butterfly, Eumenis semele. (A) The position of the scent patches (cross-hatched) on the dorsal surface of the male's forewings. (B) The male bowing to a female courtship to expose the scent patches, which the female contacts with her antennae.

The silverfish, *Lepisma saccharina,* engages in complicated precopulatory behaviour in which the male produces a package of sperm (spermatophore) and then leads the female to it with a series of silk threads that restrict her movement. This so-called leading and bridling behaviour cuylminates with the male pushing the female's ovipositor into contact with the spermatophore.

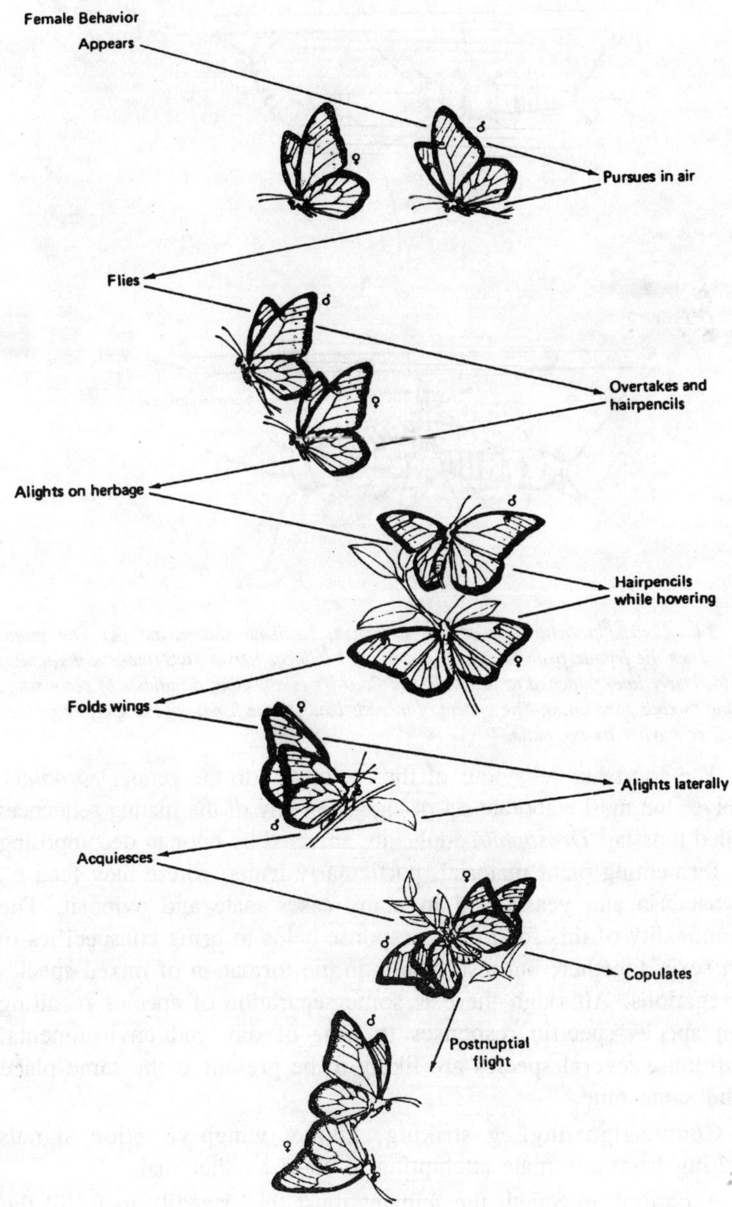

Fig. 8.5. Courtship behaviour of queen butterflies, showing the response chain resulting from an encounter between a male and a female.

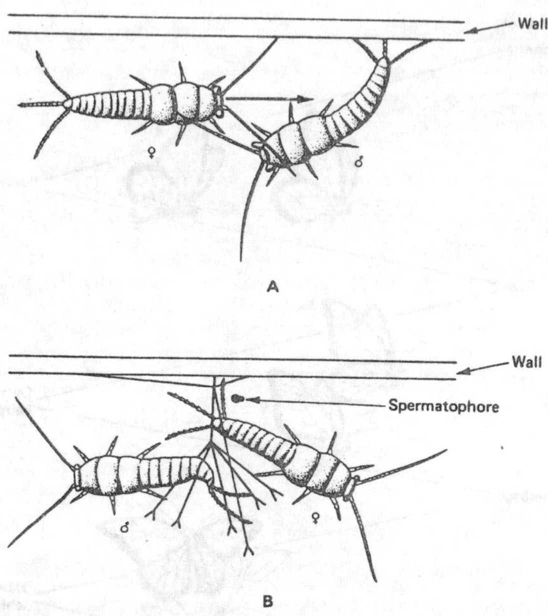

Fig. 8.6. Courtship behaviour of the silverfish, Lepisma saccharine (A) The male approaches the female from the front and the (B) induces her to pass under a main silk thread (heavy line) attached to the wall and floor by establishing a number of secondary guiding threads (fine lines). The system of threads leads to the female of the spermatophore deposited earlier by the male.

The courtship behaviour of flies belonging to the genus*Drosophila* involves the most elaborate set of signals of any of the mating sequences studied thus far. *Drosophila* adults are attracted by odor to decomposing and fermenting plant material, particularly fruits, where they feed on the bacteria and yeasts and in many cases mate and oviposit. The commonality of this food odor response helps to bring conspecifics of both sexes together, but also results in the formation of mixed species aggregations. Although there is some separation of species resulting from species-specific responses to time of day and environmental conditions, several species are likely to be present at the same place at the same time.

CountersignalingLeg striking, kikin& wingp-vibration signals resulting from one male attempting to court another male.

According to Spieth the females must feed steadily to fulfill the nutritional demands of egg production, whereas the males feed for only short perods, after which they turn their attention to mating. Since the males cannot visually distinguish between similar appearing species or conspecific males from females, they approach any passing individual with roughly the right conformation. Consequently, a system of signals has evoved that Spieth concludes has the advantage of providing the males with a means of ascertaining the receptiveness of females with a minimum expenditure of time and energy, the unreceptive females with a way to I-epel males without interrupting their feeding, and receptive females with an opportunity to sample several males thereby bringing sexul selection into operation.

TABLE 8.1.

MAJOR COURTSHIP ELEMENTS OF DROSOPHILA MALES

Orientation	turps toward another individual, slightly raising body lifts, straightens foreleg, and strikes downward against other individual; almost invariably occurs at start of coutship.
Wing vibration	oriented extends wing nearest head, then vibrates, it rapidly, interspecific variation in degree of extension, amplitude and speed of vibration, and angle of extended vane with respect to substrate, i.e.,horizontal, tilted, vertical
Wing flickling	flicks one wing sharply out, then back to resting position
Wing waving	extends one wing, then slowly waves up and down
Wing Semaphoring	alternately and repeatedly flicks wings sharply outward, then back to resting position; one wing is moved outward while the other is returning to the resting position
Wing scissoring	repeatedly and rapidly extends both wings horizontally outward and back to the resting position
Leg vibration	displaying at rear of extends and vibrates forelegs against abdomen of, usually against venter
Leg rubbing	displaying at rear, of extends and rubs forelegs to and from against abdomen of, usually venter, but some species against sides or dorsum
Cirling	perodically circles about, facing her as he moves, often from rear to front and back, sometimes completely about female

Licking	opens labellar lobes, extends proboscis, and licks genitalia; may either lick intermittently and repeatedly or continuously for a prolonged period; some Hawaiian species have modified labellar lobes which grasp of genitalia
Mounting	curls tip of abdomen under and forward, rears upward, thrusts head under wings or between her spread wings, grasps her body with his fore and mid legs, and attempts intromission

Table 8.2.

The Major Elements of the Courtship Behaviour of *Drosophila* Females

Female acceptance behaviour	
Wing spreading	Female spreads both wings outward and upward and holds them extended until male mounts
Genital spreading	Female slightly droops tip of abdomen, slightly extrudes genitalia, and spreads ovipositors apart
Ovipositor extrusion	Female extrudes ovpositor posteriorly; restricted to Hawaiian species
Female repelling behaviour	
Decamping	Female breaks contact with courting male by running, jumping, or flying
Kicking	Female kicks vigorously backward with hind legs, striking face when he courts at her rear
Fluttering wings	Female rapidly flutters wings in movements. of small amplitude; often occurs when male initiates tapping action
Abdomen elevation	Female elevates abdomen, thus raising tip high above i substrate and inhibits male courship such as kicking and leg vibration; often observed when male attempts to court feeding female; may be accompanied by extrusion

Abdomen depression	Female depresses tip of abdomen and wing tips against, substrate; inhibits male coutrship actions such as kicking and leg vibration
Extrusion	Female extends and elongates tip of abdomen, thus exposing articulating membrances around genital sclerites and simultaneously direct tip of her abdomen toward male face, usually causing male to turn quickly away and engage in cleaning behaviour

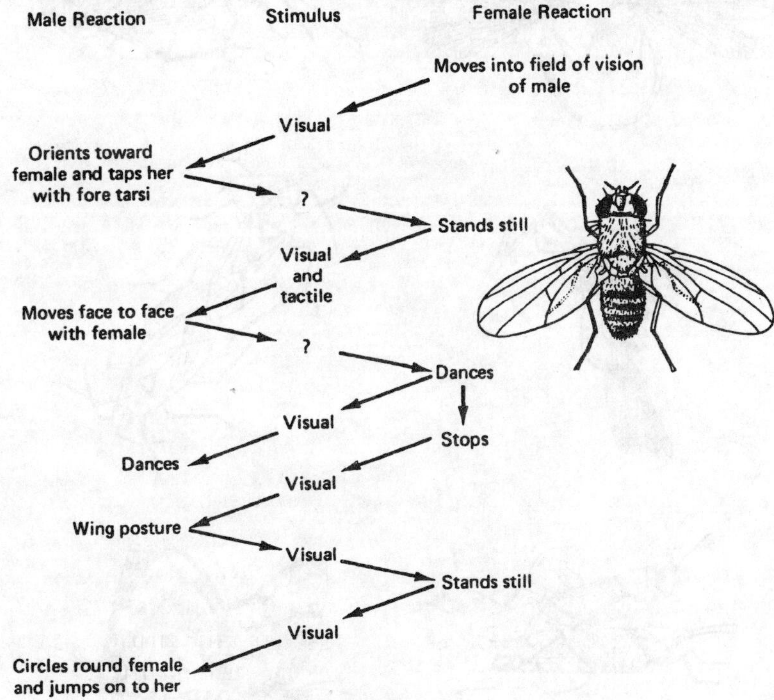

Fig. 8.7. The sequence of stimulation and response steps that characterize the courtship behaviour of Drosophila subobscura

In *Drosophila subobscura,* for example, the courtship ritual consists of a series of sexually alternating stimulation and response steps. The male begins by facing the female and tapping her with his forelegs. If the male perceives the appropriate visual and tactile stimuli from the female, he will extend his proboscis and move to a face-to-face position. The male then taps the female's head and both -begin a dance the consists of a series of side steps while still aligned face to face. As the dance progresses, the male raises his wings at right angles to the body with the leading edge tilted downward. The female responds by ceasing to dance. The male then circles his mate and finally jumps upon her and attempts copulation.

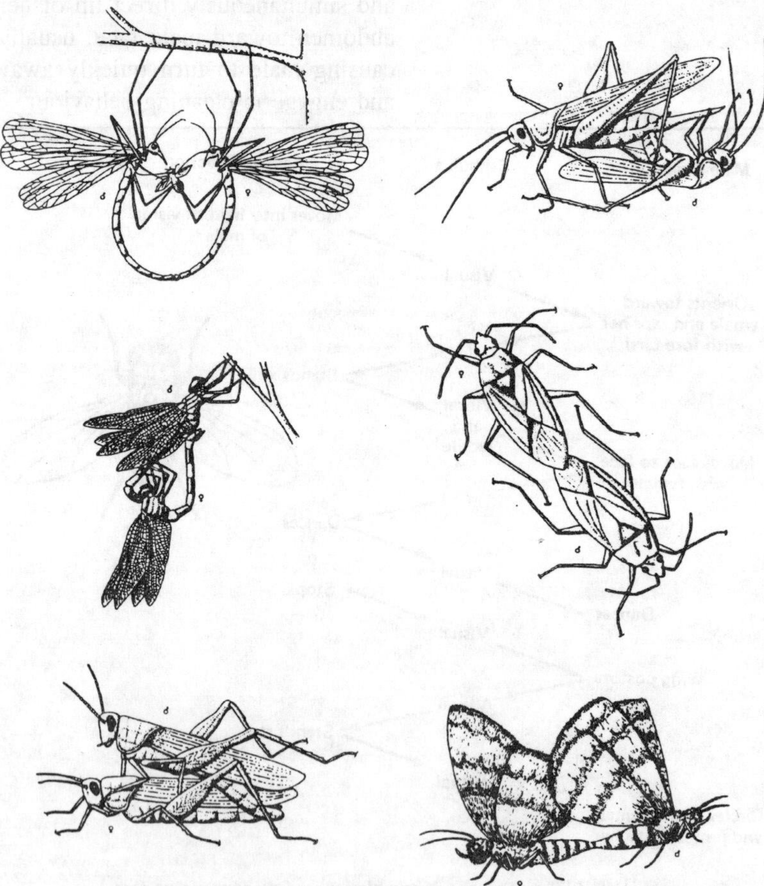

Fig. 8.8. Various positions assumed by insects during copulation.

In most .insects, successful courtship usually culminates in copulation. Various species-specific positions are employed, and the duration of coupling may range from seconds to hours. Postcopulatory behaviour is also highly variable. In many species the pair separates immediately, and the female begins to search for an oviposition site whereas the male goes off in search of another mate. In others the pair remains together for sometime. In some species the male continues to provide a food offering, which prevents the female from eating the spermatophore he has deposited, whereas in others, like the mantids, the female may actually devour her mate. The females of a few species such as the screwworm, *Cochliomyia hominivorax*; mate only once, but most mate several times, although they are usually unresponsive to the advances of males for sometime after each copulation. In a variety of species belonging to different orders, the male may remain with the female during oviposition. Some dragonflies, for example, fly with their mate as she deposits her eggs while flying over the surface of the breding pond.

Oviposition

The survival, growth, and development of immature insects depends to a great extent on oviposition in an appropriate environment. This is especially important to insects with specific diets (e.g., a particular plant, or in the case of many parasitic insects, a particular host). For example, female mosquitoes that are ready to oviposit must do so in a place where the eggs are in water or will eventually be. Although, some insects merely drop their eggs wherever, they may happen to be (e.g., some mayflies), more often they are specific as to their choice of oviposition site, locating it by means of a variety of stimuli, depending upon the kind of insect. For example, the beetle*Hylotrupes* (Cerambycidae) is attracted to the terpene odor of the wood in which it deposits its eggs. The parasitic wasp *Nasonia* locates the puparial cases of host blow flies (Diptera, Calliphoridae) by the odor of the decaying flesh in which blow fly larvae and pupae are commonly found. Insects ready to oviposit may respond to stimuli hat previously elicited no response whatsoever. For example, *Pieris* (Pieridae) butterflies show a definite preference for objects with a green colour when the are ready to oviposit, but when they are searching for food, they demonstrate no such preference. When an insect is highly selective in the choice of a site for oviposition, this does not mean that it has foreknowledge of the needs of its offspring. Oviposition in response to specific stimuli that are associated with an environmental situation in which the young can survive has, during the course of evolution, no doubt been selected for.

Brood Care

Once a parent insect has fulfilled its responsibility for placing the egg (or larva in some instances) in an appropriate environmental situation. It may simply leave. However, some continue an association with the eggs and immature stages. This association is most highly developed in the social insects ants, bees, wasps and termites) in which the brood form a core around which all activity is centered, and these brood are "reared" from egg to adult by workers. Social insects differ from social vertebrates in that a vertebrate colony is composed of a number of mating pairs and offspring, whereas an insect colony is usually the product of a single female or single male-female pair.

Many non-social insects also do more for their offspring than merely deposit the egg. Earwing females (Dermaptera) lay their eggs in burrows in the ground and guard them until they hatch. Female beetles in the genus *Omaspides* protect their brood from the ravages of invading ants. Some non-social insects go to the extent of preparing elaborate nests and stocking them with food for their young. For example, a female solitary wasp in the genus *Bembix* digs a nest in the soil with her legs and mandibles. She then captures an adult fly (or sometimes another insect) and brings it to the nest. Evans describes the prey capture

The capture and stinging of the prey occur with great rapidity. The female wasp proceeds slowly through the air or hovers over a source of flies, pouncing upon the flies either in flight or at rest; then she descends to the earth or .to some other solid object, where she quickly bends her abdomen downward and forward, inserting the sting on the ventral side of the thorax or in the neck region of the fly. Following capture, the wasp returns to the nest and deposits an egg on the fly. Thereafter, a number of flies are brought to the nest as the larva grows. Eventually, the larva spins a cocoon, pupates, and emerges from the ground as an adult. Depending on the species and the time of year, it may remain over the winter in the cocoon.

INSECTS IN GROUPS

Insects display many gradations between solitary behaviour and complex, organized social behaviour. However, comparatively few insect species are truly social *(eusocial),* a few thousand perhaps, and thses are found in only two orders, Isoptera (termites) and Hymeno-ptera (ants, bees, wasps and relatives). Matthews and Matthews provide a useful classification of intraspeci is insect associations other than sexual interludes. They divide interactions into aggregations, simple groups, primitive societies, and advanced societies *(eusocial* insects). Group behaviour is thought to provide a number of different benefits; including protection as a result of such things as collective displays and more efficient detection of potential predators, in creased efficiency in detection and utilization of food and moderation of adverse physical environmental factors. Insects that produce defensive secretions and/or display warning colouration no doubt derive increased protection by pooling their defensive capabilities.

Parental Behaviour

For both males and females, the act of mating may be only part of their investment of time and energy in the perpetuation of their genes. *Parental investment is* defined as behaviours that increase the probability of some offspring surviving to reproduce at the cost of the parent's ability to produce more offspring. Minimal behavioural investment tends to be compensated for by maximum physiological capacity to produce offspring (for example, in house flies). Conversely, maximum innvestment (such as brood care) tends to be offset by reduced production (but higher survival) of offspring. As a general rule, the investment of the female is much greater than that of the male; she not only converts most of her nutrients to the production of eggs, but she seeks a suitable site for oviposition and in some cases guards her eggs or even feeds her offspring. The male, on the other hand, produces large numbers of much smaller sperm, with less energetic investment, and attempts to use these to inseminate as many females as possible. But it is not always quite as simple as this, and it will pay us to look briefly at male parental investment before returning to that of the female.

Assurance of Paternity

Male sperm, as we have seen, are stored in the female's spermatheca and released at the time of oviposition. when females mate more than once, it is generally the sperm from the last mating that are released to fertilize the eggs. This has been termed *sperm precedence*. In instances of sexual selection involving male territoriality or nuptial feeding, it is to the male's advantage, once he has mated, to ensure that the female does not mate again before she lays her eggs. Thus a male dragonfly guards the female while she lays her eggs, ensuring his paternity of the resulting offspring. Indeed, Jonathan Waage, of Brown University, showed that the penis of certain damselflies serves a dual function : By means of a scooplike extension of the penis, any sperm present in the female genital tract is removed before the male introduces his own sperm.

Male field crickets, having attacted a female via a calling song, switch to a "courtship song;" then, after mating, to a "staying together" song, which ensures that she will not mate again before laying eggs. In the case of the hangingflies we discussed earlier, the male has invested efforts in a "nuptial gift,"' and it is to his advantage to ensure that the resulting offspring carry his genes; if the gift is large and the female fully inseminated, she enters a refractory period and will not mate again until her eggs have been laid. The male hangingfly, in fact, contributes indirectly to egg production by supplying nutrients to the female. It has recently been shown by the use of radioactive tracers that male butterflies of certain species contribute to egg production via nutrients supplied in the spermatophore. The spermatophores of some of the Orthoptera are particularly large. In the Mormon cricket 20% of the male's weight is lost in a single mating. Much of the spermatophore consists of a mass of protenaceous material that is consumed by the female following mating. Females compete vigorously for calling males, and males reject smaller females, who have been shown to be less fecund. Since rejection usually occurs after the female has mounted the male, it appears that it is at this time that the male assesses the weight of the female. This unusual exmple of "sex reversal" - competition among the females for males and male selection of females likely to produce the most offspring.

Sex reversal in which the male cares for the eggs is also known in a few instances. In giant water bugs there are repeated bouts of copulation interspesed with egg laying; these bouts are dominated by the male, who receives several eggs on his back following each mating. On one occasion a pair were seen to copulate over 100 times in 36 hours, resulting in the transfer of 144 eggs to the back of the male. While carrying the eggs, the male subjects them to necessary aeration, and he assists the young as they emerge from the eggs. Such a system ensures that the male carries eggs that bear his genes. But a male can be "cuckolded" if he mates with a female who carries sperm from a previous mating. Robert Smith, of the University of Arizona, vasectomized a male and mated him to a female that had previously mated to a male homozygous for a dominant genetic marker, a dorsal stripe. The vasectomized male received 75 eggs as a result of this mating; most were infertile, but several were fertile and gave rise to striped off spring, demonstrating that this male had been "cukolded" by another male Thus, despite this elaborate mating system, a male does run a risk when he mates with a non-virgin female.

Brood Care by Females

Since, in general, it is the female that invests the most in terms of physiological commitments to her offspring, it is not surprising that when brood care occurs, it is usually the female that is involved. Brood care had evolved in a variety of insects that have developed strategies opting for maximum protection of the offspring as opposed to production of large numbers of offspring that are "left to their own devices." Extreme examples are provided by certain cockroaches and by tsetse flies, which retain' and nourish their larvae internally, in a uteruslike structure. More commonly eggs are *"brooded"* by the female, although brooding does not usually imply the transfer of heat as it does in birds. Rather it serves to protect them from predators, egg parasites, mold, or other factors that might destroy them. Female stink bugs of several species cover their eggs and small larvae much as a hen will cover her chicks. Such eggs suffer high mortality from ants and other predators if the female is removed.

A more advanced type of parental care occurs in certain crickets in which the female prepares a burrow that she guards vigorously from intruders. The eggs are laid in a cell at the bottom of the burrow, and when the young batch, they are fed by the mother, at first with small, infertile eggs that she lays, later with food brought in from the outside. Beetles of several families exhibit brood care that in its initial stages may involve both sexes. Dung beetles (Scarabaeidae) prepare balls of dung, roll them to a suitable site, and bury them as food for the larvae. Often male and female work together to make the dung ball and bury it. In some cases, the female remains in the burrow after laying her eggs, standing guard and keeping the pellets clean and well formed. She may remain with her offspring until they are fully developed, then emerge from the ground with them. In carrion beetles (Silphidae), male and female work together to bury a dead animal, then prepare a ball of decaying flesh in which the eggs are laid. As the larvae grow, they are fed by the female with regurgitated food, much as a bird feeds its nestlings.

Brood care reaches its greatest development among the Hymenoptera, particularly in social groups such as the ants and some of the bees and wasps, which we shall consider in the next chapter. In solitary asps-from which the social Hymenoptera are believed to have evolved -the female commonly prepares a nest, provisions it. with paralyzed insects or spiders, and after oviposition seals it off in such a way that it is well-protected against predators and physical factors in the environment. We have already discussed some of these wasps briefly. Of special interest are those species in which the nest cell is not sealed off immediately but is visited repeatedly by the female, who brings in prey over a prod of days as the larva grown. *Progressive provisioning* as this is called, involves much contact between parent and offspring as well as further protection of the larva as a result of the mother's continued presence in the nest. Of even greater interest are cases of *communal nesting* that is, instances in which several females are active in the same nest, preparing and provisioning individual cells without aggression with other females in the nest. In many cases, these females are sisters or mother and daughters, and the "extended family" they represent is perhaps an important progenitor for the colonies of social species. In both cases -pogressive provisioning and communal nesting-there is much evidence that the selective advantages ralate to a reduction in the opportunities for entry by various nest parasites and predators.

PRESOCIAL BEHAVIOUR OF HYMENOPTERA

No group-of insects displays more diversity of parental care and social behaviour than the Hymenoptera. The wasps, bees and ants all have trully social *(eusocial)* representatives, but most members of the former two groups are presocial. Both the bees and the wasps display an ascending hierarchy of behaviour that many investigators believe represents an evolutionary sequence similar to that which led to the development of eusociality. Evans presented one such schema for the wasps based on both morphological and behavioural adapt-ations. The aculeate (stinging) Hymenoptera are believed to have evolved from parasitic forms, and the behaviour of many solitary, predatory wasps is clearly related to that of their parasitic ancestors, except that the ovipositor is used to narcotize their prey. In the more primitive species, the female searches for an appropriate prey, paralyzes it with her sting, lays an egg on its surface and departs. These prey, left unprotected, are clearly subject to consumption by other organisms or to accidental destruction before the wasp larva can complete its development.

The tendency of other species to conceal their prey, either before or after they have deposited their egg on it, is a form of parental care that had obvious survival benefits. Placing a single prey in a burrow in the manner of some *Ammophila* species is the full extent of parental care displayed by a number of wasps, yet it requires a great deal of effort. These species utilize single prey such as caterpillars that are large enough to fulfill the nutritional needs of their young. The progressive provisioning displayed by the sphecids, for example, not only permits the utilization of smaller prey that can be carried back to the nest in flight, but also has the potential for improving larval nutrition. The repeated visit of the female to the nest also provides an opportunity for her to come in contact with her young and opens the way to the exchange of hormones, pheromones, and gut symbionts, along with partially digested food *(trophaltazis)*, and the possibility for parental control over the development of offspring, as seen in the burying beetle *Necrophorus*.

TABLE 8.3

MAJOR STEPS IN DEVELOPMENT OF EUSOCIAL BEHAVIOUR OF WASPS (THE FAMILIES THAT DEMONSTRATE EACH LEVEL OF BEHAVIOUR ARE GIVEN IN PARENTHESES)

Step of Behavioural Sequence	*Comments*
1. Prey-egg (Pompilidae)	The female locates aprey, temporarily paralyzes it with her sting, lays eggs on the prey, and departs; the prey recovers and carries the wasp larvae which feed as external parasitoids
Prey-natural crevice-egg	The female drags the paralyzed prey to an available protective crevice wher it is left with an egg attached; the female thus provides young with a level of protection
Prey-nest-egg	Female paralyzes a prey and then constructs a nest in which it is plaxed along with an egg; this is a slightly advanced level of parental care
4. Nest-prey-egg	Same as step 3 except the nest is constructed (Pompilidae, Sphecidae) before the prey is captured; this introduces homing in that the female must return to a previously selected nest site
5. Nest-prey-egg-prey (Sphecidae)	Similar to step 4, but the addition of more prey after egg is laid introduces mass provisioning as a

	more advanced form of parental care
6. Nest-prey-egg-prey-prey (Sphecidae, Eumenidae)	Instead of mass provisioning, the nest is provisioned progressively with fresh prey, this brings the female into contact with her developing offspring' in some species, the female remains in the nest when not provisioning, thereby reducing predation, and may also clean the nest of partially consumed food
7. Prey macerated by female (Eumenidae, Vespidae)	In the process of progressive provisioning, the fresh prey are macerated by the female and fed to the larvae; this brings the female into direct contact with her offspring and provides opprtunity for trophallaxis and the transfer of pheromones
8. Female life prolonged and offspring remain with nest (Vespidae)	The prolonged female life results in overlap with the first generation offspring; which main and lay eggs in cells they add to the nest; this results in small colonies consisting of the mother and a group of undifferentiated daughters
9. Trophallaxis and division of labour (Vespidae)	Mother and daughters cooperate in nest building and the care of young, but there is no permanent division of worker and egg- laying castes; trophallaxis paves the way for queen dominance
10. Queen dominance (Vespidae)	The original offspring are all females that are incapable of producing their own female offspring, thus separating the reproductive and worker castes; intermediates may be common
11. Differential larval feeding (Vespidae)	Differential feeding of the larvae and trophallaxis lead to the production of a well-defined worker caste strongly differentiated from the queen, and a reduction in the number of intermediates.

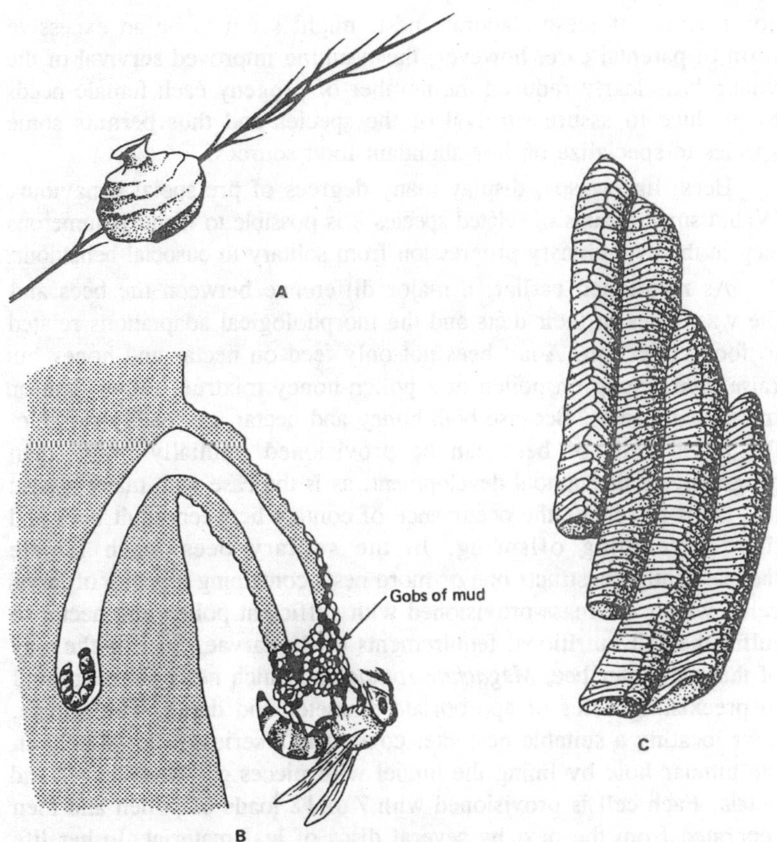

Fig 8.9. Some examples of nests constructed by solitary hymenopterans. (A) Juglike nest of the potter wasp Eumenes *(B) Section through the nest of the solitary wasp* Oplo mesas *showing the storage tunnel provisioned with a caterpillar and the down-curved entrance tube cc-istructed of mud. (C) Group of mud nest units of the pipe organ mud dauber. Trypooxyton.*

The development of patterns of behaviour that increased provisioning seems to have been accompanied by the construction of fairly elaborate neast. Among the wasps, the simplest nests consist of no more than burrows in the soil. However, the preparation, pro-visioning, and final concealment of these burrows involves a behavioural sequence that is truly tascinating to observe. More elaborate nests are fashioned from a variety of natural materials and often are quite characteristic of the constructing species. A number of wasp species use mud for nest construction, making many trips to fetch enough to build a nest suitable for a single offspring. The time and energy devoted to the construction of these elaborate nests might seem to be an excessive form of parental care; however, the resulting improved survival of the young has clearly reduced the number of progeny each female needs to produce to assure survival of the species and thus permits some species to specialize on less-abundant food sources.

Bees, like wasps, display many degrees of pre-social behaviour. Within small groups of related species it is possible to identify numerous step in the evolutionary progression from solitary to eusocial behaviour.

As mentioned earlier, a major difference between the bees and the wasps lies in their diets and the morphological adaptations related to food collection. Adult bees not only feed on nectar and honey but raise their young on pollen or a pollen-honey mixtrue, rather than on macerated insects. Because both honey and nectar are readily storable, the larval cells of bees can be provisioned innitially rather than progressively throughout development, as is the case with many wasps; this tends to reduce the occurrence of contact between adult bees and their developing offspring. In the solitary bees, each female independently constructs one or more nests containing a group of larval cells, which are mass-provisioned with sufficient pollen and nectar to fulfill the full nutritional fequirements of the larvae. Such is the way of the leaf-cutter bee, *Megachile rotundata,* which nests above ground in preexisting holes of appropriate diameter and depth. The female, after locating a suitable nest site, constructs a series of larval cells in the tubular hole by lining the tunnel with pieces cut from leaves and petals. Each cell is provisioned with 7 to 12 loads of pollen and then separated from the next by several discs of leaf material. In her life span of about 6 weeks, each *M. rotundata* female will construct 5 or 6 such nests, totaling approximately 30 larval cells.

Other solitary bees, like the soil-nesting alkli bee, *Nomia melanderr,* form. nesting aggregations. The female constructs a more. or less vertical burrow anu, like the leaf- cutter bee, constructs a series of larval cells mass provisioned with pollen. The suitability of certain patches of soil often results in the construction of a number of nests in one area, but there is no cooperation between individual females. Perhaps because of the tendency to mass provision made possible their food type, the bees do not show the variety of parental care behaviour displayed by the wasps. However, species-of *Nomia* Cons-truct composite nests consisting of a communal entrance with cells off on side branches that are constructed and provisioned by individual females. Michener classifies these species as communal and suggests that they benefit from an economy of nest construction labour. The regular back-and-forth movement of a group of females using a single entrance probably enhances the defense of the brood as well. The parental care and brood-rearing behaviour of some presocial wasps and bees is clearly only slightly less elaborate than that of eusocial species. However, the formation of large social groups.

Biological Clocks

Many moths and butterflies emerge from their cacoons at dawn when the still, somewhat moist air provides the best conditions for slowly drying their infolding wings. Insects are the most successful group of primarily terrestrial animals. As such, they are subject to substantial diurnal and seasonal fluctuations in a variety of physical factors. In the long course of their evolution, insects have developed behavioural strategies that both exploit and lessen the impact of these fluctuations. Most insects, for example, display daily cycles of activity and quiescence. They may be active at night (*nocturnal*), during the day (*diurnal*), or during the transition periods of dawn and dusk (*crepuscular*). Many insects also display seasonal patterns of reproduction, growth, development, and dormancy that are of adaptive significance. Behavioural periodicity serves as more than a means of avoiding periods of physical adversity and exploiting periods of physical favourability. As an inherited component of most living things, behavioural rhythmicity has become a significant part of coevolutionary relationships. For example, different plants bloom at different times of the year, and during the flowering period may only produce nectar and open at certain times of the day. Pollinating species of insects adapted to these plants must utilize a similar periodicity.

The simple responses to periodic changes in the environment are called *exogenous rhythms*. For example, some insects will remain inactive as long as the temperature is below some critical point. When the temperature rises above this inherited threshold, they become active regardless of the time of day. When the external stimulus is light intensity that changes regularly with the diurnal cycle of light and dark, the associated behavioural response can have a very regular periodicity. Exogenous rhythms obviously serve a multiplicity of functions but are subject to environmental variations that would not influence the behaviour of organisms with a rhythmicity driven from within.

Internally driven, or *endogenous rhythms*, are hereditary endowments that manifest themselves even when external factors remain unchanged. Endogenous cycles with a periodicity close to 24 hours are called *circadian rhythms* (*circa*, about; *diem*, day). This is the most common form of periodicity observed among insects, but rhythms with *annual* (*circannual*). lunar (*circalunar*) and even *tidal* (*circatidal*) periodicities are known. Sometimes the rhythmicity characterizes and event that occurs only once in the life of an individual, as in the case of the eclosion of *Drosophila* pupae at dawn. These timed, single events indicate clearly that endogenous rhythms are neither learned nor imposed by the environment, and the apparent innate ability of organisms to measure the passage of time has led to the use of the term *biological clock*. Behavioural periodicity can be observed in individuals and populations, and in most cases involves a combination of endogenous and exogenous components; the intrinsic clock mechanisms provides a temporal organization that is then modulated by environmental periodicity. At the level of the individual, rhythms of general activity, feeding, mating, and oviposition are commonplace.

The rhythmicity of general locomotor activity of a number of insects in relation to light/dark cycles has been observed. Cockroaches and house crickets, for example, are principally nocturnal and begin their active period soon after dusk. However, behavioural periodicity in a light /dark cycle does not necessarily means that the rhythm is endogenous. This must be determined experimentally by transferring the organisms into continuous light or continuous darkness while other variables are held constant. If the activity remains rhythmic, with a periodicity close to 24 hours, the existence of an endogenous clock mechanism not controlled exogenously by environmental stimuli is indicated, but not proved. Under constant light or darkness and constant temperature, cockroaches maintained a locomotor rhythmicity that varied between 23 and 25 hours for several weeks. Roberts also showed that the period of locomotor rhythm was shortened by an increase in temperature, but so little as to suggest virtual temperature independence.

Some insects, particularly crepuscular species, display bimodal activity patterns with peaks at dawn and dusk. When subjected to constant dark, some species will be active only once during the diel suggesting one endogenous period and one exogenous period. Others, however, display a bimodal periodicity in constant darkness. An endogenous regulator of activity would have little functional value, unless it timed the activity to coincide with a period of over-all environmental favourability. Experiments have shown however, that when endogenous oscillators are subjected to an environmental light/dark or temperature cycle, the endogenous periodicity becomes the same as that of the environmental cycle or is entrained by it provided that it is within the oscillator's range of adaptability. For example, when *Aedes aegypti* are held under constant light, they oviposit arrhythmically; but, when provided with a time marker (*Zeitgeber*) such as dark period, they oviposit synchronously at daily intervals thereafter.

Although the timing of events can be important to individuals, it is even more important to populations of mixed age groups as a means of synchronizing certain activities. This synchronization is achieved in part by once-in-a-lifetime occurrences controlled by an on-going circadian rhythm. The emergence of adult insects from their pupae is probably the best known of these phenomena, but a variety of others have been observed. Clearly, the synchronization of certain behavioural events in mixed age populations has a distinct selective advantage. For example, egg hatching at dawn could coincide with humidity and temperature conditions less likely to be injurious to the newly emerged larvae. The synchronous early morning hatching of gypsy' moth eggs, followed by the ascent of the young larvae to the upper branches of their host tree from which they drop on a silken thread, appears to be an adaptation related to their passive dispersal by wind. The synchronized emergence of new adults, resulting from a circadian pattern of pupal eclosion would enhance the mating process, on one hand but might result in extensive population inbreeding, on the other. For any single species there can be several activities that display a circadian rhythm. The pink bollworm, *Pectinophora gossypiella*, for example, displays rhythms of egg hatching, pupal eclosion and oviposition. When entrained to the same light cycle, all three show a different phase relationship to the *Zeitgeber*. These observations indicate the presence of a circadian system composed of a series of clocks, rather than a single "master clock."

The daily pattern of light and darkness serves not only as the most important *Zeitgeber* of a circadian rhythms but as the most reliable indicator of the seasons and regulator of seasonal activity. The length of the light period is always the same on any given date at any given place on the earth. The ability to measure daylength, therefore, provides an organism with an annual clock that can be used to time accurately important events in its life. The most frequently observed response to photoperiod is the seasonal occurrence of dormancy in the life cycle. Most insects are active during the summer, and therefore develop and reproduce under a regime of long days, but become dormant under short days. This type of response to photoperiod is displayed clearly by species that have several generations per year, the last of which enters a facultative winter diapause. The stimulus for diapause is often a daylength of some critical value. In most species a daylength different of 1 hour or less will determine whether development proceeds or is temporarily suspended.

The regularity of the photoperiod makes it a particularly useful advance indicator of seasonal adversity, but the daylength used to time diapause varies from species to species according. to their life cycle and the geographic location of their habitat. We usually think of diapause as a specialized overwintering state induced in many species, by the photoperiod that characterizes the insect's summer period of development. However, in hot dry areas many insects are active during the autumn, winter, or spring and pass the hot, dry period in a summer diapause induced by the short photoperiod that prevailed during their development. As all daylengths, except those at the solstices, occur twice each year, investigators have sought evidence that insects respond to the direction of the change in photoperiod rather than to a stationary period above or below some critical value as used in most laboratory experiments. However, the life cycles of most species rule out the need for information regarding the direction of photoperiod change, since their responsive stage is only present during one of the periods when the appropriate photoperiod occurs. Nonetheless, there is evidence that some species do respond to the change in daylength that occurs between different stages of development. For example, when the immatures of the red locust, *Nomadacris septemfasciata*, are exposed to daylengths over 13 hours and the adults to daylengths of less than 12 hours, they enter a reproductive diapause that prohibits reproduction during the dry season. In the bollworm, *Heliothis zea*, diapause, is induced when the larvae experience shorter days than the adults and eggs. Long-range timers or endogenous rhythms with a period close to a year (circannual rhythms) have attracted more attention as a mechanism that regulates the reproduction and migration of longer-lived animals, like birds and mammals, rather than of insects. But as Saunders pointed out, the report by Blake of a circannual rhythm that governs the seasonal cycle of the carpet beetle, *Anthrenus verbasci*, represents the pioneer work in this field.

The life, cycle of *A. verbasci* takes about 2 years for completion. Normally, 2 winters are passed in larva diapause,, with the adults

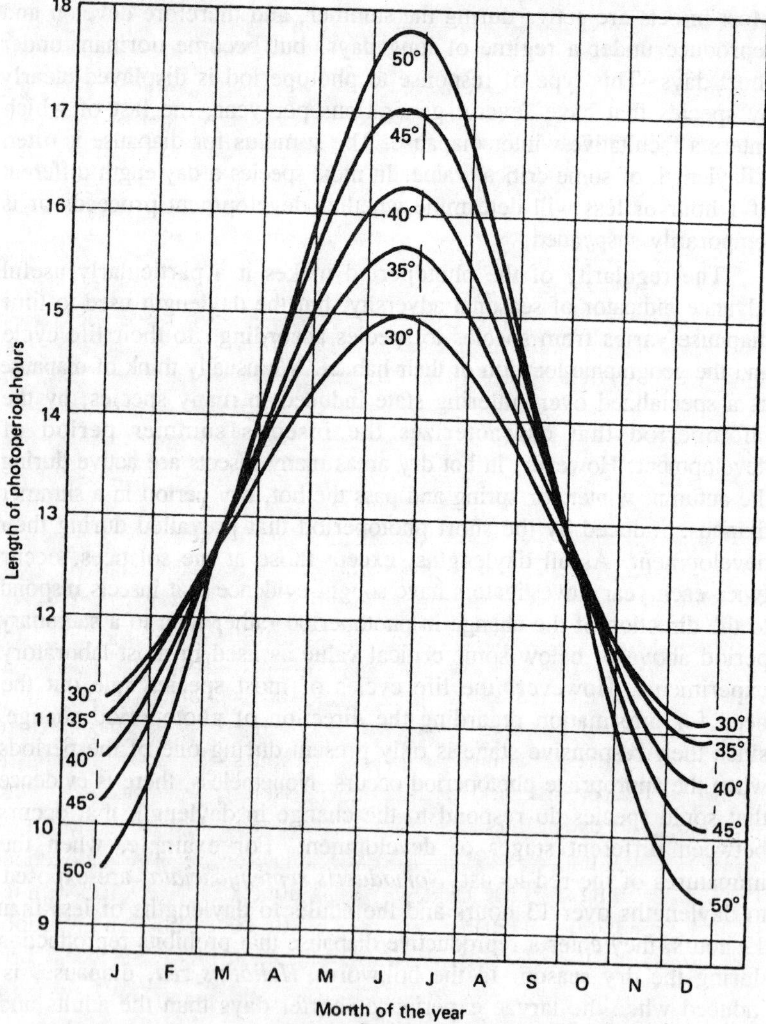

Fig 9.1. The relationship between photoperiod, date and latitude.

emerging the second spring. Blake demonstrated the endogenous nature of this rhythm by rearing the beetle in the laboratory under conditions of constant temperature, humidity and darkness. When allowed to free run under these constant conditions, and therefore without*a Zeitgeber*, a natural periodicity of about 41 weeks was revealed. However, when the larvae experienced naturally decreasing daylengths, the cycle became entrained to the environmental year and pupal development was delayed to a time that would coincide with the spring. The 2-year life cycle could be shortened to 1 year under constant temperatures of 22.5 and 25° C, but the time of pupation was still dictated by the circannual rhythm to occur during an "allowable" period. At lower temperatures, an increasing number of larvae were unable to pupate during this first period; however, instead of their pupation being delayed only a few weeks, it was delayed until the pupation period in the second year. This form of endogenous temporal organization of an event is referred to as *gating*.

The endogenous timers discussed thus far control *basic* activity and developmental patterns that, in turn, influence responses per se and certainly must be understood by anyone interested in all forms of behaviour. There are two additional types of time controllers that underlie behaviour patterns with specific functional significance. The "time memory" of the honeybee, *Apis mellifera*, and the timecompensated sun-compass orientation of a variety. of insects both appear to be under endogenous control. Beling trained bees by providing sugar syrup to them at a specific time of the day and marked some individuals while at the feeding station. Subsequent to the training period, no syrup was put out, but the time of arrival of marked bees was recorded. With this and later experiments, Beling demonstrated that the bees returned at the same time each day and the that they could be trained to come at two different times of the day provided the periods were separated by at least 2 hours. The experiments of Beling, however, did not rule out the possibility that the bees were responding to exogenous time clues such as the position of the sun.

It was not until the 1950s that the ultimate proof of an endogenous clock controlling the time memory of the honeybee. was forthcoming. Renner conducted experiments under both controlled and outdoor conditions that involved the westward relocation of trained bees. In a controlled experiment, bees transported overnight from Paris to New York (a real time difference of 5 hours) visited the

New York feeding station exactly 24 hours after the previous feeding experience in Paris. In an experiment conducted outdoors, bees transported overnight from Long Island, New York, to Davis, California (a real time difference of 3.25 hours), foraged at Davis 24 hours after the previous Long Island feeding; however, after only 3 days, there were indications of entertainment to the California light cycle.

The adaptive significance of the capability of keeping track of the temporal distributions of resources is obvious. Where this ability has been demonstrated, in the case of bees, it enables them to visit forage areas when pollen and nectar are readily available and even

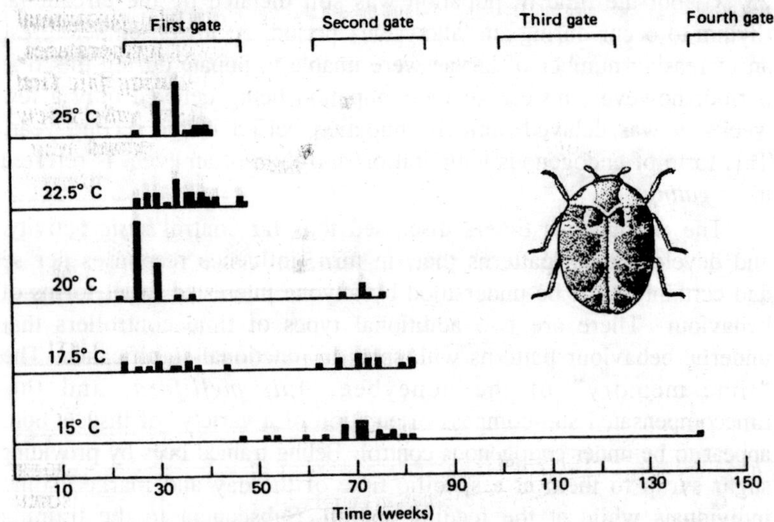

Fig. 9.2. The circannual rhythm of pupation in Anthrenus verbasci *showing the frequency of pupation times when larval development has occurred in constant conditions of temperature, humidity and darkness. A black square represents the time of pupation, to the nearest week, of an individual. Note that the larvae at higher temperature are able to utilize the first gate: at lower temperature an increasing proportion of them are required to wait until the next.*

"remember" the time relationship during short periods when foraging is curtailed by poor weather. But, as Saunders stated, "The fact that the rhythm is fairly easily extinguished without positive reinforcement, however, is also of biological importance because there is an ever-changing array of nectar sources, and there is little selective advantage in continuing to arrive at flowers long post their best." Transverse orientations are common among insects, and one form, 180 meters suncompass orientation, is used by a variety of insects to transverse open space where landmarks are scarce. Insects using sun-compass orientation throughout much of the day must have a means of compensating for changes in the sun's azimuth. Early experimental results revealed that foraging ants held captive in a dark box for several hours maintain the precapture angle of orientation relative to the new position of the sun when released. These results were counter to the possibility of time compensation. However, more recent investigations by Jander found that the black ant, *Lasius niger*, maintained its original compass bearing after release from a dark box. Similar results were obtained by von Frisch working with the red ant, *Formica rufa*, during the summer, but in spring experiments red ants seemed unable to compensate for the sun's movement.

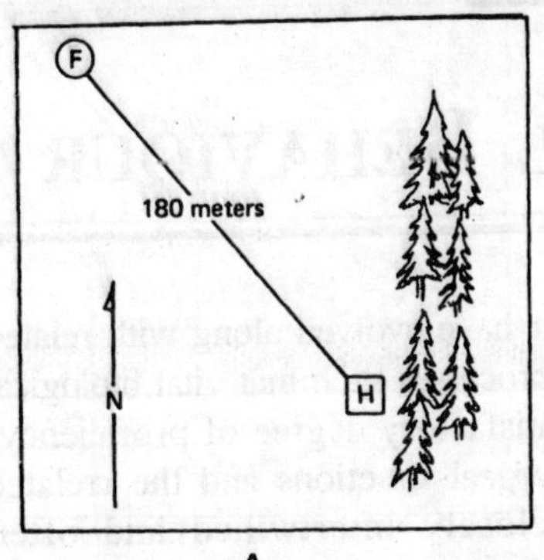

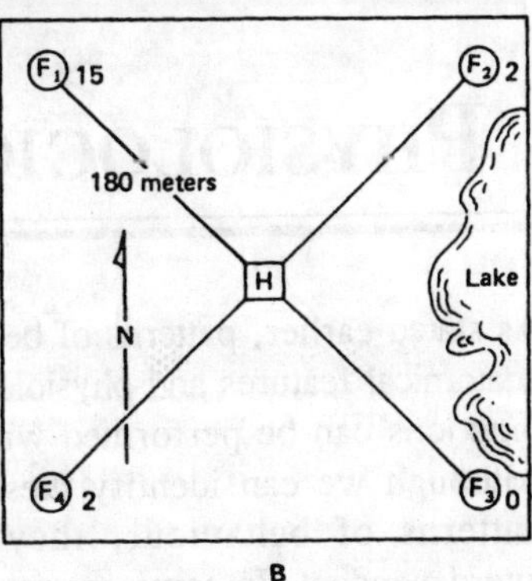

Fig. 9.3. Time-compensated sun orientation in the honeybee. (A) A bee hive H was placed in an unknown region. and a group of bees was fed in the afternoon *on a feeding table F, 180 m NW. (B) During the night the hive was translocated to another area and* in the morning *the bees had to choose one to four feeding tables 180 m NE, NW, SE, or SW, of the hive. The new landscape did not offer any familiar landmarks: the sun stood at another angle relative to the training line as in the previous afternoon. Nevertheless, most bees (encircled numbers) came to the NW: that is, the bees had calculated the sun's movement.*

Von Frisch also demonstrated time-compensated sun orientation for the honeybee. Bees were trained to forage at a feeding station west of their hive late in the day. The hive was then moved to an unfamiliar location during the night, and, when the bees were released in the morning, they foraged away from the sun (to the west) instead of toward it. The design and results of a more elaborate experiment with honeybees conducted by von Frisch and Lindauer. The work with bees, ants, and a few other insects indicates the existence of some internal timing mechanism that enables them to compensate for the sun's movement. However, more work is needed on the light-compass orientation of insects at different latitudes and seasons of the year because of the differences in the apparent rate of the sun's movement.

PHYSIOLOGICAL BEHAVIOUR

As stated earlier, patterns of behaviour have evolved along with related anatomical features and physiological processes such that vital biological functions can be performed with a satisfactory degree of proficiency. Although we can identify these biological functions and the rrelated patterns of behaviour, they are closely intertwined and often interdependent. In some species the life cycle appears to be partitioned into periods during which one functional aspect of behaviour seems to be predominant - a period of feeding is followed by migration, which is in turn followed by a reproductive period. In other species the behaviour seems to contain a series of feedback loops that result in no clear or predictable sequence of behavioural events. Clearly, an experimental analysis of the over-all pattern of behaviour would be exceedingly complex, and most behaviourists tend to incestigate some aspect of behaviour that has some basic biological interest or practical significance.

Markl and Lindauer suggested that the biological functions of behaviour could be divided between the need of indi-viduals to develop and sustain themselves, on the one hand, and interact with other individuals on order to contribute to the persistence of the species, on the other. Such a division might have some utility, but not all aspects of behaviour are assignable under this particular dichotomy. Obviously, an individual insect must locate and select an appropriate type of food not only to sustain itself, but often to provide the nutritional requirements for the production of the eggs that become the next generation.

DISPLACEMENT

The high level of motility that characterizes so many insects has long attracted the attention of behaviourists both as a source of fascination and as a subject of great practical importance. In spite of the widespread attention that insect flight has attracted, there is much yet to be learned about behaviour during flight and to the importance of flight as a cause of qualitative ans quantitative changes in populations. One hardly needs to scratch the surface of the literature on insect dispersal and migration to realize that accepted generalities have been elusive. Even a common understanding and acceptance of the terminology has failed to materialize, particularly in the case of migration. Any change of location can be called displacement. It may come about as a result of the accidental passive transport of insects by wind, water, phoresy (in association with another organism), active locomotion, or by some combination of these. In spite of the frequency with which passive transport, particularly by the wind, becomes involved in the movement of insects, there is relatively little displacement that is completely accidental and, therefore, detrimental at the population or species level. Small insects are not blown at random and do not end up in inhospitable environments as frequently as one might expect. Obviously, this was a danger that existed from the very origin of flight, and it is highly likely that species that did not evolve behavioural mechanisms to reduce in-fight accidents did not survive. On the other hand, the wind provides an inexhaustible source of external energy that insects could and have exploited with the evolution of appropriate patterns of behaviour.

The movements of insects can best be separated into those often referred to as trivial and those that are truly migratory. Trivial movements tend to be local and lacking in directionality of a type that leads to predictable displacement. The fluttering of a butterfly from plant to plant in a meadow and the intermittent pausing to feed on the nectar of flowers or to lay eggs on suitable host plants is a typical example of trivial movement. The insect tends to change direction frequently and traverse territory it has probably traversed before, rather than fly in a more or less straight line over new territory. We cannot describe trivial movements as random because they may involve a variety of active responses to various stimuli. It is during this kind of activity that insects often locate food, mates, or oviposition sites. The initial phase of these selective behaviour patterns often involves the detection of host odors or pheromones that are unevenly distributed as odor plumes. The trivial movements result in the interception of these cues, which may then lead to some oriented movements such as a positive chemotaxis or klinokinesis. The degree of displacement that results from trivial movements may be either quite substantial or rather small. Usually, insects involved in trivial flights remain within the boundary layer (the relatively thin layer of the atmospher immediatel above the substrate, where friction retards air movement and creates turbulence), and within a rather local area. Trivial flight is also characterized by numerous pauses during which insects feed, lay eggs, engage in mating behaviour, or simply rest. Flight is, of course, not a necessary component of trivial movement, and all trivial movements do not result

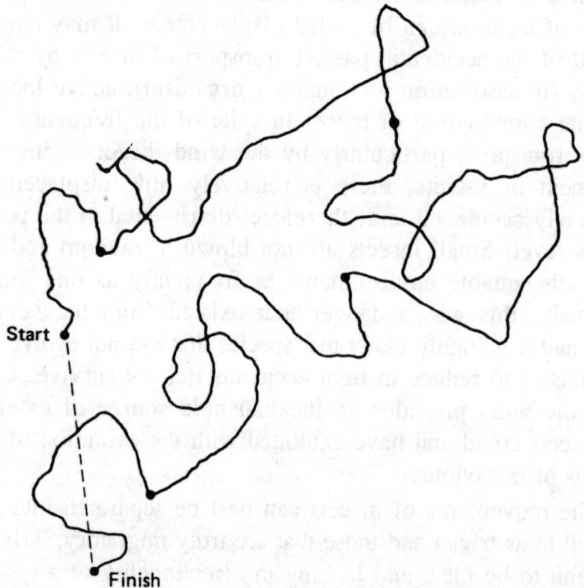

Fig. 10.1. Diagram of a hypothetical track of an adult insect engaged in trivial flight. Such flights are usually interrupted by numerous brief stop (dots). The ultimate displacement between the starting point and termination point (broken line) is usually considerably less than the total distance traversed (solid line).

in long-distance displacement. Many ground-crawling and soil- inhabiting insects substantially change their location during their daily search for food and mates although the degree of displacement may be restricted to within a relatively small home range or territory. In my view, the back-and-forth foraging of insects like wasps, ants, and bees is a specialized type of trivial movement that results in only temporary displacement, since the foragers ultimately return to the nest, which remains in one place.

Migration, on the other hand, involves behavioural patterns that lead to a departure from one havitat and movement to another. In case of aphids, it may result in movement from one host plant to another quite nearby; for other species, it may result in travel over hundreds of miles. Frequently, migration involves a behavioural pattern that leads to an escape from the boundary layer into higher elevations where the air moves horizontally at speeds that often exceed the intrinsic flight velocity of the species. Migratory movements are also more sustained than trivial movements and, in most cases, are characterized by a general straightening out of the track. Insects that migrate largely under their own power appear to be motivated by an inner drive that results in the suppression of their responsiveness to appetitive stimuli, such as food or mate odors, which would normally distract them during trivial flight. Most of the confusion that has occurred in the area of displace- ment behaviour involves the criteria for the definition of migration. Some early workers observed and recorded the mass flights of insects that often moved in a common direction with apparent purpose, or the sudden arrival of populations of insects in a new area. These investigators proposed definitions of migration clearly based on their limited experience. Some workers went as far as to suggest that true migrations are characterized by a two-way flight by the same individuals -clearly a carry-over from a basic understanding of bird behaviour; one-way travel was described as dispersal. Many investi-gators also felt that migration resulted from a sudden deterioration of a species; habitat, which caused a mixed-age population to leave in search of more favorable conditions, and that the population was in full control of the direction of its travel. Small insects such as aphids, which commonly move short distances within the boundary layer, and the apparent drifters that comprised the aerial plankton sampled by men like Hardy and Milne and Glick were not considered to be true migrants. In fact, very few species actually fulfill the early definitions of migrants.

In the case of short-lived species such as most insects, there is no biological rationale for limiting migration to a back-and- forth pattern of movement by the same individuals. Many do not live long enough to travel in both directions. However, the fact that some insects do move back and forth between different parts of their habitat has confused the issue, to say the least. Some of the best examples of regular back-and-forth travel within a local area have resulted from studies of a group of scarab beetles known as cockchafers or leafchafers. The adults of a numer of species emerge from the soil of pasture areas where pupation occurred and remain in the grass until mating has taken place. The inseminated females then fly to nearby woodlands, where they feed on the leaves of deciduous trees and develop their .eggs. Subsequently, they fly back to the pasture land where they oviposit in the soil. The result in the repopulation of previously occupied breeding grounds and little redistribution of the population to new areas. Although a rather special situation, this behaviour does constitute migration of Johnson's type II discussed a little later. Some workers have extended this interpretation of migratory behaviour to other cases of regular back-and-forth movement within a habitat. Certainly, such movements are behaviourally different from the trivial flights of the butterfly in the meadow described earlier, in that the flight pathe may be straight and the displacement predictable. However, in many cases the travel is accompanied by responses to feeding and reproductive stimuli normally ignored by migrants and consequently results in the fulfillment of basic needs normally a function of trivial flight.

Since most species sometime in their life cycles engage in dis-placement activity beyond that associated with trivial movement, we obviously need a biologically sound concept of migration. The key to understanding this aspect of behaviour, therefore, seems not to be whether the population traverses a great distance, not whether the travelers orient themselves as though they have some destination in mind, not whether the same individuals will make a return trip, but that the species periodically engagesin travel as an intergral part of its life cycle and behaviour. Kennedy has made one of the strongest recent attempts to clarify the situation by suggesting that most insect species must travel from one part of their range to another as a regular and vital part of their biology for purposes of resource utilization and gene pool mixing. Furthermore, the advantages of such travel have led to the evolution of specific behavioural adaptations that accommodate it.

Causes of Migration

The fact that insects are often observed to engage in a mass exodus from a breeding site, coincidentally with crowding or some deterioration in the quality or quantity of their food supply, has led to the conclusion that migration is simply an immediate behavioural response to the environmental conditions that exist. However, many species of insects seem to migrate as a matter of course even though they are not crowded and their habitat appears to be suitable for continued utilization. This occurs because many species actually leave their breeding place well in advance of its deterioration as an adaptive response to some early warning signals. The suggestion that migration is a sudden behavioural response to adversity is also weakened by the fact that migrants often continue to travel long after they have left the unfavourable area without testing the favourability of areas along the way. Still other species, which have several generations per year, migrate during each generation, not only the generation subjected to environmental deterioration.

Southwood concluded that migratory behaviour is parti-cularly important for species that occupy temporary habitats such as temporary pools or scattered hosts, or habitats that become periodi-cally unsuitable, as with the seasonal drying up of vegetation. Occupants of such of such habitats must be adapted to migrate at more or less regular intervals in order to survive the year-to-year variability inherent in heterogeneous environments. For these species the migratory behaviour, therefore, is best set in motion by environmental stimuli that precede the impending adversity. Photoperiod would seem to be the most reliable stimulus and one deeply involved in a number of periodic behavioural activities. However, an increase in population density, density, changes in food quality or quantity, and changing climatic conditions can all be used as advance warning signals if an appropriate response system has been evolved. From a behaviorist's point of view this may pose a problem because, late in the summer, insect population growth, high mean daily temperatures, drought, declining photoperiod, and a deterioration of the vegetation may all go hand in hand.

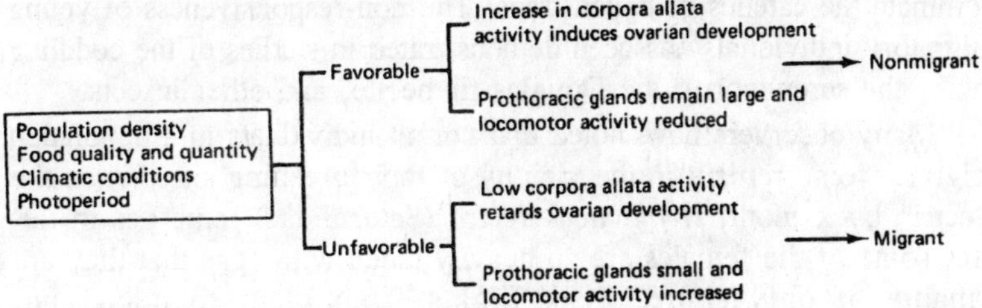

Fig. 10.2. The interrelationships between environmental conditions, hormonal activity, and locomotion that may lead to the induction of either non-migratory or migratory behaviour.

From the evolutionary point of view, it would seem that a mechanism that integrates the environmental cues with the insect's developmental physiology would have the strongest selective advantage. Experimental evidence suggests that this is accomplished by way of the envirnmental effects of the endocrine system. For example, there is an established relationship between crowding and the size and activity of the prothoracic glands. The prothoracic glands of crowded locusts are small at emergence and disappear a few day after the final molt, whereas in isolated individuals these glands are large and persist until sexual maturation is complete. Crowded individuals engage in more active locomotion than isolated individuals, and, when the latter are injected with hemolymph from crowded locusts, they too become active. Other relationships exist between environmental stimuli and activity of the corpus allatum and the development of ovaries. Poor-quality food and declining photoperiod will both result in retardation of ovaration development, a condition usually enconutered among migrants. Thus, there is a considerable degree of coordination between the development of the flight apparatus and the ovaries in relation to various environmental changes.

Because of the incompatabiliklty of a well-developed flight mechanism and fully developed ovaries, migration tends to occur when ovarian development is attenuated. The balance between migratory flight and the reproductive system may vary according to the environmental conditions, as suggested previously, but in many species this balance is a regular part of development. In quite a large number of species, migratory flights occur soon after emergence. The extent and druration of such flights may vary greatly from individual to individula depending on their developmental histories, but they occur nonetheless. During these early flights, many insects are clearly nonresponsive to appetitive stimuli, as demonstrated by the fact that older individuals tend to dominate the catches of baited traps. The non-responsiveness of young migratory individuals has been demons-trated in studies of the coddling moth, the screwworm, the Douglas fir beetle, and other insects.

Many observers have noted that not all individuals in a population migrate; some remain in the vicinity of their breeding site. When the electric buck moth, *Hemileuca electra* (Saturniidae), emerges in the fall, some of the females are so heavily laden with eggs that they are capable of only short, weak flights from plant to plant and, consequently, lay their eggs in the immediate vicinity of their pupation site. Others emerge, fly upward out of the boundary layer, and leave the area completely. In fact, these moths are recognized for their ability to fly strongly, well above the ground on windy days. Whether the behavioural differences displayed by individual moths is under genetic control or is the result of nutrition and developmental history remains unknown. In my work on the flight behaviour of the bark beetle. *Dendroctonus pseudotsugae* (Scolytidae). Hagen suggests that it is possible to identify migrant convergent lady beetles heading for hibernation sites by squeezing them to see if they contain much fat. Perhaps nutrition alone can cause the differences in behaviour that would contribute to the exploitation of both local and distant habitats. However, we shoud not rule out the possibility and selective advantages of genetic differences.

Thus, we see among the insects a confusing situationn in which some groups such as the aphids, termites and ant periodically produce winged obligatory migrants, whereas many other species produce only winged adults, some of which migrate and some of which do not. We see some migrations associated with crowding and environmental deterioration, and some that occur without environmental change. The actual cause of migratory behaviour is still not clear, but we have now come to realize that there is an endogenous motivation genetically programmed into the behavioural make-up of most, perhaps all, insect species, and that migration is clearly an ecologically and genetically beneficial from of adaptive behaviour molded by the process of natural selection. As Johnson stated, "To the universal cycle of birth, reproduction and death must be added theprocess of migration ..."

CLASSES OF MIGRATION

There is great variability in insect migratory activity. It ranges both behaviourably and ecologically from something not much different from trivial movement in terms of distance traveled to travel over very long distances. Johnson erected the following three classes of migration which provide considerable clarification:

Class I. Species with a life span limited to a single season leave their breeding site, disperse to new areas to reproduce, and die soon thereafter. The migrants make only an outward journey, but their behaviour is characterized by an impression of moving toward a goal.

Class II. Species with relatively short-lived adults that leave their breeding site and travel to a new location where they feed and their ovaries develop. After maturation, the females return to their old breeding site or a new one where they oviposit.

Class III. Relatively long-lived individuals leave their breeding site, travel to a winnter or summer resting site where they pass through a reproductive diapause. During the following season the same individuals return to their original breeding area, where the females oviposit.

Class I migrations may be extremely variable in terms of both distance travelled and duration of travel but usually occur soon after emergence and before the gonads have matured. Johnson recognized five subtypes of this class of migration, but a pair of examples should give an adequate impression of the variation that exists. A rather simple illustration is provided by the flights of ants and termites, in which winged individuals that are produced seasonally become the founders of new colonies. The winged males and females leave the nest soon after emergence and fly weakly with the wind. As the wind direction changes, the winged reproductives become displaced variously within and beyond the area where breeding is possible. Relatively few new nests need to be established to keep the area adequately populated, so the large numerical losses sustained during migration can be tolerated. Although seemingly different and certainly of a greater magnitude, the migration of the desert locust, *Schistocerca gregaia* (Acrididae) is also an example of class I migration. In tropical and subtropical areas, the desert locust must move from breeding areas that are deteriorating because of drought and resource depletion to new areas that are receiving rain and have green vegenation. These breeding areas are often widely separated and tend to be in different locations because of spatial variations in the pattern of seasonal rainiall.

The discovery that the seemingly powerfully oriented flight of the desert locust across Africa was simply adaptive travel with the wind helped immeasurably to change our view of migration. Migratory locusts are not preprogrammed to orient toward some distant goal as once thought; instead they are adapted to take advantage of the seasonal wind patterns. The analysis of films of migrating swarms of locusts revealed that the individual migrants were not necessarily oriented to their direction of travel (track). Within a swarm there are many groups of similarly oriented individuals, but throughout the swarm these groups fly in different directions. The different orientation of these groups maintains the cohesiveness of the swarm, which as a whole moves with the wind. The swarm is thereby gradually displaced downwind to zones where tropical air masses converge and generate the rainfall that stimulates plant growth in the new breeding place. The pattern of Class II migrations is illustrated by many insects that display a high degree of larval-adult divergence inn terms of habitat or food preference. Female mosquitoes, for example, must often leave the area of larval habitat from which they emerged so as to obtain a blood meal necessary for egg development. The larvae are filter-feeders in aquatic habitats, whereas the females often search for vertebrate hosts some distance from the water. After feeding and oogenesis, they return to aquatic habitats to oviposit. In the chafers mentioned earlier, the larvae feed on organic matter in the soil of pastures, whereas the adults feed on the leaves of trees to which they migrate. After maturation of their ovaries they return to the pastures to oviposit.

Class III migrations vary considerably in detail from species to species. At on eextreme, young adults emerge from their breeding site and fly in all directions throughout their habitat, sometimes aided by local winds, coming to rest in a place suitable for spending a dormant period. Following dormancy, the same. individuals migrate back to available breeding sites where oviposition takes place. The ambrosia beetle, *Trypodendron lineatuni,* for example, emerges from brood sites in logging slash and flies into forest margins in the same general area. After passing a winter diapause in the litter of the forest floor, the beetles emerge and fly out into adjacent open areas, where they locate new brood legs. On the other hand, some lady beetles one of which will be discussed in detail later, migrate long distances between breeding areas and hibernation sites.

Some of the longest and most predictable migratory flights known among the insects are of the Class III variety. The monarch butterfly, *Danaus plexippus,* in North America migrates hundreds of miles to a rather well-defined overwintering area, from which it returns to breeding areas the following spring. The vast distance covered by monarch populations had made it difficult to determine exactly how far individuals fly during each of the phases of the migration. The breeding range of these butterflies is extensive north to south, so there is considerable variation in the latitude at which they develop. The adults that result from the last generation in Canada migrate to regularly used overwintering sites in California, Mexico and Florida. The butterflies are active on warm days during the winter but engage only in trivial flights in the immediate vicinity of their overwintering site. In the spring, the overwintered adults fly northward to new breeding areas, but much less is known about the nature of the return flight. Some are believed to terminate their migration early and establish population at intermediate locations, but others are thought to return derectly to the northernmost breeding areas.

The Adaptive Migratory Behaviour

The energy required to sustain flight during an extended period of migration is substantial, and although many insects have large energy stores at the beginning of their migratory flight, there is clearly an advantage to harnessing the energy of the wind. Lipids are the fuel with the best weight-to-energy ratio and are used by many sustained fliers such as locusts, butterflies, and beetles, although some flies with substantial flight ranges use carbohydrate as their fuel. Calculations suggest that the initial fuel supply available to migrants provides some of them with a great intrinsic flight capacity, and this has been borne out by flight duration tests made with insects tethered on flight mills. We know very little about how much of their fuel supply migrating insects replenish en route, but the suppression of feeding stimuli, common at least at the start of migration, and the carbohydrate nature of most available foods suggest it may be very little. Nonetheless, some migrants such as the monarch butterfly are known to fly distances that exceed their intrinsic range as calculated from their fuel capacity and flight speed, and observations do suggest fat the inexhaustible supply of external energy provided by the wind is exploited by many species.

The general pattern of atmospheric circulation is governed by the interaction of large pressure cells variously positioned according to the seasons. Neear the ground these regional circulation patterns are modified by local climatic and topographic effects. The frequent with which local winds shift direction would make their genera exploitation risky, in that it could lead to enormous numerical losses d insects were carried to inhospitable habitats. Insects, then , must be strong enough to combat the wind or have behaviour that eitber restricts their flight to periods of relative calm or exploits winds that would normally carry them to favourable habitats.

Some insects, such as the painted lady, *Vanessa carO'* (Nymphalidae) are well known for their strong directional flights. In southern California during the early spring, mass flights of adtt painted ladies can be seen heading northward from breeding sites io Mexico. Abobtt reported that these butterflies fly in a northerly direction, regardless of the direction of the wind.

Many insects that are weak fliers also have specific patterns of behaviour that clearly enhance their opporunity to migrate with the help of the wind. Aphids are only capable of a flight speed of approximately 2 miles per hour, so are subject to displacement by even gentle winds once the let go of their substrate. Migratory individuals display a strong positive phototaxis. When they take off is response to the skylight, they fly with an excess of lift over horizontal flight. This carries them upward into the wind, which helps them to travel overland many miles. The aphids apparently beat their wings while being displaced downwind and thereby satisfy the tendency to sustain flight. This locomotor drive declines after an hour or two, a0d the aphids begin their descent. If an aphid lands on a suitable host plant, it will begin to feed and later reproduce; if it lands on 00 unsuitable plant, it will take off again. This behaviour may be repeated several times over several days and can lead to travel over many miles-Many individual aphids are lost during thses migrations, but the synchronized exodus of winged females from their summer host plants assures the survival of the species on alternate hosts throughout the fall and winter.

The importance of adaptive flight behaviour in relation to variable environmental conditions is also important and well illustrated by the migrations of the beet leafhopper, *Circulifer tenellus* (Cicadellidae), in the San Joaquin Valley of California, as summarized by Cook. The leafhoppers overwinter and pass their first generationn predominantly on wild vegetation at the southern end of the valley. In the spring, the prevailing northwesterly winds enter the valley in the area of San Francisco and are deflected southward through the valley; this is in the opposite direction of the spring leafhopper migrations. The leafhoppers are capable of flight speeds in the order of 2 miles per hour and tend to fly only when the prevailing winds have abated. This frequently occurs in the late afternoon when the warm air in the valley rises and is replaced by downslope winds from the surrounding hills. These winds create a northwesterly flow across the leafhoppers' breeding site that carries those already in flight well out innto the valley where sugar beets are cultivated. As a result, the spring migration is against the prevailing wind. Similar combinations of leafhopper flight behaviour and wind patterns at other times throughout the season allow the hoppers to move throughout the valley and ultimately end up at their hibernation sites in the southern hills in the autumn.

Studies of the pre and postdiapause migrations (Class III) of the convergent lady beetle, *Hippodamia convergens,* by Hagen revealed adaptive behaviour patterns that enable these fairly weak flying beetles not only to travel substantial distances, but also to utilize habitats with rather specific locations. In years when aphid populations are high, large numbers of young adult lady beetles emerge from fields in the lowland valleys during May and June. The general reduction in the abundance of aphids because of prior feeding by the beetle larvae leads to the departure of the young adults. About this time, large numbers of lady beetles are often observed in the vicinity of aggregation sites in the mountains. The beetles apparently leave the fields by way of vertical take-off flights on warm, calm mornings. These vertical flights, assisted by conventional currents, continue upward to a temperature ceiling of 11 to 13° C, which curtails flight. The non-flying beetles are believed to fall into warmer air that permits a resumption of their upward flight. This alternating pattern of upward flight and falling produces oscillation of movement that may have an amplitude of up to 1000 feet (305 meters). During these oscillations the beetles are carried on horizontal, westerly winds toward the mountains, where they are deposited in the zone of intersection between the temperature flight ceiling and the ground level.

Warm days during February and March in the Sierra nevada are associated with a high pressure system over southern Idaho that produces northeasterly winds aloft. The aggregation sites on the western side of the mountains are protected from these opper-level winds, but they experience conventional currents and warm upslope winds from the valley. When the temperature of the aggregation sites rises rises, the beetles break dormancy, fly upward, and eventually engage the winds aloft that carry them back to the valley. The beetles again oscillate up and down in the vicinity of the temperature flight ceiling as before but are forced to the ground as the temperature ceiling declines late in the day.

The numerical losses that occur during insect migrations are clearly high, but the benefits that accrue must more than compensate for the inflight population attrition. Insects that utilize scattered temporary habitats must produce enough progeny to ensure that a few survive the migration to new habitats. The fact that the havitats of such species are scattered unevenly throughout their range have been a strong selective force that favoured a strategy in which migration and habitat location are the functions of the winged adult. Yet, this seems inefficient in respects to all the resources consumed dwing the development of the high percentage of adults that die during the movement between habitats. On the surface it would seem to be more efficient for dispersal losses to be absorbed early in the life history, but this occurs in only a relatively few species of insects. As on might expect, those that do migrate as juveniles are rather gezieralized feeders or users of a somewhat specific, but widely distributed, food source. Those species that migrate as immatures have little capacity to navigate or terminate their travel. In order to migrate and maximise the success of establishment in a new habitat, appropriate adaptive behaviour would seem to be a necessity. Studies of the behaviour that leads to and

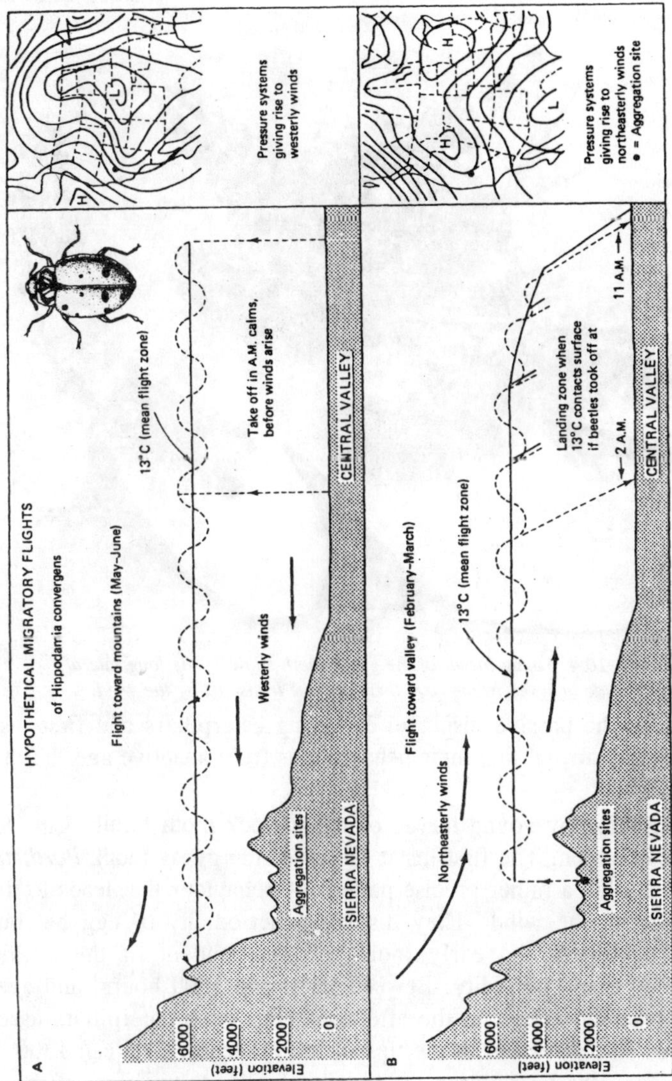

Fig. 10.3. (At left) Suspected temperature-controlled flight behaviour of Hippodamia convagens engaged in migratory flight. (A) The hypothetical pattern of migratory flights to overw+intering sites in the Sierra Nevada in May and June. (B) The hypothetical return flight to the San Joaquin Valley of overwintered individuals in February or March. The simplified weather maps indicate the dominant pressure systems at the time of the respective migratory flights.

Fig. 10.4. Young larvat of the gypsy moth showing the long lateral setae believed to improve their passive transport by the wind.

terminates the passive dispersal of young caterpillars and first instar homopterans reveal that their behaviour is truly adaptive and therefore migratory.

Migration by young larvae of the tussock moth family Liparidae is quite common. The first instar larvae of the gypsy moth, *Porthetria dispw,* display a rather precise pattern of behaviour that leads to their transport on the wind. They display a periodicity of egg hatching, which occurs in the early mornigh, independent of the au,bicnt temperature and humidity. Beween 0800 and 1000 hours, and again, but to a lesser extent, in the afternoon, the small caterpillars ascend the trees and move out to the tips of the branches. Between 1300 and 1500 hours, the larvae drop on strands of silk. At this time of the day both the horizontal and vertical air currents typically reach their greatest velocity. The suspended larvae swing back and forth until the wind is strong enough to break them loose, at which time they sail on the wind to new habitats. The long, lateral setae of the larvae increase their buoyancy and appear to be an adaptation that aids passive transport.

Significance of Migration

Insects, like most organisms, derive both genetic and ecological benefits from being able to move from one place to another. Such behaviour increases the mixing of the gene pool and hastens the spread of beneficial mutations. Ecologically, migration enables a species to vacate crowded areas or habitats, where the requisites for life are deteriorating, in favour of sparsely populated areas or habitats with an abundance of appropriate resources. As is usually the case with evolution, the persistence of a trait depends on whether or not it contributes to the survival of the species. The benefits of migration, therefore, must outweigh the associated physiological costs and numerical losses. Obviously, all insect species do not have the same need to migrate. Those with more or less permanent breeding habitats may be able to achieve adequate displacement by way of the general diffusion that accompanies trivial flight. At the other extreme, species that occupy very temporary or transitory habitats need to migrate regularly.

In order that the genetic and ecological benefits be obtained, substantial losses in the form of energy expended and of mortality must be borne. Apparently, these costs and benefits have been favourably balanced in the course of evolution. The evolution of adaptive behaviour patterns has proved to be one way to maixmize the migratory gains and to minimize the attendant losses. In fact, it would be surprising if many species of insects could survive long if they had to rely on some haphazard means of moving from one habitat to another. Even so, there would seem to be a limited number of behavioural strategies that can be exploited, even though there may be an infinite number of minor variations in the details of such behaviour.

Behavioural Ecology

The study of organisms is relation to their environment is the modern science of ecology, which has deleted in recent. years from the earlier, essentially descriptive endeavour, natural history. The inclusion of this chapter under the general heading "Structure and Function" is consistent with Odum's comment that "it is more in keeping with the modern emphasis to define ecology as the structure and function of nature." A number of general ecology texts are available. Price deals specifically with insect ecology. Andrewartha and Birch trace the historical development of insect ecology.

A basic functional unit in ecology is the *ecosystem*,, which is composed of *a community* of living (biotic), interacting organisms (plants, animals, and microorganisms) and the non-living (abiotic) components of their environment. Ecosystems vary in size and complexity, ranging anywhere from a woodland pond to the entire *biosphere* (that portion of our planet in which living forms exist). The biotic part of an ecosystem is made up of producers, consumers and decomposers. *Producers* are green plants, which synthesize food (carbohydrates and other compounds) from carbon dioxide and water by utilizing energy derived from solar radiation (i.e., *photosynthesis*). Consumers are those organisms, the vast majority of which are animals, that obtain energy and molecular building blocks by ingesting organic matter from plants. *Decomposers*, mainly bacteria and fungi, break complex organic molecules down to simple inorganic nutrients usable by producers, facilitating the continuous cycling of inorganic nutrients throughout an ecosystem.

THE LIFE-SYSTEM CONCEPT

Clark *et al.* introduce a particularly useful concept for our purpose, the concept of the life system. A life system is "that part of an ecosystem which determines the existence, abundance, and evolution of a particular population. "In other words, the life system of an insect is that part of the environment (*effective environment*) that directly influences the fate of a given population plus the population itself. Obviously not all parts of an ecosystem necessarily directly influence a given animal population, although the situation becomes rather hazy when one considers indirect influences. In view of the life system concept, an ecosystem becomes a series of interlocking life systems.

The following sections deal with various aspects of the major components involved in the functioning of a life system, i.e., population and effective environment.

Populations

Members of a given insect species are typically separated into more or less discrete groups or *populations*. Or a population may be a group of individuals of the same species delineated, for purposes of study, by a biologist. Like individuals, populations have characteristics that can be measured and described: for examples, *genetic compo-sition* (the individuals of most natural populations vary phenotypically and genotypically), *sex ratio* the proportion of females to males), *age composition* (most populations are composed of adults and immatures of varying ages), arrangement in space or *dispersion* (most natural populations tend to be composed of clumps of individuals due to irregularities in the distribution of food and shelter and the fact that individuals often attract one another), *population size* (expressed as total number of individuals), *population density* (the number of individuals per unit area or volume), *biomass* (the total weight of a population), and *dynamics* changes in numbers and or density over time). It has been long recognized that organisms have the capacity under ideal conditions to increase by a geometric progression (*exponentially*). Since this capacity for exponential increase (*biotic potential*) *is* never fully realized under natural circumstances, it is clear that there are factors in the environment (predators, limited resources, etc.) that act to prevent such increases. The collective action of these factors has been called *environmental resistance*. In the broadest terms, one may view the dynamics of a given pqpulation as representing the outcome of the interaction between biotic potential and environmental resistance.

It is the goal of population studies to understand the composition and behaviour of populations and ultimately to be able to make predictions. Such information is essential to the development of a detailed understanding of evolution and further of paramount practical importance when we consider pest organisms.

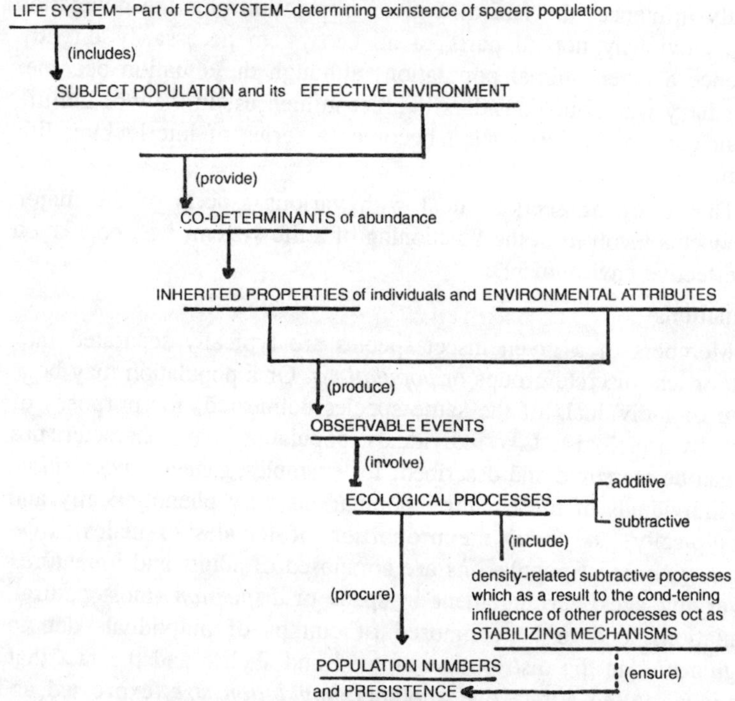

Fig. 11.1. Components of a life system.

Three basic approaches are used to study populations.

1. Analysis of population performance under controlled, but artificial, conditions in the laboratory.

2. Evaluation of populations in the field.

3. Development of theoretical, mathematical models that describe population dynamics.

Population studies in the laboratory are of necessity too simplified and only remotely representative of what must actually occur under the complexities characteristic of field conditions. On the other hand, the complexities of natural conditions make it difficult to assess the action of particular environmental factors. Further, such studies must rely on *sampling-studying a* comparatively small number of individuals from a population with the hope that the characteristics exhibited by a sample accurately represent those of the whole population. Whether his hope is realized depends upon the adequacy of sampling. Sampling methods vary with insect species, habitat, and the kind of information to be derived from the sample. Many sophisticated sampling techniques have been developed, and elaborate statistical analyses have been made easier by the use of computers. It is necessary that population studies be made over several generations. Theoretical studies are especially valuable in developing descriptive and predictive models of population performance; however, as with laboratory studies they tend to represent oversimplifications and must rely on assumptions that may or may not apply in natural situations. Fortunately, modern computers allow evaluation of increasingly complex models. All three approaches to studying populations have some value and definite limitations. Increased understanding of populations will no doubt result from an amalgamation of ideas generated by all three approaches.

Environmental Components and Populations

Population Growth

The section establishes a simple, but useful model, which helps in thinking about population growth. Assume we are evaluating the repopulation of an area from which all members of a given species have been previously removed. Since populations under ideal conditions have the capacity for exponential increase, the first step is to consider an equation that describes exponential increase. Such increase in a population after time *t is* described by the equation $N_t = N_o e^{rt}$ where N_o = population size after time t : N_o = initial population size: e = base of natural logarithms (a constant: approximately 2.7183): and r = The instantaneous rate of increase per individual in the population, which is the difference between the instantaneous birth rate b (*natality*) and death rated (*mortality*). Thus $r = b - d$ If b is greater than d, then the population is growing: if b *is* equal to d, the population is stable ($r = 0$): *if* b is less than d, the population is decreasing in size. A shows the shape of a curve that would be generated by the exponential population growth equation if r remained at a constant positive value. The population size increases in an increasing rate.

Under natural conditions. r does not remain constant, being subject to strong environmental influence. For example, r may well decrease with increasing population density. Competition for food and shelter, rates of predation, and invasion by parasites and parasitoids are examples of environmental factors that may increase as population density, increases. Looking again at the equation for exponential growt, but with r decreasing at a constant rate as population size increases. In this case, rate of population growth decreases gradually and approaches a point where it levels off. The population size at which the leveling off occurs is called the *carrying capacity* (K) of the environment. This curve is commonly called the *logistic model* of population growth.

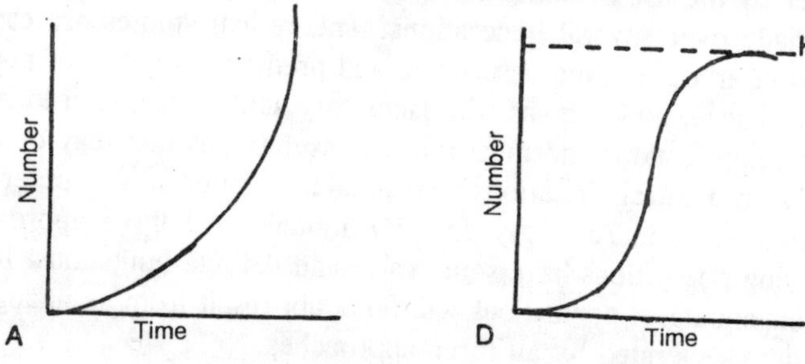

Fig. 11.2 . Population growth curves. A- Exponential population growth. B. Logistic population growth.

Although the logistic model may come close to describing popu-lation growth in some cases, it is severely limited because the assumptions upon which it is bases are rarely true in reality. Among these assumptions are equality of reproductive potential among all individuals of the population, an even age distribution with a constant proportion of individuals breeding all the time, reproduction uninfluenced by climate or other factors, and no changes in carrying capacity.

In addition to birth and death rates, emigration and immigration also influence population growth. Birth rate, death rate, and emi-gration-immigration rates are themselves influenced by a variety of factors. For example, weather, in particular temperature, influences all these rates. In addition, it can be argued that any factor that exerts an influence on one of these rates influences the others as well. For example, an environmental change, say in temperature, might cause higher mortality among insects in one stage than in another or in insects of a certain age. If this age-specific mortality happened to occur in ovipositing females, one could say that both the birth and death rates were being affected. Among the major factors that influence birth rate are average fecundity of the females, average fertility of the females, and the sex ratio. Average fecundity represents the average number of offspring that would be produced by each female under ideal environmental conditions: average fertility represents the average number of off-spring actually produced, the difference between fecundity and fertility being related to such environmental factors as quality and quantity of available food, weather components, and population density. The sex ratio is the fraction of the total population that is female. In most insects the sex ratio is 0.5, but in species where parthenogenesis occurs there may be drastic deviations from this 50-50 balance of sexes. As with fecundity and fertility, the sex ratio may be influenced by several environmental factors.

The death rate is affected by such factors as adverse weather conditions, temperature extremes in particular; predators, parasites, and pathogens; accidents; low vitality; food shortage, and lack of adequate shelter. The carrying capacity (K) of the environment also varies with many factors (e.g., availability of food, extent of predation).

Life-system Concept

Several different models have been proposed to explain the numerical behaviour of insect populations. As previously mentioned, Clark *et al.* provide a useful integrating concept, i.e., the "life-system." Our objective here is to elaborate somewhat on this concept.

Two kinds of *"ecological events"* occur as a result of the interaction of the *"codetenninants of abundance"* (*i.e.*, the "subject population" and its *"effective environment"*): *primary* and *secondary*. Primary events are those directly involved in the demographic equation explained above (i.e., births, deaths, emigrations and immigrations). Secondary, events are those that exert an influence on the magnitude, extent, frequency, or duration of primary events (quality and quantity of available food, weather components etc.). Primary and secondary ecological events may be additive or subtractive. Processes that act in a positive way on a population are additive, for example , immigration and weather conditions that reduce populations of natural enemies. The'planing of a monoculture, such as corn, is an additive process relative to species, such as the European corn borer, that thrive on this crop, as well as to insects that are parasitoids or predators of the corn-eating species. Subtractive processes (e.g., emigration and adverse weather conditions) have a negative effect on a population, causing the death of individuals and/or a decrease in the nature of progeny produced. The planting of corn would constitute a subtractive process for insects that were originally present, if they could not survive in a corn agroecosystem.

Additive and subtractive ecological events may be either density independent or density-related (i.e., the effects of the action of a given ecological process on a population may or may not be related to the density of that population). Subtractive density- related processes are of special interest since they may act, in some instances, as regulators of the level of abundance; that is, as a given population increases, a point is reached where further growth is inhibited by some factor.

Long-term Numerical Changes

Over the long term, as populations interact with their effective environments, there are fluctuations , in population size. Some populations fluctuate irregularly apparently in response to changes in environmental components such as food supply and weather. Other populations tend to fluctuate regularly about a mean level of abundance. As mentioned above, this may be a reflection of the action of some subtractive density related process that is serving to regulate the level of abundance. Insects with a reproductivee period restricted to particular time or times of year tend to display regular, seasonal population peaks associated with reproduction.

It has become more and more apparent that, in a given life system, certain "key" ecological processes with age-specific effects determine major population trends, while other processes exert some-what lesser effects. Elaborate "multifactor" studies have been carried out for a number of insect species. The objective of these studies has been to derive "life tables" that contain information as to population densities' at different times during the life cycle and age-specific information regarding the "key" ecological processes that account for mortality. The development of a truly representative life table requires the sampling of a population over many generations. Another approach that has been used where preliminary studies have indicated a few key influences involved in a life system in the *key factor method*. In this type of study population density is measured at only one point in. each generation. This approach requires much less sampling and enables investigators to concentrate on critical periods of time in the life cycle when the "key" process or processes are active without spending much time on other periods.

ENVIRONMENTAL COMPONENTS

Various components of the environment that have been found to be significant in their influence on insect or other animal or plant populations are discussed in this section. Any combination, or all of these components, may at some time act to varying degrees upon a given population. When one of them approaches or exceeds the species-specific limit of tolerance, whether expressed in terms of survival, development, fecundity, and so on, it becomes a limiting factor. That is, it becomes the environmental component that is directly responsible for limiting the extent of survival, degree or rate of development, fecundity, and so on. In the field it is often very difficult to pinpoint a given environmental component as a limiting factor since, obviously, several components are likely to be interacting to produce the "effective environment" of any population. For the same reason, it is difficult to relate studies of environmental effects under the carefully controlled

TABLE 11.1

LIFE TABLE FOR SECOND GENERATION OF THE DIAMONDBACK MOTH ON EARLY CABBAGE

Age interval	*Numbers Per 100*	*Mortality*		
		Causative Factors	*Per 100 Plants*	*Per cent*
Eggs	1580	Infertility	25	1.6
LarvaePeriod 1	1555	Rainfall	1199	77.1
Period 2	356	Rainfall	36	10.1
		Parasitism by M. plutellae	52	14.6
Period 3	268	Parasitism byHinsularis	69	25.7
Pupae	199	Paratism by D. plutellae	92	46.2
Moths	107	Sex (49.5%)	1	1.0
Females × 2	106	Photoperiod	78	73.6
"Normal" females × 2	28	Adult mortality	20	71.4
Generation totals			1572	99.5

conditions of a laboratory to what actually occurs in the field. Another problem further complicates the picture. Environmental components, in particular temperature, moisture, and light, are not uniform throughout an ecosystem. For example, the temperature of one part of a plant may be quite different from that of another part. Thus, at least in many instances, to obtain a truly accurate picture, one must measure the temperature in specific parts of an ecosystem (e.g., bottom side of a leaf). Realization of this problem has led to the development of the concept of "microenvironment," which implies the recognition of distinct horizontal and vertical (spatial) and temporal differences in environmental components within an ecosystem. Figure 11.2 portarys such differences in terms of relative humidity and water vapour pressure at different levels above the ground (vertical) and at 'different tiltes during the 24-hour cycle (temporal).

Weather

Weather results from the combined action and influence of all the physical factors of the environment at any given time. It varies continually hroughout days, weeks, months and years and exerts an influence on insect abundance, longevity, rate of development, and so on, from one year or season to the next. Climate, on the other hand, is the average course or condition of the weather in a locality over a period of several years. Weather changes rapidly, often violently, while climate tends to remain pretty much the same or change very slowly over a period of many years. The main elements of weather are temperature moisture, and light, although several other physical environmental factors are known or thought to exert a degree of influence on insects. Various materials and methods used in measuring and interpreting physical aspects of the environment are described in Platt and Grdffths.

Temperature

Insects are basically poikilothermic- that is, their body temperature tends to be the same as ambient temperature. However, this net necessarily mean that an insect's body temperature is always the sanle as that of the environment. For every insect species there is a fairly well-defined range of temperature within which it is able to survive' Exposure to temperatures above the high or below the low extremes of this range results in death. The range of tolerable temperatures, varies from species to species. Within a species, and with the physiological state of an individual. Thus, there are times or stages during the life cycle when an individual may be able to survive much lower temperatures that at other times would kill it. exposure to many insects are able to survive much lower temperatures For example in the fall and winter than in the spring or summer. Tropical spepes are generally less tolerant of cold than those in temperate zones. Terrestrial insects usually have a somewhat wider range of teloperature tolerance than do aquatic insects, and not surprisingly the range of temperature variation in terrestrial habitats is usually substantially greater than that in aquatic habitats.

The range of survival relative to temperature for most insects probably lies somewhere between 0 and 50°C, although it is likely that no one species can thrive throughout this entire range. There are, however, exceptional species that are able to survive at temperatures well-beyond these extremes. For instance, some dipteran larvae apparently thrive at temperatures of 55°C or higher, while certain species of beetles go through their entire life cycle in ice grottos at temperatures slightly below and slightly above 0°C. The firebrat, *Thennobia dornestica*, can live indefinitely at temperatures of 42°C and higher. It typically inhabits such places as ovens, hotwater pipes, and similar *"hot"* environments. If insects of a given species are exposed to a temperature gradient, they will move until they reach the *"preferred temperature,"* at which point they will tend to congregate. Near the upper and lower tolerable limits of temperature, insects become dormant- In the range between these limits, they are active.

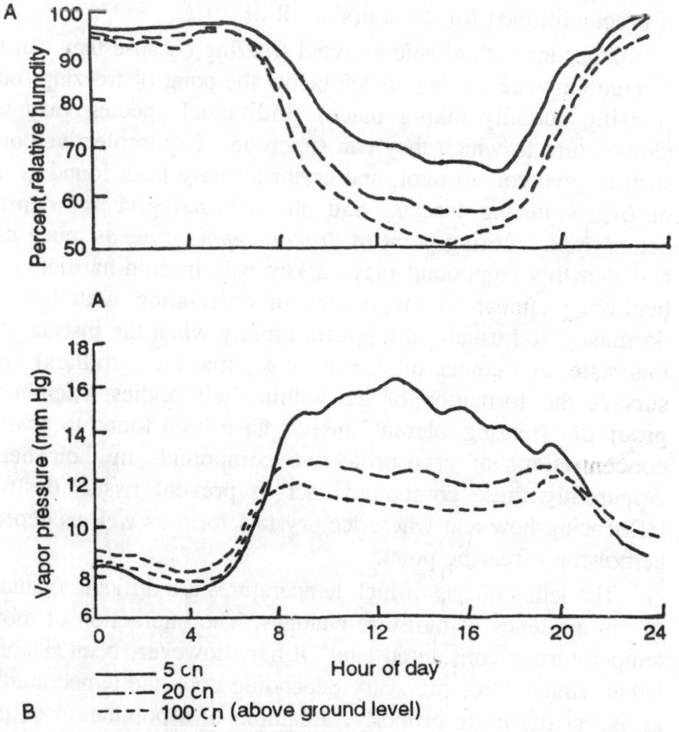

Fig. 11.3. Changes in relative humidity (A) and water vapor pressure (B) at different levels above the ground and at different times of day.

The actual cause or causes of death at the limits of the temperature range are not clear. At the lower the submicroscopic structures of cells may be disrupted by the formation of ice crystals or the metabolic balance may be thrown off. At the upper limit protein denaturation, metabolic imbalance, disruption of ordered molecules, and desiccation are likely to be involved. The phenomenon of insect cold-hardiness has been reviewed by Salt Asahina, and briefly by Baust and Morrissey. Downes discusses adaptations of insects in the Arctic. Many insects that become dormant in temperate regions are able to survive low temperatures for considerable periods of time. Most of these insects are dormant in a stage that is more cold hardly than the preceding one. Some are capable of long exposure to low temperatures and display a certain amount of cold acclimation, but succumb to freezing of the body fluids. For example, *Aedesaegypti* larvae reared at 30°C are killed by exposure to -0.5°C for 17 hours, but survive such an exposure if preconditioned for 24 hours at 18 or 20°C.

Other insects are able to avoid freezing because they can withstand supercooling (i.e., being cooled below the point of freezing, but without freezing actually taking place). Individual species vary as to the temperature to which they can supercool. Cryoprotective com-pounds such as glycerol, sorbitol, and erythritol have been found in the tissues of overwintering insects. Salt showed that glycerol depresses the hemolymph freezing point of *Bracon cephi* larvae as much as 17.5°C and that this compound plays a key role in cold-hardiness. Glycerol begins to appear in the tissues in correlation with the advent of dormancy and usually disappears rapidly when the insects come out of this state. A number of insects (e.g., many caterpillars) are able to survive the formation of ice within their bodies. Members of this group of "freezing-tolerant" insects have been found to possess higher concentrations of cryo-protective compounds in their hemolymph. Apparently these compounds act to prevent tissue destruction by influencing how and where ice crystals form as well as depressing the hemolymph freezing point.

The lethal effects of high temperatures are difficult to study because of the influence of moisture changes. The interaction of moisture and temperature is considered later. It has, however, been established that lethal temperatures may vary depending upon the temperature to which an insect or, more properly, a sample of a population of insects has been exposed previously. Such high tempe-rature acclimation has been demonstrated in *Calliphora and Phormia* (Diptera, Calliphoridae), and other. Acclimation to both high and low temperatures may or may not occur in the same species. Like cold acclimation, high- temperature acclimation is likely to be of value of insects under natural circums-tances, since seasonal and daily high temperatures are usually preceded by a gradual transition from somewhat lower temperatures. Acclimation at both ends of an insect's tolerable range of temperatures maybe looked upon as promoting the insect's survival against the effects of extreme daily and seasonal temperature fluctuations.

Temperature also effects the duration of life. For, example; a clear relationship exists between the duration of life in male and female *Drosophila subobscura* and temperature. Temperature may also affect survival by influencing the rate of utilization of food reserves when food is present in limited quantities. This is particularly evident in blood sucking insects such as the tsetse flies. *Glossina spp*. (Diptera, Muscidae), which depend on stored food reserves between meals. Increases in temperature shorten the survival period between meals. Obviously, if a fly uses up its reserves from one meal before it is able to obtain another, it will perish.

Temperature exerts a strong influence on the reproduction and rate of development of insects. As with lethal limits of temperature, insects also have definite tolerable ranges of temperature in terms of reproduction and development beyond which neither wall occur. For example, the temperature range in which the eggs of the beetle *Ptinus* (Coleoptera, Ptinidae) will develop is between S and 28°C. *Pediculus* (Anoplura, Pediculidae) fails to lay eggs below 25°C. For a given species the range in which development will occur is probably somewhat broader than that in which reproduction will be successful. Within the tolerable ranges, egg development, oviposition rate, and the rate of larval and pupal development usually increase with increasing temperature. For example, the duration of pupal life of the mealworm beetle, *Teneibio monitor* (Coleoptera, Tenebrionidae), is decreased by 180 hours (from 320 to 140) as the temperature is increased by 12°C (from 21 to 33°C).

The specific ranges of tolerance and influence of temperature on rates of reproduction and development vary among members of the same species. In addition, the span of ranges varies from species to species. Within each range of tolerance is an optimum zone in which the rates of reproduction and development are maximal. For example, the oviposition rate of *Toxoptera graminum* (Hemiptera-Homoptera, Aphididae) increases with increasing temperature to a maximum of approximately 25°C and then falls off. Most laboratory studies of the effects of temperature on reproduction and development have been carried out at constant temperature. The results of such studies do not necessarily reflect what would occur under uncontrolled field conditions.

Periodically fluctuating temperature, which is characteristic of field conditions, tends to induce higher rates of development than would occur at constant temperature. For example, "Grasshopper eggs kept at a variable temperature showed an average acceleration of 38.6% and nymphs an acceleration of 12% over development at comparable constant temperature."

The distribution, horizontal and vertical, of an insect species is often greatly affected by temperature. In temperate zones the northern extreme of a given insect's distribution is commonly deter-mined by low-temperature extremes. When northern limits are determined in this manner, there is usually a zone somewhat below the extreme limits in which the overwintering stage is killed but which is repopulated during the warm season. Proceeding southward from such an area, a greater and greater percentage of the overwintering individuals survive. For example, the corn earworm, *Heliothis zea* (Lepidoptera, Noctuidae), in eastern North America must become completely reestablished during the warm season each year in Canada and to a progressively lesser extent in the United States proceeding southward. The ability to become cold-hardly also plays an important role in determining the northernmost

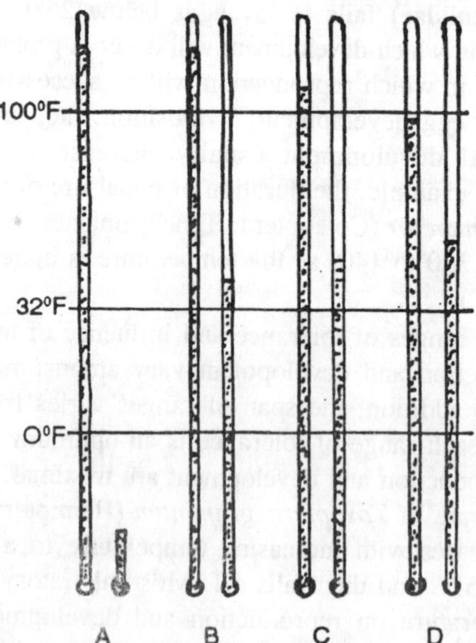

Fig. 11.4. Tolerable temperature ranges for various aspects of a hypothetical insect's life. The left-hand thermometer of each pair registers the maximum tolerable , temperature: the right-hand one, the minimum tolerable temperature.

limits of distribution. The number of generations per year often varies between the northern and southern regions of an insect's range. For example, the corn earworm completes a generation approximately every 36 days as long as weather permits. Thus in its northern range it may only complete two or three generations per year, whereas in the southern portion it may complete several more, breeding the year round. One would expect a gradation in the actual number of generations between the northern and southern extremes of the range. Temperature also affects, to a greater or lesser extent, the rate of dispersal of an insect species.

We have already seen the various ways temperature influences insects. We now want to consider the actual temperature of an insect and the factors that may influence it. We have established the idea that the temperature, or any of several other parameters, may vary substantially even within a small area (e.g., different parts of a plant). Likewise, the temperature of an insect in one part of a habitat may not be anywhere near the same as one in another and may not be the same as the ambient temperature. On the other hand, the temperature of an insect under controlled laboratory conditions usually reflects the ambient temperature. The temperature of an inset, depends on the sources of heat gain and loss operating under a given set of circumstances. The major sources of heat gain are solar radiation and metabolic, heat. Solar radiation may cause the temperature of an exposed insect to be significantly different from the ambient temperature. The effect of solar radiation on the temperature of an insect is influenced by such factors as size, larger insects being more affected than smaller ones; colour, darker colours absorbing more radiation than lighter ones; shape, the more surface directly exposed to radiation, the greater the absorption; and orientation with respect to the sun, some insects orienting such that a large or small amount of body surface is exposed.

Metabolic heat results from the breakdown of complex organic molecules. Part of this energy is stored in the high-energy bonds of ATP; the remainder is released as heat. In the absence of solar radiation, this is the sole source of heat and can be quite significant in heat balance, particularly during flight or in clusters of gregarious forms. Sources of heat loss from an insect include evaporation, con-vection, conduction, and long-wave radiation. Evaporation of water from an insect has a cooling effect since heat is required to propel a molecule of water from the body surface. Evaporation is the major cause of heat loss in the absence of solar radiation. As stated already that the rate of evaporation of water from an insect is dependent partly on the size of the insect. Since smaller insects have a larger ratio of surface area to volume, they have a grater tendency to lose water through evaporation than larger ones. The other causes of heat loss — convection, conduction, and long-wave radiation - are significant in the absence of solar radiation when the temperature differential between an insect and its surrounding is usually greater than in the presence of solar radiation. Air movement may accentuate the heat loss by contributing to the maintenance of a steep gradient between an insect and its surroundings. Dense covering of hairs and scales, on the other hand, may serve as an insulating layer and retard heat loss.

Moisture

The wave content of insects varies from less than 50% to more than 90% of total body weight. Variation occurs both between different species and between different life stages of the same species. Soft-bodied insects such as caterpillars tend to have comparatively large amounts of water in their tissues, whereas many insects with hard bodies (i.e., relatively thick cuticles) tend to have somewhat lesser amounts. Active stages commonly have a higher water content than dormant stages. In most instances it is critical that water content be maintained within certain limits, which are influenced by several other environmental factors (e.g., temperature, pressure, air movement,

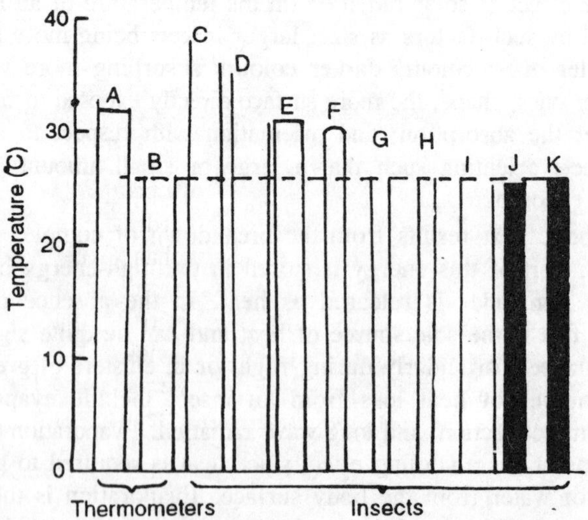

Fig. 11.5. Effect of radiation on the body temperature of selected insects. A. Thermometer painted black. B. Air temperature.

available surface water). If the limits of tolerancee under a given set of circumstances are exceeded, an insect either perishes or many of its activities are seriously impaired.

Environmental moisture factors of major significance are preci-pitation, humidity, condensation, and available surface water. Rainfall is the most common and widespread form of fluid precipitation. Snow is the most common form of solid precipitation: hail and sleet are less common forms. The annual and seasonal amounts of precipitation are primarily determined by the movements of large masses of air and by topographical characteristics. Thus, there are very "wet" and very "dry" regions and innumerable gradations between. Humidity refers to the amount of water vapor in the air and depends on temperature and atmospheric pressure. Condensation (dew, fog, and white frost) occurs when the atmos- phere becomes saturated with water vapor. Saturation is the result of the relative humidity approaching 100% or the temperature dropping below the dew point (the point at which the relative humidity becomes 100%).

Available surface water is related to all the other moisture factors and to the nature of the substrate (soil, leaf surface, bark, and so on). It is well-known that soils vary in their water-holding capacity and the rapidity with which water runs off or soaks in. All these moisture factors influence the water balance of terrestrial insects. What, then ore the environmental factors that influence, the water balance of aquatic insects? The "wetness" or "dryness" of an aquatic environment is a function of the osmotic pressure. Thus insects living in fresh water must cope with a comparatively "wet" environment; those in brackish and salt water (e.g., many of the salt-marsh forms, such as the mosquito*Aedes sollicitans*) are living in a very "dry" environment

Compounding the water-balance problem in insects is the fact that under other than carefully controlled laboratory conditions the moisture factors continually change. Obviously, an insect living in a given locale must be able to survive the extremes of these changes. As with temper-ature and the other weather parameters, one must think in terms of microenvironments. For example, the amount of rainfall measured at the edge of a forest hardly reflects the actual amount of water reaching an insect living in a tree hole or on the underside of a leaf. All the moisture factors vary both temporally and spatially. For example, relative humidity varies with location, time of day or year, topography, Vegetation, and so on, and commonly tends to be comparatively high during the night and lower during the day. It may also be different at different heights above the ground.

As with temperature, there is an optimal moisture range in which a given species thrives. Mortality may occur under conditions of excessively low environmental moisture content for the active stages of most insects, and under conditions of excessively high moisture for many Death under very dry conditions is generally due to content excessive water loss. Under conditions of excessive moisture the causes of death are more variable and may be direct or indirect. For example, drawing may be the result of excessive moisture, as is the case with overwintering pupae of the moth *Heliothis zea* during wet years in with the eve southeastern United States. Survival is indirectly affected by very wet conditions that favour the spread of viral, fungal, and bacterial diseases and by any negative effects the excessive moisture might have on the, food of a given insect species.

The fall webworm. *Hyphantria cunea*, the armyworm, *Pseudaletia unipuncta*, and the gypsy moth, *Porthetria dispar*, succumb most readily to viruses when the weather is warm and the humidity is high. Whether

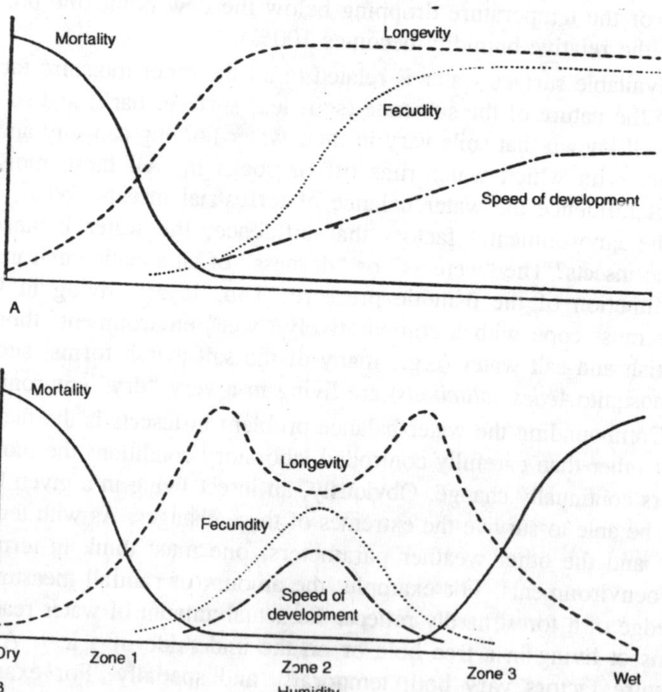

Fig. 11.6. Influence of humidity on various aspects of a hypothetical insect's life. A. Insect not harmed by high humidity. B. Insect adversely affected by high humidity. Zone 1. lethal dryness: Zone 2. favourable moistness: Zone 3. lethal wetness.

high humidity affects the host or the development of the pathogen is not clear. However, many viruses do not develop rapidly unless temperatures of 21 to 29.4°C and relative humidities of 50 to 60% are experienced.

If excessive moisture does not kill an insect, it may seriously affect the length of its life. For example, newly emerged adult migratory *locusts*, *Locusta migratoria*, live longer the lower the humidity. Since environmental moisture content may determine survival. It is commonly a major factor along with temperature in determining the geographic distribution of an insect species.

The High Plains grasshopper reproduces and develops in an area of about 50,000 square miles, and from this center the adults may spread over an area perhaps twice as large. The region of endemic infestation lies in the short-grass belt of the High Plains where the average winter temperature generally falls between 28° and 38°F and the average annual precipitation ranges from about 15 to 18 inches. That the High Plains grasshopper flourishes in only a part of the short-grass belt indicates that climatic conditions, rather than host availability, limit the range of the insect.

Extremes of environmental moisture content directly influence many of the activities of insects, including feeding, reproduction, and development. Spruce budworm larvae stop feeding when the air becomes saturated with water, and the tsetse fly, *Glossina tachinoides*, does not feed on its vertebrate hosts when the relative humidity is above 88%. Newly emerged adult migratory locusts do not produce eggs below about 40% relative humidity. Generally low humidity adversely affect the rates of oviposition which increase as humidity increases. The rate of development may be decreased by extremes of moisture content or development may be halted altogether. Under very moist conditions silkworm larvae fail to pupate. According to Bursell the incubation time for eggs of the spider beetle *Ptinus*, under a constant temperature of 20°C *is. 15* days at 30% relative humidity and 10 days at 90%. He further points out that generally higher humidities are more favourable for embryonic stages than low humidities. Two sets of hypothetical curves summarize the points made in this and the preceding paragraphs.

The effects of environmental moisture content are often strongly modified by other weather factors. Temperature and moisture, in particular, interact to a large extent in their effects. Thus temperature exerts a relatively great effect on insects at the extremes of moisture conditions and *vice versa*. For example, the boll weevil is more tolerant of higher temperatures at comparatively low humidities than at high humidities. Another good example of the interactions of temperature and moisture is their combined effect on the rate of development of insects. As mentioned earlier, air movement, atmospheric pressure availability of surface water, and other factors may also influence the effects of moisture conditions on insects.

Insects are adapted in a number of ways and to varying degrees to cope with changes in environmental moisture conditions. Dormant stages are often well suited for exposure to drought. The eggs of many species of mosquitoes (*Aedes*, *Psorophora* and others) can withstand prolonged drying in air. Many insects become dormant in response to different environmental conditions and in this state are able to withstand long periods of drought. For example, the potato beetle.*Leptinotarsa decemlineata*, becomes quiescent in response to dryness and can survive in this resting, desiccated state for months. Such a response ensures that when eggs are laid, the larvae will be exposed to environmental conditions more favourable for'survival. Hinton describes a chironomid (Diptera, Chironomidae) larvae, *Polypedilum vanderplanki*, that is able to survive almost complete dehydration for several years. These insects show no visible signs of metabolic activity and are described as being in a state of *cryptobiosis*.

Most insects offset the influence of dryness and other factors promoting water loss by drinking water or taking it in with food.

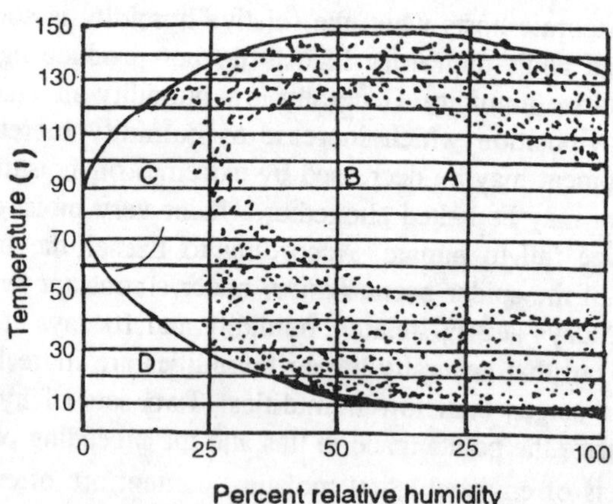

Fig. 11.7. Interrelationship of temperature and, humidity as they affect the rate of development of a hypothetical insect. A. Region of most rapid development. B. Region of favourable development. C. Region of retarded development. D. Region of no development.

Time is important in the survival of active insects under adverse moisture conditions. Many can survive extensive desiccation for extended periods. Some insects that live under extremely dry conditions, such as mealworm beetle larvae (*Tenebno molitor*, Tenebrionidae, Coleoptera), are able to utilize metabolic water (i.e., water that becomes available as a result of the metabolic breakdown of food materials). Other insects, such as some Thysanura (silverfish and relatives), are able to absorb moisture directly from the atmosphere.

Light

Light is of direct important to insects more as an environmental point of reference than as a survival factor since its parameters (Photoperiod, illuminance, wavelength etc.) are more or less constant and it is seldom, if ever, directly lethal under natural conditions. In the nonequatorial region of the earth there is a regular change in photoperiod due to the tilt of the earth's axis of rotation 23 1/2° from vertical to the imaginary plane that passes through the sun and the earth's orbit. Regular change in photoperiod serves as an annual clock for insects and is used by many to maintain synchrony with the seasons and their host plants. Photoperiod is one of the major stimuli that induces diapause. The daily cycle of dark and light with crepuscular (dawn and dusk) periods in between also serves as a clock by which the feeding, mating etc., are regulated. As with temperature and moisture, the. reactions of insects to photoperiod and other light parameters vary both among different species and among different life stages of the same species.

Different wavelengths of reflected light are commonly utilized by plant-feeding insects in host location. The position of the sun and degree of polarization of light in different parts of the sky are important to many insects in orientation and navigation. The effect of light on both aquatic and terrestrial plants may indirectly influence the activities of insects. For example, the amount of light reaching submerged aquatic vegetation will affect oxygen- generating photosynthesis and in turn affect the oxygen concentration in the water, which then influences aquatic insects.

Other factors

Other environmental factors that under some circumstances influence insects include currents in air and water, gases dissolved in water, air composition, electricity and ionizing radiation.

Air and water currents are determined to a large extent by physiographic conditions. Air movement is modified by trees and other vegetation and by anything else that may block or redirect it. Currents in water are influenced by such factors as water volume, slope of stream bed, and temperature differences between the surface and various depths. Wind is a very effective agent in the distribution of insects-aphids, leafhoppers, and others being blown for hundreds or even thousands of miles. Air movement may be directly responsible for the death of insects in two ways. First, severe wind and heavy rain together may cause mortality. Second, movement of air above a surface where evaporation is occurring (e.g., insect cuticle) increases the gradient of water vapor concentration and hence tends to increase the rate of evaporation. Other factors being constant, the rate of evaporation is proportional to air movement. On the other hand, air movement may be beneficial if humidity is high.

Water currents often determine which species of insects will live in a given area. For example, the various general of mayflies (Ephe-meroptera) may be classified into still or rapid-water forms. The legs and bodies of these insects are appropriately adapted (e.g., legs capable of clinging and streamlined bodies associated with fast-moving water). Black fly larvae fasten themselves to stones or other stationary material in the water. Several caddisflies (Trichoptera) attach their cases to sub-merged objects. Many aquatic insects (e.g., mosquito larvae) are unable to survive in moving water. Another important aspect of currents in the aquatic environment involves the circulation of dissolved gases, salts and nutrients. The insect fauna in a given location are often determined to a large extent by the amount of dissolved oxygen. For instance, caddisfly and mayfly larvae may be found under conditions of relatively high oxygen concentration, midge and black fly larvae (Diptera; Chiro-nomidae and Simuliidae, respectively) are somewhat lower concentrations, and certain mosquito (Diptera, Culicidae) and other fly larvae at very low concentrations. Dissolved oxygen is determined by water movement, wind, water splashing, photo-synthesis in aquatic plants, and so on. Other dissolved gases that may be of importance are carbon dioxide (a highly soluble waste product of cellular respiration) and nitrogen.

The gaseous composition of air is remarkably constant and is probably not a significant limiting factor for terrestrial insects and other animals. However, the gas content in cavities in flowers may be quite different from the surrounding air, and a large number of insects live in such cavities. Further, the composition of air in the middle of a thick canopy of vegetation is not necessarily the same as in open air, nor is it necessarily the same throughout the day since temperature and the photosynthetic activities of plants vary during the course of a day. For example, measurement of the carbon dioxide concentration above fields of wheat and clover at different times of day revealed that carbon dioxide decreased toward the middle of a day and reached a maximum between midnight and 6 a.m.

Electrical factors have seldom been taken into account, although they may have a direct effect on insects. Under natural conditions, the ionization of air and atmospheric potential may vary and may affect certain activities of insects. For example, the ionization of air has been found to modify the flight activity of a blow fly. *Calliphora sp.* An increase in the number of ions causes a temporary increase in activity; for example, flight in *Drosophila is* abruptly reduced for a short period of time by sudden exposures to a potential gradient of 10-62 volts/cm. Under natural conditions the atmospheric potential falls rapidly between the ground and a few meters above the ground.

Electromagnetic radiation bombard the earth continuously. Radiation in the visible and near visible region plays many important roles in life processes; for example, it affects photosynthesis and is involved in vision. Radiation of shorter, more energetic wavelengths also influences living organisms. This highly energetic radiation arises from cosmic, solar, and terrestrial sources. Most radiation from extra-terrestrial sources is absorbed or reflected by the atmosphere and deflected by the magnetic fields, but a significant amount gets through none the less. Cosmic radiation probably varies considerably from time to time as a result function of changes in the earth's magnetic fields. The occurrence of nearby supernovae (exploding stars) and so on. Such changes in the intensity of cosmic radiation may have played (and may continue to play) a major role in biological evolution by inducing drastic increases in mutation rates at times during the earth's history. Most terrestrial sources of highly energetic radiation occur in trace amounts throughout the earth's crust. However, since the beginning of this century, man has learned how to release immense quantities of radiation by "splitting the atom." The inherent dangers of this activity are well-knows. Entomological interest in high-energy radiation stems from

1. The usefulness of radiation as a basic research tool, for example, radioisotopes are used as tracers in the study of biochemistry, and radiation is used to induce physiological morphological, and genetic changes with the hope of further understanding biological processes.

2. The usefulness of insects as model biological systems in evaluating the harmful effects of radiation.

3. The applied value of high-energy radiation in inducing sterilization or deleterious genetic changes in insect pests. For information and literature sources regarding the influence of high-energy radiation on insects.

FOOD

This section deals with the ways insects may be influenced by variations in quantity and quality of food resources. As a group, insects are essentially omnivorous. As individual species, however, they exhibit much variation, some being extremely selective and perhaps relying on only one or a few kinds of food (including host plants and animals and prey) and others taking advantage of many kinds of food. Whatever, the habits of a given species may be, abundance and quality of food may play an important role in survival, longevity, distribution, reproduction, speed of development, and so on.

Quantity of Food

Animal populations that consume all or most of their food resources are few compared with those that do not. Thus "absolute" shortage of food is probably not an important limiting factor for most populations. However, such shortages may occur in patches throughout the distribution of a given population. In these circumstances there is an "effective" shortage of food.

There are many possible causes of "absolute" and "effective" shortages of food. Among them are large numbers of individuals per unit quantity of food (intraspecific competition), more than one species consuming the same food material (s) (interspecific competition), species that influence the food of other species Without consuming it, and other environmental factors. The first instance might occur, for example, among insects during the actively growing larval stages. When there is a relatively small number of individuals per unit quantity of food, there is enough for all to grow to adulthood. However, as numbers increase, a point is reached where there is insufficient food for all individuals present to grow to maturity, only those that develop most rapidly reach adulthood, the slower developers do not. Obviously, two or more species consuming the same food will reduce the total amount available for any one of them.

Species that do not actually consume the food supply of another may exert a positive or negative influence on that supply. For example, many of the sanitary practices of humans, such as incineration of garbage and treatment of waste materials, destroy the food supply of many insect species, especially cockroaches and flies. On the other hand, failure to carry out these procedures increases the same food supply, enhancing the survival of insects that thrive in such materials. Microbes that are pathogens of an insect that is the prey of another may reduce the population size of the prey species sufficiently to influence the predator species. An epizootic of the fungus *Entomophthora so* reduced the numbers of the caterpillar *Plutella* that the predators (*Angitis* spp. and others) suffered severely from a shortage of food where it had been adundant before the outbreak of disease.

A similar relationship may exist between a plant species, the insects that feed on it, and microorganisms that are pathogenic to members of the plant species. In fact, any environmental factor, biotic or abiotic, that has the effect of reducing populations of particular plants or animals will probably cause the reduction not only of animal populations that utilize these plants or animals for food but also of the parasites and predators of these animals. Monophagoas insects are more likely to be affected by such reductions in food supply that polyphagous species. Examples of causes of "effective" shortages of food include accidental separation from the food source, certain behavioural traits, and effects of feeding activities on animal hosts. It is not difficult to imagine an ectoparasite starving to death when separated from its host. Tsetse flies (Diptera, Muscidae) remain close to tall bushes and will feed on vertebrates that are in the vicinity of these bushes, but will not feed on the same or other vertebrates in open grassland Where a single or a few blood-feeding insects might successfully feed to satiation on a host, larger numbers may elicit an avoidance or destructive response on the part of the host, resulting in very few, if any, successfully feeding. Thus, although a host may have ample blood for several hundred tsetse flies, mosquitoes, and so on, it may tolerate the feeding activities of only a small fraction of that number.

An absolute shortage of food could result from the food plant or anima being completely destroyed within a localized region, but it is unlikely that total destruction of a food plant or animal could occur in this way. In response to a food shortage, individuals may survive but be much smaller than they would have been with more food. However, as numbers of individuals increase, a point is eventually reached where fewer and fewer individuals are able to survive, and finally none survive to adulthood. Another frequently encountered result of food shortage is cannibalistic behaviour. One well-known species in which cannibalism is known to occur is the confused flour beetle. *Tribolium confusum* (Coleoptera, Tenebrionidae). Cannibalism may also occur when there is overcrowding, accidental injury to an individual, or during the vulnerable period immediately following ecdysis but before the cuticle has become sclerotized (i.e., the teneral state). Several adaptations that promote survival under conditions of food shortage have evolved, particularly in response to regularly occurring shortages. Probably one of the most important is migration. Insects that respond to food shortages by migrating are much more likely to discover a fresh food source than those that do not. Many adult insects, fruit flies and house flies. For example, lay their eggs in situations where the food supply is in excess relative to the numbers of individuals feeding on it. The behaviour of the adults in egg deposition essentially guarantees abundant food for their offspring. Polyphagy on the part of a parasite, predator, or herbivorous insect also helps ensure against the likelihood of being exposed to dangerous food shortages.

Quality of Food

Egg production and larval development are especially susceptible to variations in the nutritive quality of food. Survival, longevity, and size may also be strongly influenced by the quality of available food. Many insect species store sufficient nutrients during the larval stage to accomplish adult activities (copulation, egg production, and oviposition). The adult lives of these species are of comparatively short duration, and they commonly do not feed at all. For example, mayflies (Ephemeroptera), which live only long enough to copulate and deposit their eggs, rely entirely on larval reserves. In other species, larvae may store nutrients sufficient for egg production, but the adults must ingest water and carbohydrates to survive. Many mosquitoes and other true flies (Diptera) fall into a third category in which adults usually need to ingest a complete diet (especially protein) in order to sustain life and produce eggs. For mosquitoes and other blood-feeding forms, blood meals afford the necessary nutrients. The queens of the social Hymenoptera and termites also fall into this category. These insects lay eggs for almost all of their adult lives and require food constantly. Commonly, this food is provided by a worker caste, which in turn may obtain food by foraging.

An example of the effect of quality of food on the rate of development is given by Folsom and Wardle. Both bananas and horse manure are suitable foods for house fly maggots. However, at approximately 21°C, the maggots complete their development on horse manure one to nearly two weeks sooner than one bananas. The quality of ingested food in some instances influences the outcome of development; for example, the differences between workers and queen honey bees depend entirely on the diet that each receives during larval development. Both receive the same food for the first two days of larval life — royal jelly, a substance secreted by glands that open into the mouths of workers. After the third day, larvae destined to become workers receive a diet containing increasing amounts of honey, whereas the queen larvae continue to be fed royal jelly. Another example of food quality affecting development is found in aphids (Hemiptera-Homoptera, Aphididae). Changes in the quality of food may induce the appearance of winged forms and migratory behaviour.

NICHE

The place where an organisms lives is its *habitat*. This "place" may be an entire field or forest, the shoreline of a stream, the under-sides of leaves of a particular kind of plant, among others. A given species is typically found living in essentially the same kind of surroundings throughout its distribution, although there may be variation within the limits of tolerance of the species. The degree of suitability of a given habitat will vary with the extent to which it satisfies the needs within these limits of tolerance. Each species of the community of organisms living in a given habitat requires certain resources (e.g., food, shelter, breeding sites, favourable temperature, favourable humidity, space and time) in sufficient amounts and of sufficient quality to survive and reproduce. This is, every species occupies a particular physical location at a given time and does a given thing (eats, copulates, rests etc.) at that place and time. A compilation of all needed resources, both in qualitative and quantitative terms describes the *ecological niche* of a species. A community is composed of individuals of different species segregated into different niches.

Insects commonly occupy a wide variety of niches in almost every kind of terrestrial and freshwater habitat. About the only habitats not broadly colonized by insects are those within the ocean; although many insects from different orders are found in intertidal marine habitats, and some are found on the open ocean (e.g., several species of water striders, *Halobates*, Hemiptera, Gerridae). However, there are no known marine insects that spend their entire life cycle submerged. Janzen provides an interesting discussion of the possible reasons why insects in particular have been able to occupy so many different niches.

OTHER ORGANISMS

Other organisms include individuals of the same or different species as part of each other's environment. The topic thus divides into intra-and interspecific interactions.

Intraspecific Interactions

The ways in which members of the same species interact are related in part to population density. There seem to be advantages associated both with relatively low and relatively high densities. Examples of circumstances in which high population density may be advantageous include mate fording and survival of potential predation. In a situation where the probability of fording a mate is decreased owing to low population density, the result would be fewer fertilizations and hence a lower average fertility. Whether a given population density is advantageous or disadvantageous is relative and depends upon other environmental influences. This is particularly apparent with regard to such available resources as food and shelter. The maximum population of a given species an area can support depends on the abundance of these resources in that area. When resources are limited, *intraspecific competition* may become increasingly pronounced as the maximum population is approached and may result in the death or emigration of individuals. Other environmental influences may, however, serve to keep a population well below a level where competition for limited resources would occur.

Interspecifc Interactions

Interspecific interactions may be conveniently divided into competition, symbiosis, predator -prey interactions, herbivore-plant interactions and indirect interactions. Interspecific competition comes about when the needs of two or more different species for a given resource (food, shelter, etc.) coincide—when their niches overlap. In situations, where two species with essentially identical life needs are brought together, one species may be expected to have a competitive advantage and eventually to eliminate the other. Stated another way; "no two species can occupy the same niche at the same time for very long." The segregation of the different species in an ecosystem into different niches is explained on the basis. of the operation of competitive exclusion. A good example of competitive exclusion is the outcome when two species of flour beetles (*Triboliurn castaneum* and *T. confusum*) are placed in the same container of flour. If the container is maintained under conditions of high humidity and temperature, *T. castaneum* invariably wins out. However, maintaining the beetles under conditions of low humidity and temperature results in a "victory" for *T. confusum.* In the absence of the other, either species can be maintained indefinitely under wet and warm or dry and cool conditions.

Symbiosis is used here to mean a close association between two different species. This association may be mutually advantageous (*mutualism*), disadvantageous for one of the species (*parasitism*), or advantageous for one without harm to the other (*commensalism*). There are many examples of mutualistic associations between insects; one is seen when ants actively care for and protect aphids, which in turn extrete honeydew that is ingested by the ants. The relationships, between fungus-growing ants and fungi are good examples of mutualism between insects and other kinds of organisms. Additional examples include the relationships between microbes and insects relative to digestion and nutrition. A recent review deals specifically with the intracellular symbiotes of the Hemiptera-Homoptera.

There are numerous examples of mutualistic relationships between plants and insect where the plants provide food for an insect that in turn pollinates the plants.

Among the organisms that parasitize insects are insects themselves, microorganisms, mites and nematodes. In some instances microbes and nematodes parasitize both insects and vertebrates. In these cases the insects may act as *vectors*, carrying parasites to their vertebrate hosts.

Well over 1000 microbes, most of them pathogens (disease-causers), have been described in insects, and new ones are being added regularly. According to N.A.S. the current list includes "90 species and varieties of bacteria, 260 species of viruses and rickettsiae, 460 species of fungi, 255 species of protozoa. "These microbes may gain entrance into insects orally or via wounds in the integument, or they may be capable of actively penetrating the integument (particularly fungi). In some instances pathogens that have gained entrance may be passed *transovarially* (via the egg) to offspring, as are certain arboviruses in mosquitoes.

Interest in pathogenic microbes associated with insects has largely been focused on their potential use in biological control. During the past *30* years or so, insect microbiology has grown rapidly as an entomological speciality.

Among the bacteria that infect insects, the best known is *Bacillus thuringiensis*, a spore-former that has been used with some success in biological control. It is pathogenic for nearly 200 species of pest insects, particularly Lepidoptera. Another member of the same genus, *Bacillus larvae*, causes American foulbrood, a serious disease of honey bee larvae. In addition to members of the genus *Bacillus*, certain species of *Clostridium* and *Streptococcus* are also insect pathogens. Many bacterial diseases of plants are mechanically transmitted by insects. Certain bacterial pathogens of vertebrates are also transmitted by insects, for example, those that cause plague (*Yersinia pestis*) in humans.

Viruses are obligate cellular parasites composed in part of DNA or RNA. Those associated with insects are generally not as well-known or understood as the bacteria. They are claccified on the basis of the part of the host cell in which they develop, the presence or absence and morphology of an inclusion body, and the kind of nucleic acid (DNA or RNA) present. Some insect viruses produce granular inclusion bodies; most produce crystalline polyhedral bodies in the nucleus or cytoplasm of an infected cell. Virus particles may be alone in an inclusion body or in packets. Several viruses that are pathogenic for insects have been identified and described. Most have been found among Lepidoptera, although several also are known from the Hymenoptera, Diptera, Coleoptera and Neuroptera. It is interesting that a virus may act in conjunction with a bacterium to produce a disease syndrome not produced by the virus or bacterium separately. Such is the case in two silkworm diseases, gattine and flacherie, *Streptococcus bombycis* and *Bacillus bombycis*, respectively, being the bacteria involved. Insects, especially aphids and leafhoppers (Hemiptera-Homoptera), are important vectors of viruses pathogenic for plants. Insects also serve as vectors of several viruses that attack humans and other vertebrates, notably the ***arboviruses*** (arthropod-borne viruses), including those that cause yellow fever, dengue, and encephalitis.

Microbes somewhat similar to bacteria, but lacking cell walls, *mycoplasmas*, have recently been found to cause the "yellows diseases" of plants, such as aster yellows. Leafhoppers (Hemiptera-Homoptera, Cicadellidae) are involved in the transmission of these organims. Some rickettsiae are insect pathogens. In size they lie somewhere between viruses and bacteria, but, unlike viruses, they are capable of independent metabolism in vitro. Those rickettsiae that are pathogenic for insects are very slow in killing their hosts. They have been grown in mammalian-tissue culture and have killed white mice upon injection. Owing to slow kill of insects and potential danger for mammals, they are unlikely ever to be used in insect control *Rickettsia prowazekii* (causes epidemic typhus) and *R. prowazekii mooseri* (causes murine and endemic typhus) which are pathogenic for humans, are vectored by body lice and fleas, respectively.

There are more species of fungi that are known to be pathogenic to insects than of any other group of microbes. These *entomogenous* fungi have been described from several groups of fungi. Species in the genus *Beauveria* have bene used in attempts at biological control. However, the success of fungus inflections in insects (i.e., whether they become established and kill an insect) depends to a great extent on weather conditions, and hence these microbes would likely be undependable as agents of biological control. Although insects are apparently not vectors of fungi that cause human or other vertebrate diseases, they do serve as mechanical vectors of fungi pathogenic to plants. An example is the fungus that causes Dutch elm disease, which is vectored mainly by the European elm bark beetle, *Scolytus multistriatus*. Madelin discussed fungi that are parasites of insects. A large number of protozoa, especially *Microsporidians, are* known to kill insects, but, like rickettsiae and fungi, they act very slowly. No doubt many of those slow-acting microbes weaken their hosts and make them more susceptible to the effects of other environmental components. Insect pathogens have been described in the protozoan phyla Sarcodina (amebas), Mastigophora (flagellates), and Sporozoa (sporozoans). The microsporidian *Nosema bombycis* (Sporozoa) causes the "pebrine" disease of silkworms. The elucidation of this relationship by Louis Pasteur in the nineteenth-century stands as a classic in microbiological research. Other well-known microsporidian insect pathogens include *Nosema apis* and *N. pyraustai*, which attack the honey bee and European corn borer, respectively. A mosquito, *Culex enaticus*, parasitized by the microsporidian *Thelahania minuta.* Protozoans are common partners in mutualistic relationships with insects; we have already discussed those found in the gut of termites, which provide cellulase and enable their hosts to digest cellulose. Several protozoa pathogenic for humans and other vertebrates are vectored by insects. Examples include the malarias (*Plasmodium spp.*) vectored by *Anopheles spp*, mosquitoes (different forms of malaria occur in birds, monkeys and humans). American trypanosomiasis (Chagas' disease) caused by *Trypanosoma cnuzi* and vectored by blood-sucking bugs (Hemiptera, Reduviidae), and the two forms of African sleeping sickness caused by *T. rhodesiense* and *T. gambiae* and vectored by tsetse flies (Diptera, Muscidae, *Glossina spp*). The serious disease of cattle, *nagana*, which has retarded the development of major parts of Africa, is caused by the protozoan *T. brucei*, also vectored by tsetse flies.

Mites (Arachnida, Acarina) are very small arthropods, many species of which parasitize insects. For example, the larvae of members of the family Erythraeidae are parasites of insects and other arthropods and have been found attached to wing vens and other locations on the insect body. *Acarapis woodi* (Scutacaridae) causes the acarine disease of bees. This species either lives in the tracheae or on the external parts of the bee's body and weakens the host to the point where it can no longer fly and eventually succumbs. About 100 species of nematodes (phylum Aschelminthes, roundworms) have been described as being associated with approximately 1500 insect species. In most instances, these "entomophilic" nematodes damage and eventually kill their host. Nematodes show some promise in the biological control of insects. A number of species that attack humans, for example, filarial worms, (*Wuchereria bancrofti* and others), and other vertebrates, for examples, dog heartworm, spend part of their life cycles in insects (mosquitoes for the examples here), which serve as their vectors.

Many relationships between two or more insect species or between insects and other organisms are commensal. For example, probably many of the microbes associated with insects neither harm nor particularly help their host but gain food and a place to live. Phoretic relationships are good examples of commencalism. In a phoretic relationship an individual of one species attaches to an individual of another and gains a mode of transportation. Insects may be transporters or riders, or both. Some chewing lice (Mallophaga) attach themselves

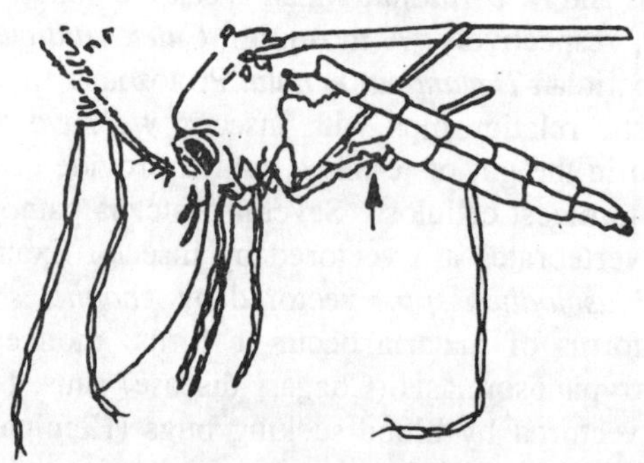

Fig. 11.8. Mosquito, Psorophora *sp., carrying the eggs (indicated by arrow) of the torsalo fly, Dennatobia hominis.*

by their mouthparts to 'louse flies (Diptera, Hippoboscidae), some of which are also parasites of birds, and in this way move form one host to another. The torsalo fly, *Dermatobia hominis,* deposits eggs on other flies, such as mosquitoes, black flies, and house flies. When these insects come into contact with a potential vertebrate host (including man), larvae emerge from the eggs and penetrate the skin. Clausen discusses phoresy among entomophagous ("insect-eating") insects.

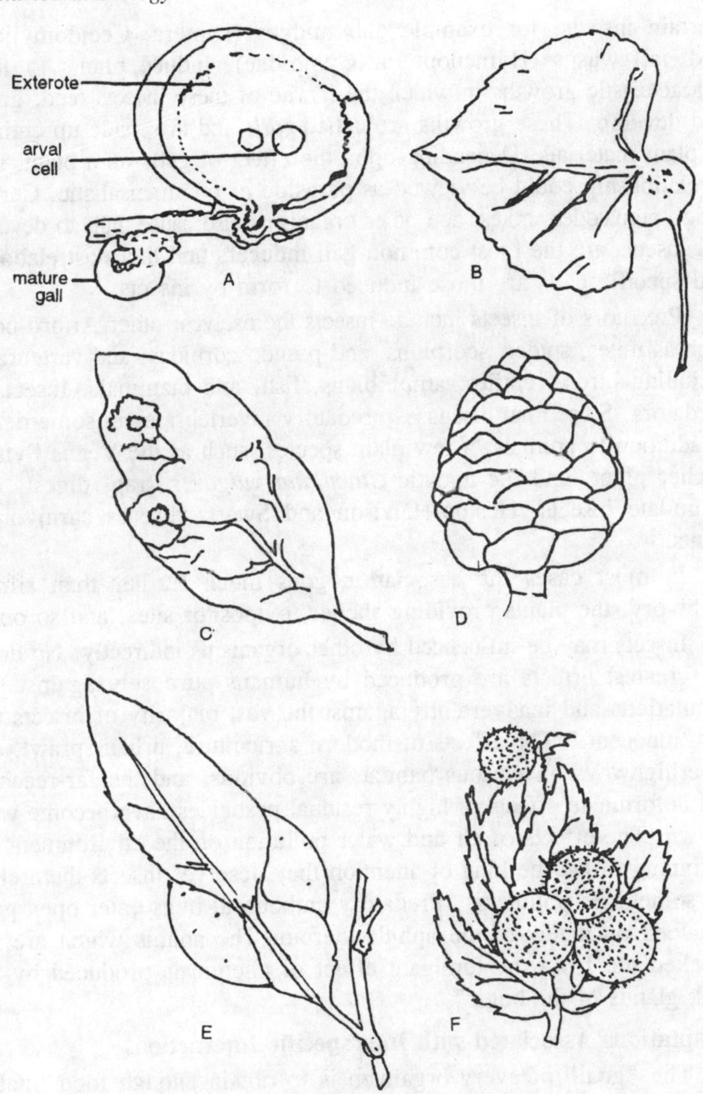

Fig. 11.9. Insect galls, A. California gtdlfly, Andricus californicus *(hymenoptera: Cynipidae). B. Transverse poplar gall aphis,* Pemphigus populiamuversus *(Homoptera) on stem* of *poplar leaves.* C Andricus pauersonae *(Hymenoptera: Cynipidae) on leaf of blue oak. D. Pine-cone willow gall caused* by Rhabdophaga strobiloides *(Diptera; Cecidomyiidae). E. Willow apple gall caused by the sawfly* Pontania pomum *(Hymenoptera: Tenthredinidae). F. Spiny rose gall caused by* Rhodites puslulatoides *(Hymenoptera; Cynipidae).*

Certain insects, for example gall midges (Diptera, Cecidomyiidae) and gall wasps (Hymenoptera, Cynipidae), induce plants to form characteristic growths in which the larvae of these insects feed, grow, and develop. These growths are called *galls* and are made up entirely of plant materials. Depending upon the effect of galls on a plant, such a relationship could be viewed as parasitic or commensalistic. Certain fungi, nematodes, mites, and other organisms also cause galls to develop, but insects are the most common gall inducers and the most elaborate and specific galls are those induced to form by insects.

Predators of insects include insects themselves: other Arthro-pods, such as mites, spider, scorpions, and pseudoscorpions; and vertebrates, including birds, reptiles, amphibians, fish, and mammals. Insects as predators. Sweetman discusses predatory invertebrates in some detail. In addition to animals, a few plant species, such as the Venus flytrap, pitcher plant, and the aquatic *Utnculana vulgar s*, trap, digest, and assimilate insects. Heslop-Harrison and Swartz discuss carnivorous plants.

In most cases the association goes much further than simple herbivory, the plants providing shelter, ovipositor sites, and so on.

Insects may be influenced by other organisms indirectly. No doubt the greatest effects are produced by humans purposely against pest populations and inadvertently against the vast majority of insects that are "innocent." The effects of modern agriculture, urban sprawl, and superhighways on various habitats are obvious, and the far-reaching and unfortunate effects of highly residual pesticides have become well-known. The effects of air and water pollution on the environment are beginning to get the kind of attention they deserve. Insects themselves are sometimes polluters: "Predatory anthocorid bugs enter open galls and feed on a few of the aphids therein. The aphids which are not attacked die from the fumigant effect of chemicals produced by the stink glands of the bugs."

Adaptations Associated with Interspecific Interactions

The "goal" of every organism is to obtain enough food (matter and energy) to maintain itself long enough to reproduce, passing its genes to the next generation. As an organism proceeds from conception to reproductive maturity, it must constantly obtain food and at the same time avoid becoming food for some other organism. Organisms, that are unable to do this successfully, for whatever reason, are mal-adapted and are, in the long term selected against. Although a number of environmental factors are no doubt involved in the selection process, examination of specific adaptations often leads to the identification of specific selecting agents. Such is the case when we examine adaptations associated with many interspecific interactions. Organisms that are closely associated ecologically often act as agents of selection reciprocally: that is, they act as selecting agents on one another. There is good evidence that many organisms have done so for long periods of geologic time. These organisms are said to have *coevolved* or to be *coadapted*.

Examination of several examples where coevolution has played a role reveals at least two types of coevolutionary interactions. Two (or more) different species may have coevolved to the extent that they benefit ope another in the quest for reproductive success: their relationship thus is mutualistic. In this case the partners have become (or are becoming) more and more successful in their interaction leading to sustained or improved reproductive success for both. Alternatively, the participants may have engaged and continue to engage in a kind of genetic warfare in which one member "evolves" a mechanism of offense providing increased access to the other as food, only to have the other "respond," in the evolutionary sense, with a defense, and so on through time. Such is the case in interactions between parasites (and parasitoids) and hosts, predators and prey, and herbivores and plants. In this section, examples of several coevolutionary adaptations are examined. An excellent example of coevolution that has resulted in a mutualistic relationship is that which exists between the bull's- horn acacia, *Acacia comigera*, and the ant *Pseudomyrmex fern ginea*. Janzen describes this relationship as follows:

The bull's-horn acacia... is a representative swollen-thorn acacia with well-developed foliar nectaries, enlarged stipular thorns, and small nutritive organs (Beltian bodies) borne at the tip of each leaf segment. The colony of *P. femiginea* living in the enlarged stipules obtains sugars from the foliar nectaries, and oils and proteins by eating the Beltian bodies.

The workers patrol and clean the surfaces of the acacia, and bite and sting animals of all sizes that contact the plant. The workers maul any other species of plant that contact the acacia and in many cases, any that grow under the acacia. The colony attains a very large size and up to 25 per cent of the workers may be active on the surface of the acacia both day and night. The larger the colony becomes, the smaller is the damage sustained by the plant from defoliators. The colony enhances its own probability of survival by protecting the acacia on which it is completely dependent for food and domatia. Pollinating insects and the plants they pollinate also provide excellent examples of adaptations associated with long coevolutionary relationships.

Sexual reproduction in flowering plants is accomplished by the transfer of pollen from the another of a male flower to the stigma of a female flower. When a pollen grain contacts a stigma, the male germ cell in the pollen grain unites with the female germ cell or eggs, and a fertile seed develops. When the seed is exposed to the proper conditions in or on an appropriate substrate, it will give rise to a new plant. The transfer of pollen form a male to a female flower is accomplished primarily by the wind or by the activities of insects that associate with plants. Examples of wind-pollinated plants include cereal plants such as wheat and corn and many species of trees. The flowers of these plants are generally small with weakly developed petals, do not produce nectar, and produce dry pollen grains, which are easily picked up by the wind.

The relationships between plants and their insect pollinators are mutualistic in that the plants provide sugar-rich nectar and/or pollen for insects, which in turn serve as accessory plant "sex organs" in transmitting gametes from the male to the female plant (or flower). Recently, nectar of certain plants has been found to contain nutritive substances, such as certain amino acids and lipids, in addition to sugar. Insect-pollinated plants have evolved traits that make them attractive to effective insect-pollinators. In many cases the result has been a one-to-one relationship between a single plant species and a single insect species. An example of such a relationship is that between the yucca plant and yucca moths. An adult female moth uses its specialised mouthparts to gather the pollenia of the yucca plant into a ball. This ball is then scraped across the plant's stigma, accomplishing cross-pollination. The dependence of the yucca plant on the pollinating activity of the moth is demonstrated by the failure of the plant to develop pods in the absence of the moth. The yucca plant provides a home for the moth larvae, which remain within the plant until ready to emerge as adults.

Distinct correlations can be made between the anatomical and physiological characteristics of the flowers of a given species and the anatomy, physiology, and behaviour of their insect pollinators. Among the characteristics of flowers attractive to insects are

1. The production of particular scents.
2. Colour, size, and shape of petals.

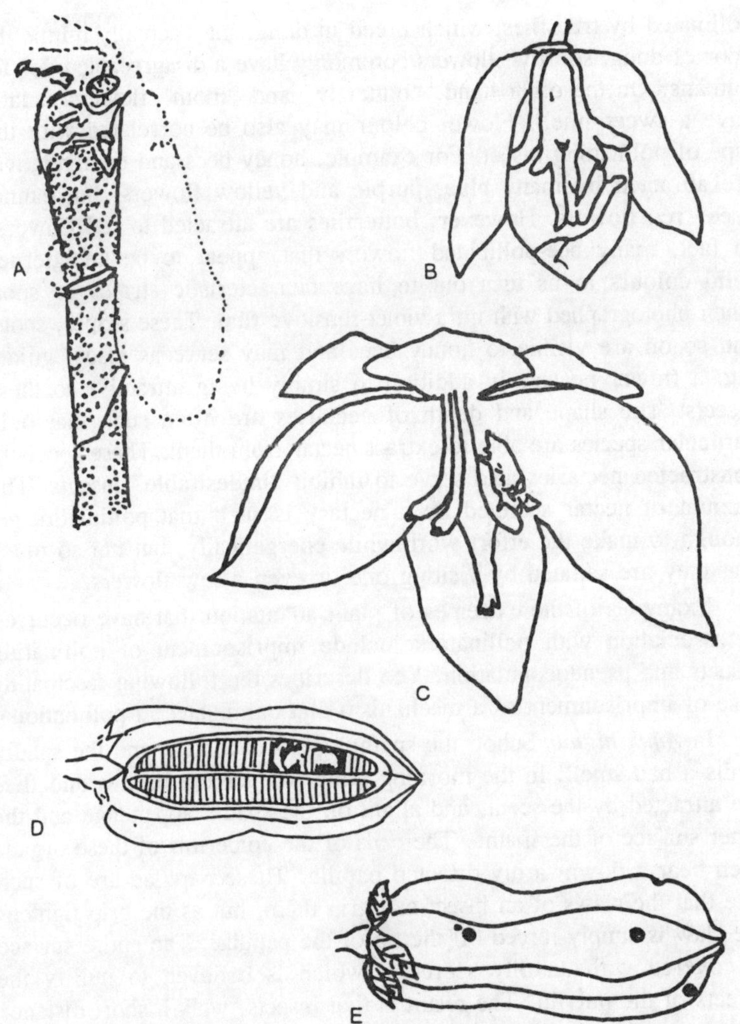

Fig. 11.10. Yucca moth and yucca plant. A. Female moth gathering pollen. B. Female scraping the pollen ball across the plant's stigma. C. Female ovipositing (several petal removed). D. Larva within mature pod (portion of pod removed). E. Pod with exit holes and constrictions caused by larvae.

3. Patterns of stripes of spots on petals.
4. Whether petals are separated or not.
5. Shape of flower.

Scent production is usually very important in attracting a potential pollinator and often in determining behaviour following landing. Flowers pollinated by true flies, which breed in dung, may actually mimic the odor of dung, so "fly" flowers commonly have a disagreeable odor for humans. On the other hand, "butterfly" and "moth" flowers usually have a sweet smell. Flower colour may also be correlated with the type of pollinating insect. For example, honey bees and their relatives are attracted by many blue, purple and yellow flowers, but cannot "see" red flowers. However, butterflies are attracted to red flowers. In fact, many bee-pollinated flowers that appear to be unpatterned solid colours to us turn out to have characteristic stripes or spots when photographed with ultra-violet-sensitive film. These stripes, spots, and so on are visible to honey bees and may serve as visual guides into a flower nectary in addition to simply being attractive to these insects. The shape and depth of nectaries are often such that only particular species are able to extract nectar from them. These specially constructed nectaries also serve to inhibit "undesirable" insects. The amount of nectar secreted by a nectary is such that pollinators get enough to make the effort worthwhile energetically, but not so much that they are satiated by visiting one or even a few flowers.

Examples of the extremes of plant adaptation that have occurred in association with pollinators include imprisonment of pollinating insects and pseudocopulation. Yeo describes the following fascinating case of imprisonment as a mechanism that culminates in pollination :

In *Amm nignun* Schott the spathe opens overnight and the spadix emits a bad smell. In the morning dung-frequenting beetles and flies are attracted by the scent, and alight on the spadix appendage and the inner surface of the spathe. The cells of the epidermis of these organs each bear a downwardly directed papilla. These papillae are of such size that the claws of an insect can grip them, but as the grip tightens the claw is simply forced off the tip of the papillae. The entire surface is covered with an oily secretion which is believed to nullify the effects of the pulvilli. The result is that insects, walk a short distance and then suddenly fall. The heavier ones take wing as they fall but the smaller ones are too slow, and drop through the ring of bristle-like sterile florets into the "prison." At this time the stigmas can be pollinated by pollen carried by the incoming insects. The following night the stigmas cease to be receptive: pollen is then shed into the chamber and dusts the insects. By the morning the sterile florets, previously smooth and oily, have become wrinkled so that insects can walk on them. The papillae on the spathe and spadix also shrink, and the insects can escape.

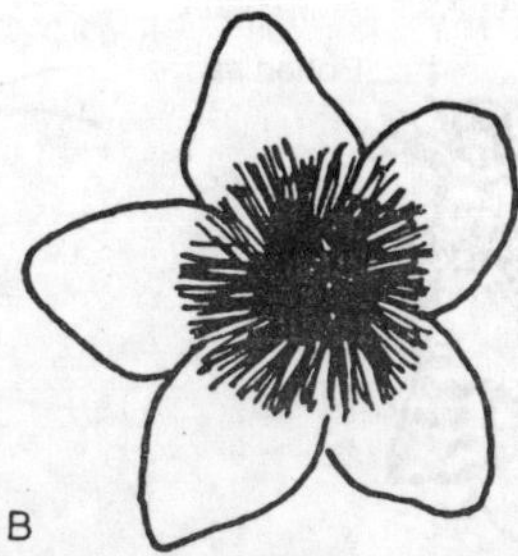

Fig. 11.11. Marsh marigolds as they appear to humans (A) and to insects sensitive to ultraviolet light (B).

Certain orchids (*Ophrys*) produce stimuli that attract their specific pollinators (particularly Diptera or Hymenoptera) by releasing copulatory behaviour. These orchids produce scents that mimic the cffects of sex pheromones as well as stimulating the insects visually and tactilely. The most common insect pollinators are various members of the orders Coleoptera. Lepidoptera, Diptera and Hymenoptera. Among the common adaptations of pollinating insects are elongated mouthparts, that facilitate obtaining nectar from flowers with deep nectaries, plumose (featherlike) hairs on the body to which pollen clings, and various specialized pollen-collecting and/or transporting structures such as the corbiculae on the hind tibiae of honey bees, and their relatives and pollen brushes on the hindlegs of most bees.

Another good example of the evolutionary "fine tuning" that can occur between 'mutualists is seen in the association between attine ants and their fungus gardens. As ants prepare a fungus garden, they add their own fecal material, which benefits the fungus. The fecal material contains proteolytic enzymes and 'various nitrogenous materials that play vital roles (i.e., protein digestion and enhancement of growth) in the metabolism of the fungus. In turn, the fungus contributes cellulase, which benefits the ants by catalyzing the digestion of cellulose. Such close metabolic interdependency is characteristic of many mutualistic associations.

Parasites and hosts apparently pass through successive cycles of "parasite attack new host defense," the parasite tending to become increasingly benign and the host more tolerant, perhaps eventually leading to a commensalistic or even mutualistic outcome. For example, parasites that invade the insect hemocoel and commonly encapsulated. The presence of such a capsule around a parasite may several limit the parasite's activities by inhibiting mobility or interferring with feeding

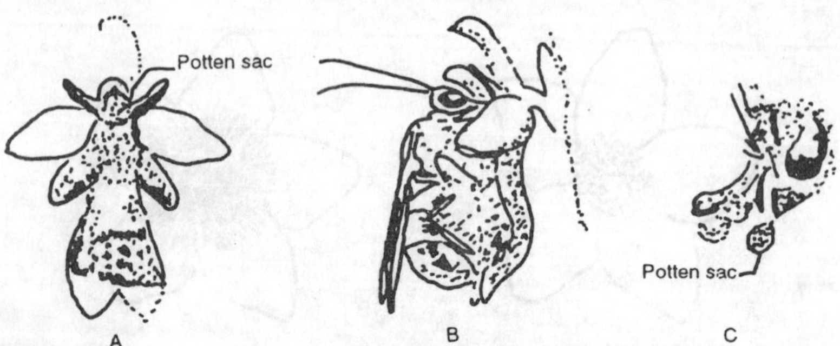

Fig. 11.12. The orchid Ophrys insecdfera, *which visually resembles a female bee. B. A bee attempting to copulate with the flower. C. As the result of attempted copulation. pollen sacs become attached to the bee's head.*

and/or gaseous exchange. On the other hand, some parasites secrete materials that block capsule formation, Duffey contains information on chemicals in insects that have an antibiotic effect. Whitcomb *et al.* consider insect defenses against microorganisms and parasitoids. A remarkable example of an extrmely close adaptive adjustment between parasite and hpst is the relationship between the rabbit fleas *Spilopsyllus euniculi* and *Cediopsylla simplex* and their rabbit hosts. The reproductive behaviour an physiology of these fleas is strongly influenced by the rabbit's reproductive hormones. Egg maturation only occurs on pregnant doe rabbits and has been shown to be stimulated by the host's corticosteroids. Estrogens and other hormones also contribute to egg development and influence oviposition. Larvae develop in the rabbit nests in which the young rabbits are born. Linkage of the sex cycles of the fleas and rabbit hosts ensures that the reproductive activity of the fleas occurs such that newborn flea larvae end up in the host's nest.

That predators of insects and their insect prey have exerted strong selection pressures on one another is clearly evident in the means predators have evolved to capture prey and the avoidance mechanisms of potential prey. Several examples of coevolutionary adaptation involving insects as predators and insects as prey have already been given in earlier chapters. Here we consider examples of insect adaptations in response mainly to selection pressures by insectivorous vertebrates, in particular protective colouration, from, and pattern; and coevolutionary adaptations in bats and moths. Examples of protective form, colouration and pattern include crypsis, asposematic colouration, mimicry, and spots. Thus, although we will emphasize form, colouration, and pattern in this discussion, it must be remembered that "appropriate' behaviour has also come about as a result of selection pressure applied by predators.

Crypsis refers to various combinations of form, colour and pattern that facilitate "hiding" from potential predators. Resemblance to various inedible, even repulsive, objects like thorns, or bird droppings; colouration and shading that cause an insect to blend into the background; and transparent wings that allow the background to show through all belong in the crypsis category. A classic example of crypsis (and one that has contributed significantly to our understanding of natural selection) is *industrial melanism.* Industrial melanisnm refers to a phenomenon first observed in the peppered moth, *Biston betulana*, in England. These moths are nocturnally active and during the day they rest on lichen-covered tree trunks. Collection records of peppered moths described them as light-coloured, an appearance that provided them with camouflage when they rested on the tree trunks. Dark (*melanic*) forms began to appear around the industrial center of Manchester and aventually came to be more common than the light-coloured forms. It was hypothesized that the change in predominant phenotype (fronn fight to dark) was associated with the overall darkening of tree trunks due to industrial pollution. Such darkening was thought to lessen the selective advantage of light-coloured moths while favouring the survival of dark forms. Birds were assumed to be the agents of selection. Kettlewell demonstrated experimentally that birds did, in fact, prey more on uncamouflaged forms; light-coloured forms had a definite selective advantage in unpolluted areas. He also showed that moths tended to rest on a substrate that matched their body colouration, indicating that they could discriminate between light and dark backgrounds. With the advent of pollution controls, light moths are beginning to appear again in industrial regions.

Aposematic or *warning colouration is* sometimes called *"advertising"* in the sense that an insect tastes very bad (i.e., is unpalatable)· stings, or does something similarly disagreeable to a predator and communicates this ability visually by colours and patterns that contrast blatantly with the background. Vertebrate predators Soon learn to avoid these insects on the basis of a few unpleasant encounters. An aposematically coloured insect may also be advertising falsely in that although it looks like (mimics) a harmful insect, it is really palatable and harmless. Aposematically coloured insects are usually boldly patterned in shades of orange, red, or yellow contrasting with black and stand out against the greens,. and browns that are characteristic of the environment. Unpalatability is commonly due to the presence of chemicals in the hemolymph that have been derived from host plants. For example, the monarch butterfly and certain true bugs and beetles, which feed on various species of milkweed plants (Asclepiadaceae),. accumulate chemicals (specifically *cardiac glycosides*) from these plants. These chemicals not only render the insects unpalatable to vertebrate predators (especially birds) but also act as emetics (i.e., they make a predator vomit). Although all monarch butterflies are aposematically coloured, an individual may or may not be unpalatable depending on the level of cardiac glycoside in the particular milkweed plant it fed upon as a larva. In an interesting coevolutionary turnabout, certain insecti-vorous birds have circumvented the monarch's chemical defense by learning to reject or ingest individuals on the basis of taste. In this instance aposematic colouration would tend to be disadvatageous for the insects since it would render them more visible to predators.

Fig. 11.13. The monarch butterfly, Danaus pkdppus (A), serves as the model for its Baterisan mimic, the viceroy butterfly, Limenitis archippus (B).

Mimicry, as used here, refers to the dose resemblance (in form, colour, pattern, or otherwise) between one insect, the *mimic*, and another insect or a plant part, the *model* (*insects* may mimic thorns, leaves, etc.). Various forms of mimicry have been identified in insects, among them Batesian, Mnllerian and Wasmannian. *A Batesian mimic* is palatable (and otherwise harmless), but is protected somewhat by virtue of its similarity to an unpalatable (or otherwise harmful) model. An oft-cited example is the viceroy butterfly (*Limenitis archippus*), which is a Batesian mimic of the monarch butterfly. Batesian mimics are commonly less numerous than their models. This is interpreted as advantageous on the basis that large numbers of aposematically coloured but palatable individuals would reduce the avoidance learning in predators. *Mullerian mimics* differ from Batesian in that both mimics and models are unpalatable (or otherwise harmful). Several species that bear close resemblance to one another may comprise *a Miillerian mimicry complex*, all members gaining advantage by virtue of the fact that the number of different colours and patterns predators are required to learn to avoid are reduced; that is predators need learn only one pattern to result in protection for all the insects in the complex. Wasmannian mimics are insects that live in close association with ants and that have come to closely resemble their hosts. In this case the models (i.e., ants) are considered to be the selecting agents, the guests who fail to resemble their hosts sufficiently being attacked. Many insects (e.g., certain moths, butterflies and caterpillars) bear spots at various locations on their body. These spots often closely resemble eyes of vertebrates and perhaps, in some instances, eyes of other insects. Many moths, which have eye spots on the hindwings, are otherwise cryptically coloured when resting on their usual substrate. If the first line of defense, crypsis, fails and a predator strikes, the forewings are thrown forward, suddenly displaying the eyespots. Such behaviour has been shown experimentally to frighten and repel insectivorous birds. The eyespots resemble eyes of birds (e.g., owls) that prey on the insectivorous birds. Small spots are commonly found along the edges of the wings of many butterflies. These have been shown to serve as pecking targets and by virtue of their location away from vital parts of the body may provide protection by diverting the peck of a predator and allowing time for escape.

A superb example of predator prey coevolution is the association between insectivorous bats and members of certain families of night-flying moths, in particular Noctuidae, Arctiidae, and Geometridae. Bats locate prey by emitting pulses of sound beyond the range of human sensitivity (ultrasonic). As these sounds bounce off various objects, living and nonliving, the bats hear the echo and use this information to guide their flight and to locate flying prey insects. Details of the discovery and elucidation of this echo-locating ability are recounted in Griffin. Tympanic organs that perceive the echo-locating cries of bats have evolved in several moth families. The coevolutionary "battle" has proceeded a step further in certain Arctiid moths, which possess microtymbal organs on the metathorax. When a bat approaches one of these moths, trains of sound pulses are generated by the microtymbal organs. These sound have been shown to in effect, "jam" the bat's echolocating system and hence interfere with its ability to catch the moth. Herbivorous insects and plants have played major roles in one another's evolutionary history. Several structural and behavioural adaptations of herbivorous insects are described elsewhere.

Plants have responded, in the evolutionary sense, in a variety of ways to the continued onslaught of herbivorous insects. Among the adaptations that provide defense against insect herbivores are numerous structural and biological characteristics, but the major defensive adaptations involve chemicals.

Structural characteristics that interfere with insect attack (feeding and/or oviposition) include though cuticle, hard seed coats, velvetlike pubescence, and a variety of spines and thorns. Recently certain plants have been found to be covered, at least in part, with highly specialized, minute, sharp-pointed, hooked hairs (*hooked trichomes*). These hairs hook into the integument of caterpillars (*Heliconius spp*) feeding on *Passiflora adenopoda* or leafhoppers feeding on certain strains of field

Fig, 11.14. to moth (Female). Automeris io, *with forewings thrown forward, displaying eyespots.*

beans, immobilizing and puncturing these insects, which eventually succumb to starvation and desiccation. Limited growing seasons, nutrient-poor sap (relative to herbivorous insects), and mechanisms that allow rapid dispersal of seeds (which increases difficulty in food location for seed eaters) are examples of various biological means by which plants "combat" herbivores.

Many chemicals found in plants have no apparent role in plant metabolism, but are present in comparatively concentrated amounts. In several instances, these *secondary plant substances* (*secondary metabolic products* have been shown to be of value-to-the plants by influencing the behaviour or physiology of herbivorous insects. That is, they sometimes act as allomones. Secondary plant substances may have toxic, repellent, deterrent, or hormonal effects on insects. The toxic effects of certain plants have long been known, and several *botanical insecticides* still ford use today. Examples include *nicotine* (derived mainly from *Nicotiana tobacum*, the common tobacco plant), the *pyrethrins* (from various species of *Chrysanthemum*), and *rotenone* (from *Denis spp*. and many other legumes). Citronella and cedar oil are examples of insect repellents derived from plants. Deterrents of various sorts have been identified. These may be substances that are ingested and influence feeding or such things as resins that physically interfere with feeding.

Substances with molting-hormone activity have been found in several ferns (Polypodiaceae) and two families of gymnosperms. Many different *Phytoecdysones* have been isolated and analyzed; the most common is *fiecdysone*, the major insect-molting hormones. Many phytoecdysones are more potent than insect hormones. These substances protect plant by interferring with insect development. Juvenile-hormone activity has also been identified in certain plants, especially balsam fir and eastern hemlock. *Iiivabione, a* juvenile-hormone mimic from balsam fir, is very similar in chemical structure to juvenile hormone. Like the phytoecdysones, juvabione and other plant substances with juvenile-hormone activity cause pathological effects, such as inhibition of metamorphosis and sterilization of adults. Juvenile-hormone activity in plants was dis-covered by chance when the bug *Pynizocoris apterus* failed to complete development in cages the bottoms of which were covered with a particular kind of paper towelling. The hormonally active paper towelling turned out to be produced from balsam fir. Recently, a secondary plant substance with antijuvenile hormone activity has been identified from the *plant Ageratum haustonianum.*

Many insects have *"fought back"* against plant defenses. An insect (or nay herbivore) that breaks through a given plant's defenses obtains a double advantage; it fords a new source of food and does not face competition from other herbivores that have not broken through the plant's defenses. One mechanism that has provided some insects with protection against secondary plant substances has been the development of microsomal Mixed-Function Oxidases (MFOs) secreted in the midgut. These enzymes degrade a wide variety of substances; for example, they are active against pyrethrins. However, in the case of *Chrysanthemum* (producer of pyrethrins), the plant has responded with the production of a substance called *sesamin*, an MFO inhibitor. Interestingly, MFO systems are best developed in polyphagous insect species, which are most likely to be confronted by a variety of secondary plant substances. Some insects not only have broken through plant defenses but also have come to use secondary plant substances to their own advantage. For example, as previously mentioned, the monarch butterfly accumulates cardiac glycosides, which render his insect unpalatable to predators. For other insects secondary plant substances serve as kairomones.

INDEX

C

D

Q

R

S